T0231194

Strategic Software Engineering

Strategic Software Engineering

An Interdisciplinary Approach

Fadi P. Deek
James A.M. McHugh
Osama M. Eljabiri

Auerbach Publications
Taylor & Francis Group

Boca Raton   London   New York   Singapore

Published in 2005 by
Auerbach Publications
Taylor & Francis Group
6000 Broken Sound Parkway NW, Suite 300
Boca Raton, FL 33487-2742

International Standard Book Number-10: 0-8493-3939-1 (Hardcover)
International Standard Book Number-13: 978-0-8493-3939-4 (Hardcover)
Library of Congress Card Number 2005041000

Library of Congress Cataloging-in-Publication Data

Strategic software engineering : an interdisciplinary approach / Fadi P. Deek, James A.M.
McHugh, Osama M. Eljabiri.
    p. cm.
Includes bibliographical references and index.
ISBN 0-8493-3939-1 (alk. paper)
    1. Software engineering. I. Deek, Fadi P. II. McHugh, James A., 1994- III. Eljabiri,
Osama M.

QA76.758.S765 2005
005.1--dc22   2005041000

Taylor & Francis Group
is the Academic Division of T&F Informa plc.

Visit the Taylor & Francis Web site at
http://www.taylorandfrancis.com

and the Auerbach Publications Web site at
http://www.auerbach-publications.com

Contents

Dedication

With love and appreciation to Maura Ann,
my wife and best friend.

Fadi P. Deek

To my wife, Alice,
my sweetheart and guiding light.

James A.M. McHugh

To my mother, Hind,
for instilling in me values
for which I will be eternally grateful.

Osama M. Eljabiri

Preface

Software is a disruptive technology that has changed how almost every sector of human society and the economy works. Software is now pervasive; it is a component of almost every industrial product or at least essential to the development of such products. Software capabilities lie at the core of the new national and international information-based economy. This mission criticality of software imposes increasingly stringent demands on business organizations that depend on software systems or are responsible for software development. The Darwinian nature of modern business competition makes software development a struggle for survival in an unpredictable environment characterized by intense pressures for rapid development; decreased time to market; flexible and easy-to-use applications; and low cost. It is now more important than ever for software developers, project managers, and business organizations to understand and implement diversified, multidisciplinary software development environments in their organizations.

Strategic Software Engineering: an Interdisciplinary Approach addresses these needs by offering a view of software engineering as a strategic, business-oriented, interdisciplinary enterprise, rather than as a primarily technical and scientifically focused process. We view software technology as a tool for achieving business goals in collaboration with all the affected stakeholder communities. Although we address many of the technical and scientific aspects of development extensively, this is done in a way that is broadly accessible. We critically review software development models and processes. We consider how software has been created in the past and with what shortcomings as well as what new paradigms are emerging that reflect how development should be done. We provide a strategic, business-oriented assessment of the forces that have influenced the development of software process models in order to better understand what measures or directions should be taken to further improve them. We extensively address the relation between problem-solving techniques and strategies for effectively solving real-world problems. Finally, we consider the impact of interdisciplinary factors on software development, including the critical role of people and financial factors.

This book is designed for students, faculty, and practitioners with an interest in a broad, eclectic, business-driven view of software engineering principles, methodologies, and development models. The diverse backgrounds of the authors, which encompass traditional computer science, information systems, information technology, and business applications, have helped us create an integrative approach that we believe is highly compatible with the new trend towards interdisciplinary curricula in computing and business schools in the United States and elsewhere. The book is particularly suitable for upper level and graduate courses in software engineering with a management information system, business, information technology, or computer science emphasis. It should also serve as a useful resource for business or systems analysts. Software project management leaders in business organizations should find it a helpful reference in contemporary areas such as software process diversity and interdisciplinary software development.

Introduction

This book has a focus different from those of other texts on software engineering. It proposes and develops a view of software engineering as a strategic, business-oriented, interdisciplinary enterprise, rather than as the primarily technical or scientific process described in traditional presentations. We extensively address many of the technical and scientific aspects of software development in a way that is accessible to a broad audience. The discussion of strategic software engineering is divided into three sections. Section 1 provides a detailed, critical review of software development models and processes (Chapter 1 through Chapter 4). This is then followed by a strategic, business-oriented assessment of how process models have evolved over time and what directions should now be taken to improve them (Chapter 5). Section 2 (Chapter 6 through Chapter 10) focuses on the relation between problem-solving techniques and strategies for effectively solving real-world problems. Section 3 addresses the impact of interdisciplinary factors on software development, including the critical role of people and fiscal effects (Chapter 11 and Chapter 12) and concludes with a brief look at so-called specialized systems development (Chapter 13). An overview of each chapter follows.

Chapter 1 ("Software Development Strategies: Basic Planning and Control") introduces and critiques the basic software development process and the key risk-reduction models. We observe how these and later software process models share (in varying degrees and evolving over time) a number of characteristics, beginning with an emphasis on requirements engineering; the use of a multistage development decomposition derived from the waterfall model; documentation requirements; stakeholder involvement; project management; a consideration of objectives related to economic or business constraints; and implicit or explicit adoption of recognized best practices in development. Their shared characteristics reflect the universal human, technical, and economic constraints under which software development operates. For example, recognition of best practices is a recurrent theme in the evolution of every engineering field. In software development, these practices include separation of concerns, deferring design decisions when possible, focusing on stakeholder goals, and, more recently, the application of use cases to identify requirements.

The historical evolution of process models has played a significant role in how models have diversified over time, with later approaches building on earlier ones and with technological advances enabling new approaches. We consider first the basic life-cycle models that introduced structured planning and development and applied basic engineering organizational and planning principles to the development of software. The Waterfall Model was the most influential of these. Incremental and iterative models were introduced to reduce the cycle time for development. These include the Evolutionary Development Model and the early Iterative Enhancement Model, which served as a practical method for achieving stepwise refinement. Incremental development facilitated early solution of implementation problems and reduced risk associated with the late integration of components.

Investing in any business involves risk, as does developing a software product. We thus next critique the basic models that addressed risk in software development such as the prototyping and spiral models. Prototypes are widely used in engineering; examples include rapid, throwaway, exploratory, and embedded prototypes, etc., as well as techniques such as the use of presentation prototypes, breadboards, mockups, and pilot systems. Benefits of prototyping include obtaining early feedback from users and motivating user involvement, which help to avoid failure of user satisfaction.

The most famous risk reduction strategy is embodied in Boehm's spiral model, which relies heavily on prototyping but is also designed to allow incorporating other process models into its cycles. Each spiral development cycle is like a mini-life cycle with its deliverables and assurance processes intended to minimize risk. We also consider the Win–Win spiral variant that uses a stakeholder approach to determine the objectives–constraints–alternatives for each cycle of the spiral. Finally, we examine the Cleanroom Model; this is based on incremental development under statistical quality control and formal correctness principles and uses statistically based software testing intended to yield a certifiably reliable software product.

Chapter 2 ("Software Development Strategies: Tools, Objects, and Reuse") examines computer-supported tools for software development and models that emphasize the fundamental concept or principle of reusability. Reuse is a decisively important idea in software engineering because it reduces risk and development costs. The chapter describes process models that capitalize on the idea of reuse, beginning with object orientation. The central motivation underlying the use of objects is that they represent a natural way to model phenomena and correspond to the most fundamental of cognitive elements: the concept or object. The conceptual nature of objects underlies their ability to be designed for reuse. At one level, we consider how objects can be systemically used throughout the development process.

We then provide an overview of the Rational Unified Process and its comprehensive suite of CASE tools for object-oriented development. Commercially available reusable system components or commercial off-the-shelf components represent reuse at a different scale at a much higher scale of functionality. Finally, even when objects or COTS components are not applicable, for a large number of systems, the issue of reuse presents itself in the reengineering of existing systems, which would be totally prohibitive to develop *ab initio*. The large extant systems to which this approach is applied are typically legacy systems and are effectively recycled by being modified or adapted to update their performance characteristics and interfaces. We also briefly touch on another important instance of reuse: namely, the reuse of design patterns for solutions to problems.

Chapter 3 ("Software Development Strategies: Process Improvement") examines the theme of software process improvement, in which the goal is to take a proactive role in creating better software development models. One approach to achieving this is to use simulation models to better understand the internal dynamics of process models, such as how changes in one process parameter can affect other process parameters. Another approach is to address more explicitly and carefully the human factors involved in development, including cognitive, psychological, and social factors that come into play at different stages of development. The establishment of explicit standards for software development and for related organizational and managerial practices, as is done in the Capability Maturity Model, is a further tactic that has been taken to improve the overall excellence with which software best practices are applied and improved. Software development excellence can also be promoted by improving the professional and technical abilities of the individual developers, as typified by Personal Software Process, and the teams to which they belong. We consider each of these approaches.

Chapter 4 ("Software Development Strategies: Reinventing How It Is Done") examines a number of more recent trends in software process models. An especially remarkable example is the open source movement, which represents a paradigm shift in how software is developed. It even has some of the characteristics of a disruptive technology—that is, a technological development emerging from outside the mainstream of scientific development that radically challenges the existing technological paradigm. Agile Development is not quite as radical but reflects a new order of lightweight process model intended to reduce what some perceive as the unwieldy process overhead in other approaches. Rapid Application Development has a similar objective of expediting the return time on product delivery.

Workflow models, akin to the production line models common in manufacturing, view business environments as networks of collaborating agents in which information is transformed as it moves between agents. They attempt to automate the enactment of these processes. Aspect-oriented models address difficulties with object orientation that arise because phenomena such as concurrency and scheduling tend to straddle objects, making the application of the central principle of separation of concerns problematic. Each model is part of a continuing exploration into how to develop software systems effectively.

Chapter 5 ("An Assessment of Process Life-Cycle Models") discusses the purpose and role of software engineering processes. It includes critiques of existing models and proposals for evaluating models. The critical role of time as a factor in development is considered. The lack of an adequate integration between software and hardware technology, on the one hand, and business and social disciplines, on the other, is identified as a persistent shortcoming undermining the ability to attack real-world problems optimally. We then identify a series of questionable assumptions that have affected the development of software process models, including a tendency to assign primacy to the role of internal software factors; the relative independence of software development from the business process; separation of the software project as management enterprise from the software development process; and a restrictive choice between process-centered versus architecture-centered development. These assumptions tend to reduce the role of people, money, interdisciplinary knowledge, and business goals in terms of their impact on the problem solution.

The elements of a redefined software engineering process are then identified based on the integration of critical activities; required major interdisciplinary resources (people, money, data, exploratory and modeling tools, and methodologies); organizational goals; and the impact of time on an ongoing roundtrip approach to business-driven problem solving. The redefinition includes limitations identified in the literature related to business evaluation metrics, the process environment and external drivers, and process continuation, as fundamentals of process definition.

Chapter 6 ("The Problem-Solving Process") considers the relation between classic problem-solving concepts and software development, particularly in a business environment. A basic point concerns the advantages that accrue from exploiting diversity as a tool in problem solving when diversity refers to the differences in cultural or personal background; professional experience; problem perspective; understanding; or technical and disciplinary capability. Diversity is a frequently overlooked resource that offers a unique opportunity for achieving a broader, more integrated approach to solving problems. Failure to capitalize on it undermines the ability of software development to address the complexity of real problems. A related issue is that, because of their technical background, computer scientists may be prone to overemphasizing the centrality of technical capability; however, the correct identification of business goals is often the critical factor for effective development, with business goals providing the criteria and framework according to which the suitability of software systems can be properly assessed. Such an approach is user centered or customer driven. It acknowledges the decisive importance of user perception and assumes solutions should come from a thorough understanding of user needs.

We examine the impact of problem-solving concerns and principles on the development process because software development is closely linked to the concepts and strategies of problem solving. A review is presented of the basic ideas regarding problem solving and some of the kinds of problems that arise specifically in business environments, such as how to meet standards; selection from a set of alternative solutions; satisfying customer expectations; goal evolution; and improving organizational process. Finally, a brief review of the theory of problem solving, its concepts, methods, strategies, and their relation to approaches used in software development is given, together with some classic approaches used in business problem solving.

Chapter 7 ("Software Technology and Problem Solving") examines how the introduction of information processing has changed the way in which people and organizations address problems. Chapter 6 considers how problem-solving approaches are closely related to how software development is done; Chapter 7 addresses how the availability of software tools influences how problem solving is done. Software serves as the critical enabling technology that automates routine problem-solving activities and interactions, facilitates visualization, supports collocated and distant collaboration, etc. Because software is enabled by technology, advances in problem solving have become coupled with the rapid advances in technology. Software tools are now pervasively used to support classic problem solving tasks from data exploration to communication. A similar pervasive adaptation of software and business processes is seen in the rapid evolution of business operations represented by the e-business revolution, which is reshaping entire industries.

We also consider the impact of the dramatically increasing portability of computing on business processes and the effect of enhanced digitally driven connectivity on development issues such as product cycle time. The flip side of the coin to the enabling power of computing technology concerns its limitations. Although software has provided business managers with capabilities that enhance continual growth and created added business value, revolutionizing communication, portability, and connectivity, software does not represent a complete solution. The challenges to software-driven approaches to problem solving include the diversity of user requirements; the difficulty of capturing requirements; the complexity of business and decision-making processes; the lack of business experience and background among software specialists and developers; and the tight coupling between computer information systems and the people who use them. We consider some of the difficulties involved in adapting software to individual differences and changing organizational environments, as well as difficulties that arise because, naturally, end users are not programmers.

We consider how the introduction of new software systems in complex organizations is problematic for various interdisciplinary reasons. The effective business value that a software system adds to business performance tends to be neither explicitly addressed nor adequately quantified because the traditional focus in software development is on technical metrics intended to assure the technical quality of the software product. We observe that, although project management and fiscally driven factors are part of the software engineering process, they are often not well integrated into the process. Thus, a gap remains between the discipline of management information systems and the software development disciplines, with MIS looking at solutions from a managerial perspective and technical concerns being more influential for software development.

Chapter 8 ("Evolution of Software Development Strategies") further examines how the focus in development has shifted from the technical to the business context. The technical aspects of software development have become increasingly easy. Frequently used code common to many applications such as that for GUIs has already been developed. Web-based collaborative environments provide excellent platforms for rapid communication among experts and developers independently of location. Increasing automation enables even nontechnical users to customize applications to meet special requirements or user preferences. The central challenge to software development today is not to create new code, but to survive an extremely competitive marketplace for software solutions that are on time, on budget, and on target.

Other challenges include accommodating user power, market share, the anytime–anywhere factor, return on investment, and the impact of technology on competitive advantage in development. The close coupling between software and business context is now recognized as a primary factor. This recognition has emerged gradually. In the early era of management isolation, attention was primarily devoted to the technical side of software systems with little emphasis on the business side of development strategy. During the era of business evaluation of software engineering, managers began to take control of the software process with development performance assessed through the expected business outcomes of the product. The current *maturity era* of software engineering is characterized by a high degree of collaboration and partnership between the computing and business domains. The rationale is to create value from diverse needs, backgrounds, and interests in effective collaborative environments. There is significant pressure to incorporate into software development strategies exogenous concepts from financial, managerial, and psychological perspectives, which are being recognized as critical in development.

Chapter 9 ("Diversification of Problem-Solving Strategies in Software Engineering") examines factors that have promoted the diversification of software process models. The intention is to understand more clearly the problem-solving process in software engineering and to identify criteria that can be used to evaluate alternative software-driven problem-solving strategies for differing projects' requirements. A review of software process modeling is given first, followed by a discussion of process evaluation techniques. A taxonomy for categorizing process models, based on establishing decision criteria, is identified that can guide selecting the appropriate model from a set of alternative models on the dual basis of the process model characteristics and the software project needs. The idea is to facilitate adaptability in the software process so that the process can be adapted to special project needs.

The subject of Chapter 10 ("Strategies at the Problem-Engineering Level") is concerned with the correct and complete definition of problems. In a business context, this includes recognizing the managerial, economic, human, and technical aspects of the problem. This requires considering all stakeholders—internal and external, individuals, groups, communities, departments, partners, and other organizations. The expected outcome of problem engineering is a problem definition that reduces uncertainty, equivocality, and ambiguity to a minimum.

Basic methods that can identify relevant interdisciplinary resources include reverse engineering of existing strategies and knowledge bases and finding relevant resources—for example, by using problem decomposition techniques appropriately. The important data collection phase entails generating the stakeholders list; identifying the rationale for change; measuring the risks of change; identifying the root causes of the dissatisfaction with the current situation; surveying for benchmarking and setting evaluation criteria; identifying what the stakeholders are looking for in a solution as well as limitations on the solution; and identifying the tools and techniques available for gathering requirements. After problem-solving data has been carefully examined, verified, evaluated, and structured, it is ready to be presented in a standardized or formal way.

Multidisciplinary thinking helps us understand problems better and therefore solve problems more effectively. The previous chapters address this at the *process* level, examining process structure, process models, process activities, and problem analysis as basic components of the problem-solving process. Chapter 11 ("People and Software Engineering") examines multidisciplinary drivers for development in terms of the *people* dimension. Traditionally, software engineering has considered people as a relevant resource only if they were explicitly involved in carrying out software development tasks. In interdisciplinary software engineering, the concept of people as a resource extends beyond those immediately involved in development to all the individuals who play a significant role in the problem-solving process, regardless of whether they are officially affiliated with the development team. This inclusive concept of human actors comprises those informal but critical human resources without whose cooperation the problem cannot be adequately solved: those engaged through a process of collaboration rather than formal affiliation—stakeholders as customers, managers, and group clients.

The software business is no different from any traditional business: one must invest money and assets in order to generate returns. Software development represents a strategic investment whose purpose is to create a marketable generic software solution or to solve an in-house business problem. Thus, the production of software can be viewed as an economic as well as an engineering process. Chapter 12 ("Economics and Software Engineering") examines various aspects of the role of money and its many surrogates in software development.

To begin with, software-driven problem solving uses money as an input resource to produce a solution. Money subsequently serves as a key performance indicator calibrating the success of the solution or product. However, money does not adequately reflect what is invested or what is expected in return. Software investments entail capital costs, development time, a variety of developer and managerial talents, development effort, and so forth. The expected returns can be expressed in terms of attaining the maximum possible value-creation objectives, including market share, company and product image, technological leadership, etc. This chapter discusses the economic aspects of software engineering and the fundamental role that financial resources play in the software problem-solving process. We also present a fairly detailed review of software cost-development techniques such as COCOMO and the use of function point analysis.

Software development is a complex process driven by factors that are related to problems as well as to solutions. The problem-related factors determine the criteria for the characteristics of the expected solution and help system designers tailor solutions to specific problems. The solution-related factors delineate possible options, assist in making projections, and facilitate scaling and mapping the solutions to problems. It remains an open issue as to whether the preferred software engineering approach should be to develop *generic prescriptions* for common problems (*generalization*) or derive *domain-dependent solutions* to specific problems (*specialization*). Generic approaches are like general-purpose strategies intended to give broad development guidance for an unrestricted class of applications. Generic software development is an incomplete strategy for solving problems because it only supplies guidance for solving problems, not actual solutions to problems at hand. In contrast, specialized approaches are tailored or adapted to a specific type of application. They provide development guidance closely related to the kinds of problems prominent in that category of application. Chapter 13 ("Specialized System Development") examines specialized systems, defining specialized system development, its drivers, advantages and drawbacks, and explores the different types of specialized system development.

About the Authors

Fadi P. Deek received his B.S. in computer science in 1985; his M.S. in computer science in 1986; and his Ph.D. in computer and information science in 1997, all from the New Jersey Institute of Technology (NJIT). He is dean of the College of Science and Liberal Arts, director of the Information Technology Program, and professor of Information Systems and Mathematical Sciences at NJIT, where he began his teaching career as a teaching assistant in 1985. He is also a member of the graduate faculty—Rutgers University Ph.D. Program in Management. Dr. Deek maintains an active funded-research program. His research interests include learning and collaborative systems, software engineering, programming environments, and computer science education.

Dr. Deek has published over 100 papers in journals and conference proceedings and he has given over 40 invited and professional presentations. He is also the author of seven book chapters and coauthor (with J. McHugh) of the book, *Computer-Supported Collaboration with Applications to Software Development* (Kluwer Academic Publishers, 2003). Dr. Deek has received numerous teaching, research, and service awards: The NJIT Student Senate Faculty of the Year Award, given to him in 1992 and 1993; the NJIT Honors Program Outstanding Teacher Award in 1992; the NJIT Excellence in Teaching Award in 1990 and 1999; the NJIT Master Teacher Designation in 2001; and the NJIT Robert W. Van Houten Award for Teaching Excellence in 2002. He has also been awarded the NJIT Overseers Public and Institute Service Award in 1997 and the IBM Faculty Award in 2002.

James A.M. McHugh received an A.B. in mathematics (with a minor in philosophy) from Fordham University in 1965 and the Ph.D. degree in applied mathematics from the Courant Institute of Mathematical Sciences, New York University, in 1970, where he completed his thesis under

National Academy of Science member J. Keller. He has been a member of the technical staff at Bell Telephone Laboratories, Wave Propagation Laboratory; director of the Ph.D. program in computer science at NJIT; and acting chair of the Computer and Information Science Department at NJIT. He was advisor of a thesis on pattern recognition that won the Rutgers University Dissertation Award for Outstanding Doctoral Dissertation.

Dr. McHugh has published over 40 papers in refereed journals and conferences. He is author of the book, *Algorithmic Graph Theory* (Prentice Hall, 1989). He is coauthor (with Chang, Wang, and Healey) of *Mining the World Wide Web* (Kluwer, 2001; Japanese edition, 2003). He is also coauthor (with F. Deek) of *Computer-Supported Collaboration with Applications to Software Development* (Kluwer Academic Publishers, 2003). Dr. McHugh received the Excellence in Teaching Award from NJIT in 2002. His research interests include algorithmic graph; string processing algorithms for bioscience applications; pattern recognition; mathematical analysis and modeling; computer-aided problem solving; Web-based applications; and collaborative technology. Currently, Dr. McHugh is a tenured full professor in the Computer and Information Science Department at NJIT.

Osama M. Eljabiri received his M.S. in information systems in 2001 from NJIT and an M.S. in banking and financial sciences (majoring in information systems) in 1999 from the Arab Academy for Banking and Financial Sciences in Jordan, with distinction. He is a candidate for the Ph.D. degree in Information Systems. Mr. Eljabiri is a lecturer of computer science, information systems, and information technology at NJIT. He teaches, develops and coordinates software engineering courses, and directs the senior project capstone courses in which he manages relationships with numerous industry customers, from Fortune 500 companies to small businesses to public sector and research institutions. Prior to joining NJIT, Mr. Eljabiri held various executive positions at multinational corporations where he led business and IT-driven projects, industrial automation, ISO and BPR quality assurance, and software development projects. His managerial experience has exposed him to the real-world business problems and solution strategies that he brings into the classroom.

Mr. Eljabiri received NJIT's Excellence in Teaching Award in 2001 and the College of Computing Sciences' Excellence in Teaching Award in 2003. His research interests include empirical and object-oriented software engineering; software architecture; interdisciplinary problem solving; requirements engineering; software economics; business process reengineering; project management; data mining; and Web engineering. Mr. Eljabiri has published his work in conferences and journals and is the coauthor of a book chapter in the *Computer Science and Engineering Handbook*.

Section I

The Process and Its Models

Chapter 1

Software Development Strategies: Basic Planning and Control

1.1 Introduction

Software engineering is a cognitive reaction to the complexity of software development. It reflects the inevitable need for analysis and planning; reliability and control of risk; and scheduling and coordination when embarking on any complex human endeavor. The planning and organized effort required in developing software products is not unlike that required in many other activities. As a very simple example, one could compare developing a software product to starting on a journey—both begin with preparation. For a journey, the first decision is to decide the destination. Then, before the journey begins, plans are made so as to arrive at the destination within a reasonable time and at an acceptable cost, with an understanding of the length and constraints of the journey. In doing this, one may evaluate alternative routes to the destination, consider environmental conditions, identify and evaluate potential risks or dangers, and so on.

Similarly, developing a successful software solution involves establishing a destination or product goal; carefully examining alternative designs for the system; identifying potential risks; demarcating milestones along the way; identifying what activities must be done in what sequence or those that may be done in parallel; and identifying needed resources—including human resources, financial resources, information, tools, and strategies. More complex endeavors require more complex planning. Pretested patterns for performing activities, learned from experience and proven helpful, are universally used in commerce and engineering.

For example, extensive standard protocols are followed when constructing a building. The purpose of the building and justification for construction, its detailed architectural design plans, engineering and structural constraints, budget, and scheduling must be clarified or documented. The building design may be highly original or it may rely on preexisting design templates and even prefabricated components. Specific design patterns proven to be useful as solution templates for different kinds of problems may be drawn upon during the design stage of the development. In architecture, such design templates vary with the building type and use. Naturally, the stakeholders in the enterprise must be in agreement, from the customer who has contracted for the building to the architect, builder, and municipal agencies that enforce implementation standards like zoning and building codes, etc.

In software engineering, a variety of similar development protocols or models for organizing development effort have also evolved over time. All these models share certain characteristics. They identify stakeholder goals; specify key activities to be followed according to a certain sequence; work within time constraints; and are based on what has been learned from past experience. For example, at the design stage in software engineering, comparable, successful, reusable design patterns have been recognized, such as those compiled by the so-called Gang of Four (Gamma et al. 1995), just as has been done in architecture.

Similarly, in software engineering, proven useful practices for solving problems become part of so-called best practice, just as in other fields of engineering. A wide array of strategies for organizing the process of software development has emerged over the past four decades. In a sense, these strategies represent pretested patterns for successful development under different conditions. The strategies share generally similar objectives, but reach their goals by different routes. These development strategies are called *software development life-cycle models* or *process models*. They address in an encompassing way the entire, cradle-to-grave, software development process. The notion of a software process model is more general than the related idea of a method or technique, which tends to refer to approaches or tools used in specific stages of the development process.

This chapter introduces and critiques the basic development process and risk reduction models. We observe how these and later models share (in varying degrees and evolving over time) a number of characteristics, beginning with an emphasis on requirements engineering; the use of a multistage development decomposition derived from the Waterfall Model; documentation requirements; stakeholder involvement; project management; a consideration of objectives related to economic or business constraints; and implicit or explicit adoption of recognized best practices in development. Their shared characteristics reflect the universal human, technical, and economic constraints under which development operates. For example, recognition of best practices is a recurrent theme in the evolution of every engineering field. In software development these practices include separation of concerns, deferring design decisions when possible, focusing on stakeholder goals, and, more recently, the application of use cases to identify requirements.

The historical evolution of software process models has played a significant role in how models have diversified over time, with later approaches building on earlier ones and technological advances enabling new approaches. The basic life-cycle models that introduced structured planning and development and applied basic engineering principles to the development of software are considered first. The Waterfall Model was the most influential of these. Incremental and iterative models were introduced to reduce the cycle time for development. These include the Evolutionary Development Model and the early Iterative Enhancement Model, which served as a practical method for achieving step-wise refinement. Incremental development facilitated early solution of implementation problems and reduced risk associated with the late integration of components. Investing in any business involves risk, as does developing a software product.

Thus, the chapter next critiques the basic models that addressed risk in software development, such as the Prototyping and Spiral models. Prototypes are widely used in engineering; examples include rapid, throwaway, exploratory, embedded prototypes, etc., as well as techniques such as the use of presentation prototypes, breadboards, mockups, and pilot systems. Benefits of prototyping include obtaining early feedback from users and motivating user involvement, which help to avoid failure of user satisfaction. The most famous risk reduction strategy is Boehm's Spiral Model, which relies heavily on prototyping but is also designed to allow incorporating other process models into its cycles. Each spiral development cycle is like a mini-life cycle, with its deliverables and assurance processes intended to minimize risk. The win–win spiral variant, which uses a stakeholder approach to determine the objectives–constraints–alternatives for each cycle of the spiral, will be considered. Finally, focus shifts to the Cleanroom Model, which is based on incremental development under statistical quality control and formal correctness principles; this model uses statistically based software testing intended to yield a certifiably reliable software product.

1.2 Characteristics of Software Development Strategies

The software development process models described in this chapter share a number of characteristics. These include an emphasis on the role of requirements engineering; the use of a multistage decomposition approach derived from the Waterfall Model; documentation requirements; stakeholder involvement; project management; objectives related to economic or business constraints; and the implicit or explicit adoption or embedding of recognized best practices. Each of these characteristics will be considered.

All the models, aside from the primitive code-and-fix approach, are problem-solving approaches that apply *requirements engineering* to help solve problems based on varying degrees of problem specification. The models implicitly or explicitly adopt some variation of the four-stage *Waterfall Model*, partitioning the software development into phases such as analysis, design, coding, and maintenance, although the strict linearity of the sequence of stages may not be preserved. The models typically rely heavily on *documentation* and conceptual artifacts such as diagrams as tools for planning development, monitoring its progress, and assuring its quality. The artifacts also provide a degree of traceability for the entire development process, which is a precondition for system testing, modification, and maintenance, as well as for process improvement.

The use of requirements engineering necessitates user or *stakeholder involvement* to ensure that the software product is a valid solution to the underlying problem; however, the level of stakeholder involvement varies considerably across the approaches. Because software development strategies are needed specifically for solving nontrivial problems, the process models also require some type of *project management* in order to manage the complexity of the development process efficiently. The problems addressed by requirements engineering and software development arise in business or organizational contexts in which the bottom line is to produce a profitable software solution that satisfies customer needs in a cost-effective manner and with appropriate quality. An efficient solution to the problem adds economic value to the organization. The economic success of an application is measured in terms of metrics such as profit maximization, cost reduction (Boehm 1984), or customer satisfaction. These *economic goals* are reflected or represented in software process models in terms of project deadlines, budget constraints, and the efficient use of resources (Liu & Horowitz 1989).

The shared characteristics of software process models reflect the shared human, technical, and economic constraints under which the models operate as they try to guide development projects in mapping application problems to software-driven solution using an orchestrated set of tasks.

This chapter briefly considers how these factors have persistently affected process models:

- The need for a well-defined problem definition as an input to the software development process underlies the need to use requirements engineering in process models. Indeed, the need for a well-defined problem definition is what distinguishes the pre-software-engineering era in which code-and-fix approaches prevailed from that in which well-engineered solutions are derived from well-understood problems. Also, increasing emphasis has been put on clear problem definition combined with increasing user involvement; the problems are recognized as user problems regardless of whether the user is internal or external to an organization.

- The tasks needed to produce a well-engineered solution define the second shared factor. Although the nomenclature and details of task decomposition differ, the *analysis–design–coding–testing–maintenance* paradigm appears in most models. However, the relationships between the tasks vary substantially, with tasks sequential in some models, iterative in others, functionally independent or related by transformations, static or dynamic.

- The third shared factor is the role that stakeholders play throughout the development process. Stakeholders can range from users of the software product under development to individuals who decide on the system's requirements to system developers. This factor represents the people dimension of the process and affects every process phase, regardless of the degree of automation, because people are never absent from the process.

- The fourth shared factor is the documentation deliverables that are an essential feature of every software process model. Automated mechanisms like CASE tools may reduce the number of manual deliverables; however, these same tools can also increase the overall amount of documentation. The IBM Cleanroom Model is an example of a system in which automatic transformations across process phases are done using mathematical specification techniques rather than by referencing manual artifacts; this results in a significant reduction of documentation, but does not eliminate it.

- The fifth shared characteristic is that the essential outcome of the development process is economic value because no market exists for economically infeasible software products. As a consequence, cost-reduction and business benefits are the most common measures of effective software production, though this outcome may encompass effects beyond the direct economic impact of the product. The economic objective underscores the importance of project management in process modeling because efficient utilization of resources requires effective project management.

A decisive, historically driven phenomenon that has affected the definition of software models has been the recognition or discovery over time of a variety of principles or *best practices* for software development that have subsequently become embedded in development models. The recognition of such best practices is a recurrent theme in the evolution of every engineering field. Indeed, the best practices in each field often echo those in other fields.

Perhaps the most basic best practice or principle is what is called *separation of concerns*, which recommends intellectually segregating from one another the consideration of different problem-solving issues. This principle is reflected in the separate stages of the software life cycle, each of which focuses on a different part of the development problem. The life-cycle stages also reflect the practice of *deferring decisions* wherever possible to keep the development options as flexible as possible. For example, system design decisions are deferred until the issues of problem analysis and specification are clarified, and so on. Another best practice, related to the pivotal role of users, is to focus on the underlying product objectives, concentrating on the *goals of stakeholders* rather than prematurely examining functional mechanisms for achieving those objectives.

The application of *use cases* during requirements analysis has also become a recognized best practice in more recent models and is prominently embedded in development models like the Rational Unified Process. Of course, the stakeholder goals should drive the identification of the use cases; these goals are more dispositive of what a product should do than of the expected tasks a system should perform because goals are more immediately related to stakeholder intent (Blank 2004).

Some specific best practices have been recognized for the systems analysis stage. For example, in the case in which the system to be developed is intended to replace an existing system, best practice recommends *not* modeling the design of the computerized system on the existing (nonautomated) system. Otherwise, one is likely to reify the structure of the existing system, whose functions could probably be provided more effectively using a design created with computer support in mind. The reason for this is that in-place systems evolve to reflect or adapt to the extant technological, human, and organizational context; a move to (increased) computerization is almost certain to benefit from a very different system or workflow architecture (Blank 2004).

A notable instance of this practice is related to the increasing preference for flat organizational hierarchies. The desired flattening can be achieved by eliminating or streamlining intermediate organizational layers using computer support—a highly important design strategy called *disintermediation*. Disintermediation refers to the elimination or reduction of third-party intermediaries between the client or customer and the server or supplier of goods or services. Such a supply-chain compression of intermediaries is prominently applied in the Internet. Disintermediation is widely recognized as a major factor in the productivity increases that have resulted from computerization (Blank 2004).

The variation in their shared characteristics is the most important source of variation among the software process models. However, in addition to their shared elements, process models also exhibit a number of significant differences rooted in factors like the enabling technology underlying the model; the nature of the problems addressed or the problem-solving approach adopted; interdisciplinary considerations; etc. A context diagram illustrating the important factors affecting the diversity of process models is given in Figure 1.1.

The historical evolution of models has played a major role in how models have diversified over time. Naturally, ideas about how to define models evolved, with later approaches building on earlier ones. Significantly, technological advances enabled new approaches. For example, RAD (Rapid Application Development) was enabled by the introduction of CASE tools and 4GL techniques, and the development of the Internet enabled or accelerated Web-based approaches such as the open source movement. Indeed, some models have been based on the enabling technology as the critical factor.

Models have also reflected underlying problem-solving approaches and not just the general character of the problems. For example, some approaches were based on structured design and others on object-oriented design; some were linear and others iterative; some used sequential workflows and others concurrent workflows. Dependency on the characteristics of the problem-solving methodology naturally affects the kinds of solutions produced because the problem-solving approach adopted by a developer affects how the problem is modeled.

Approaches have also varied with the kind of problem addressed or the problem domain, as well as problem size, structure, and complexity. Some models have been tailored to specific problem domains, and others have been kept relatively generic. Some models were developed with large systems design in mind (DeRemer & Kron 1976); others were developed for small-scale projects. Problem structure varied, often according to its relation to an organizational pyramid; very structured problems arose at the operational level of an organization, semistructured problems at middle-management levels, and unstructured problems at the upper-management or strategic

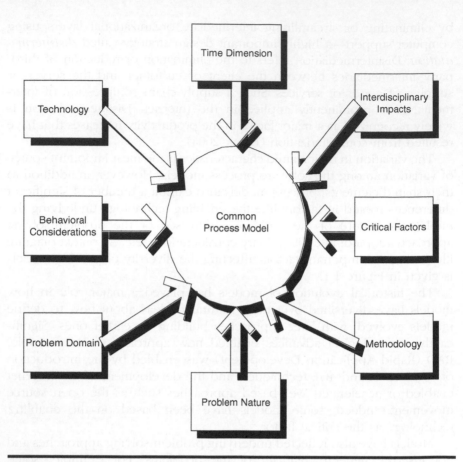

Figure 1.1　Context diagram for software process models.

level. The native organizational level in turn affected the degree of problem uncertainty and equivocality faced by developers (Daft & Lengel 1986).

Problem complexity is related to problem structure and size, and software-related organizational effects, such as the recognized relation between organizational complexity and the impact of technical change (Keen 1981), affect problem complexity and model design. Process models are strongly affected by what people believe to be the critical considerations in managing development. Thus, some models have focused on tasks and task decomposition as the essential element in solving problems, and others have identified people as the essential element and taken a people-centered approach to project management (Abdel–Hamid & Madnick 1989). Risk management was the critical factor motivating the Spiral Model. Interdisciplinary contributions have led to the inclusion of managerial (Abdel–Hamid & Madnick 1989); financial (Ropponen & Lyytinen 2000; Boehm 1984, 1988); and psychological factors (Leveson 2000) in models. Behavioral and social considerations have been notable in recent models and are a primary motivation for incorporating a system dynamics view of software development in process modeling; earlier models that lacked these enhancements were more static in structure (Abdel–Hamid & Madnick 1989; Chase et al. 1994).

1.3 Life-Cycle Models

This section begins the discussion of the different major software development process models. It reviews the basic life-cycle models that first introduced structured planning and development and that applied basic engineering principles to the development of software.

1.3.1 The Waterfall Model

The *Waterfall Model* (see Table 1.1) was one of the first and most influential of the process models. Originating about 1970, it has had a significant historical influence in the evolution of subsequent models and has become the basis for most software acquisition standards (Boehm, 1988). This model was an improved version of an earlier process model called the *Nine-Phase, Stage-Wise Model* (see Bennington 1956 or 1983 and Madhavji et al. 1994). The Nine-Phase Model was a one-directional, sequential model that was enhanced by the waterfall model through the

Table 1.1 Profile of Waterfall Development Model

Category	Specifics
Evolution of goals	Solving stage-wise problems with feedback and explicitly planned development phases
Methodology	Sequential and structured with feedback control
Technology	Not critical
Critical factors	Tasks such as requirements or specification and feasibility analysis and estimation
Interdisciplinary effects	None
Behavioral considerations	None
Problem nature	Large-scale projects
Application domain	General

introduction of bidirectional relations between the successive model stages, corresponding to feedback elements in the development process.

The Waterfall and the Stage-Wise models addressed problems that had been recognized in the most primitive method, the so-called *code-and-fix* approach, which merely iterated through a series of write-code and fix-code steps. The problem with this rudimentary tactic was that after a few iterations, the code would tend to become increasingly poorly structured and consequently increasingly expensive to fix. Furthermore, the implemented products were often poorly matched to the user requirements (Boehm 1988). These problems led to recognition of the need for explicit model development phases as was done in the Nine-Phase Model.

Although the Waterfall Model emphasized the need for feedback between stages, it used a relatively local type of feedback, confining "the feedback to successive stages to minimize the expensive rework involved in feedback across many stages" (Boehm 1988). The Waterfall Model also introduced the notion of prototyping (Madhavji et al. 1994; Boehm 1988). The partitioning of problems into manageable pieces was a significant methodological advance, especially for the design of large or complex systems, as was recognition of the need for feedback loops and the use of basic prototyping in the software life cycle (Boehm 1988).

The different phases in the Waterfall Model incorporate the critical best practice of separation of concerns mentioned previously. In this case, that practice localizes a given class of problem solving issues to a particular phase of the development life cycle. Each phase produces a document as its product. The document summarizes the project work done up to that point so that, after that phase, it is the document "consulted without rethinking any of the decisions that went into it" (Hamlet & Maybee 2001). This is characteristic of the principle of separation of concerns. It helps the software developer maintain "intellectual control of the process" (Hamlet & Maybee 2001). Indeed, the motivation underlying the problem partitioning provided by the life cycle is to reduce the complexity of the problem sufficiently so that the developer can gain a measure of intellectual control of the problem. Of course, this also demands intellectual discipline of the developers. They must resist the temptation to address issues outside the current area of concern. For example, when addressing database requirements with an end user, the developer must ignore such out-of-phase issues as data storage representation.

The Waterfall Model was widely used because it formalized certain elementary process control requirements. It provided an explicit schedule that included quality-control steps at each process completion (Yamamichi et al. 1996). Significantly, this model became "the basis for most software acquisition standards in government and industry" (Boehm 1976, 1981, 1988). Later, in a related vein, the German defense organization introduced

Table 1.2   Profile of V-Shaped Development Model

Category	Specifics
Evolution of goals	Modified version of Waterfall with increased focus on quality assurance and accountability across development phases
Methodology	Sequential
Technology	Not critical
Critical factors	Traceability is established by linking development effects between later and earlier development phases
Interdisciplinary effects	None
Behavioral considerations	None
Problem nature	Large-scale projects
Application domain	General

a modified version of the Waterfall in 1992 called the *V-Shaped Model* (see Table 1.2). This model included validation and verification processes by associating testing activities with the analysis and design phases.

According to standard terminology (IEEE 610.12-1990), *verification* addresses whether a system was built or developed correctly, that is, whether the partial products delivered at each stage satisfied the preconditions defined at the start of that stage. *Validation* addresses whether the right system was built in the sense of satisfying stakeholder goals. The V-Shaped Model also clarified the iteration and reworking steps that tended to be hidden in the Waterfall Model (Madhavji et al. 1994). Thus, it provided the important managerial characteristic of *accountability* by ensuring that earlier stages, such as requirements, high-level design, and low-level design, were properly accounted for in the later compliance stages of acceptance and integration testing and unit testing. Together with project documentation, this helped guarantee traceability between implementation and testing.

Shortcomings of the Waterfall Model included its lack of risk assessment, slow or unresponsive structure, and its inadequacy for object orientation. Furthermore, although the model created a project management structure, it did not provide a guide for activity transformation across phases, thus limiting its ability to handle changes arising during development. Another limitation was the model's view of the development process as similar to a fixed, engineering-based, manufacturing process, rather than a dynamic, problem-solving process that could evolve over time as development experience was gained and learning occurred (Pfleeger 1998). The simple, bidirectional relationship between successive Waterfall phases was insufficient to capture the learning that results from user feedback and involvement.

Another concern was that the model's mandated, document-driven standards often compelled developers to produce "elaborate specifications of poorly understood user interfaces and design-support functions," which was then too often followed by the "design and development of large quantities of unusable code" (Boehm 1988). Boehm (1996) formulated some of these criticisms in a particularly compelling manner. Concerning the inadequacy of written specifications for characterizing the look and feel of a user interface, he quipped that one "prototype is worth 100,000 words." He also observed that the fixed requirements encouraged by the document-driven character of the model tended to lead to so-called *gold-plating*, which refers to inclusion in the system design of overly elaborate or inessential functions. The fixed requirements also inclined towards rigid *point solutions*, which are "optimized around the original problem statement." Boehm (1996) critically observed that the Waterfall's milestones were a misfit to an increasing number of project situations.

Humphrey and Kellner (1989) critiqued the model's failure to address the pervasiveness of change in software development; its unrealistically linear and orderly sequence of software activities; its inability to accommodate developments like rapid prototyping or language advances smoothly; and for providing "insufficient detail to support process optimization." The Waterfall documents used at the earlier specification and design stages frequently lack a level of clarity sufficient to allow effective fault discovery or ensure quality; the result is that errors may be overlooked until final testing. At that late point, correction becomes much more difficult with attendant complex revisions that tend to affect quality adversely (Yamamichi et al. 1996). Despite its drawbacks, the Waterfall Model remains the superclass of many process-modeling approaches in software engineering. Its fundamental notions of problem and solution decomposition and a sequential step-by-step approach with feedback can be improved, but remain essential to managing the complexity of software development.

Lott (1997) describes an interesting variant on the Waterfall, which applies to situations for which the project is contracted incrementally. An initial stage of the development scopes the work, identifies so-called *thin requirements*, and possibly develops a basic interface prototype using a rapid development tool such as Visual Basic, or even a model on paper. The completion of this work constitutes the completion of the contract up to that juncture. At this point, the developer or contractor relationship can be terminated by either party. This strategy represents a software development version of *due diligence* under which, prior to committing to an entire project, each side spends the requisite "time to fully understand the people and the business" (Lott 1997).

Lott's *staged approach* to waterfall-style development allows either party to opt out of the arrangement at preidentified stages, a strategy somewhat reminiscent of the risk-reduction approach used in the Spiral Model. In contrast, in the conventional Waterfall Model, the contractors and developers are essentially compelled "to estimate cost based on limited information" (Lott 1997). This constraint can put either party at a disadvantage. In a fixed-price contract situation, the software developer assumes most of the risk because underestimating cost may lead to a substantial loss. In a time-and-materials contract, the customer for whom the software is developed assumes most of the risk because he or she may pay considerably more than expected if the estimated development costs are exceeded. Risks associated with this approach include unstable budgets and theft of intellectual property. Another risk is what some call (facetiously) "stealth technology transfer" in which the customer uses the product and knowledge acquired in the first stage to acquire the developer's expertise (Lott 1997).

1.3.2 Incremental and Iterative Models

Incremental and iterative models, also called phased development models (Graham 1992), share the common objective of reducing the cycle time for development. Although the terms tend to be used almost interchangeably, distinctions are sometimes made. Iteration entails, as the word implies, a repeated series of attacks on a problem. Each attack or *iteration* is like a miniature development life cycle. Iterative development tends to mean developing a prototype of the *entire product in the first phase* and then repeatedly improving the product in subsequent phases of successive refinement until an effective system is created (Pfleeger 1998). The *incremental* approach also enacts a series of iterations, but the successive iterations are understood as adding incremental functionality to the product. Incremental development tends to be viewed as building a *part of the intended system* in each of a sequence of partial releases until the entire system is completed.

The incremental and iterative models might be compared to depth-first and breadth-first approaches. In a depth-first (incremental) approach, a new functional behavior of the system is implemented in detail at each stage. In a breadth-first (iterative) approach, the set of functions is initially implemented in a broad but shallow manner; many functions are included but only tentatively realized. These shallow functions are then refined as development proceeds. However, as already observed, the usage of these terms is by no means consistent in the literature. For example, the Iterative Enhancement Model of Basili and Turner (1975) is quite similar to the incremental models that Graham (1992) reviewed. Similarly, although so-called *evolutionary development* is usually viewed as an incremental version of the Waterfall Model (Graham 1992), Pressman (1996) categorized incremental development as a subclass of the Evolutionary Model.

Consider the Evolutionary Development Model, which was a reaction to difficulties with the Waterfall Model (McCracken & Jackson 1982). In this approach, "increments of system capability" are released (Boehm 1996) with subsequent stages of development based on user and developer experience with earlier releases. The initial release of the system must not be trivial and must provide "sufficient capability to serve as a basis for user exercise and evaluation" (Boehm 1996). A potential difficulty with evolutionary development is that the initial release may be so far off target that users fail to use it and may even lose confidence in the entire development process. Evolutionary Development also suffers from the same tendency as the Waterfall Model by potentially creating an "inflexible point-solution" (Boehm 1996), with the result, for example, that the initially prescribed software architecture may not scale to the entire system.

As already observed, incremental development models develop the entire system as a "series of partial products, generally with increasing functionality" (Graham 1992). The idea is to develop a succession of small, self-contained systems that eventually converge to a final completed system. The *delivery* of such systems is said to be incremental if these partial products are delivered to users as they are developed, which has been called *evolutionary delivery* (Gilb 1988). The major advantage of evolutionary delivery is the extensive opportunity provided for user feed-back, thus allowing recommendations to be folded back into the development process (Graham 1992).

Each incremental step must include not only implementation, but also testing, documentation, and training. Indeed, each step is intended to constitute a mini-life cycle, complete with its own functional product, manuals, requirement specifications, review reports, etc. Incremental development reflects a recognition that it is often only at the end of development that one clearly realizes how a project should have been defined, designed, and implemented in the first place. This applies to the developer who creates the system as well as to the users who, when finally seeing a completed system, may only then realize that this is *not* the system that they had expected, even though they may have been closely involved in specifying the system. Such surprising user behavior can occur because, just as for the developer, "user knowledge also grows throughout the development process" (Graham 1992).

Of course, surprises could be avoided if the complete system specifications were frozen from the beginning as they are in the Waterfall Model, but this would reduce the benefits that accrue from the growing user and developer knowledge that occurs precisely as a consequence of the incremental development. Another beneficial side effect of incremental or evolutionary delivery is that it brings the new system into an organization inch by inch, thereby decreasing organizational disruption and allowing users to gain familiarity with the use and benefits of the system gradually, without requiring a steep learning curve. This practice can significantly promote user acceptance, a concern that is typically one of the key problems in the successful adoption of new systems.

Graham (1992) contrasted incremental development unfavorably with the monolithic character of the Waterfall Model. The Waterfall approach fixes requirements, costs, and schedule at the earliest point in order to be able to meet "contractual restrictions" (Graham 1992). The monolithic life-cycle approach also postpones the major system test to the end of development; because of the dual impact of the magnitude of testing and scheduling deadlines, this can lead to an opportunistic contraction of the system test. According to Graham, such a monolithic approach is suitable only for "small systems, of short duration, where the requirements are well known at the beginning of development and unlikely to change."

It is important when doing incremental development to "keep the increments as small as possible, provided they will provide a useful function to the users" (Graham 1992). The requirements must be frozen during each incremental step; however, because the steps are incremental, unlike in the Waterfall Model, this is comparable to freezing "ice cubes instead of icebergs" (Graham 1992)—a droll analogy. Graham also alludes to Boehm's classic observation that "developing software requirements is like walking on water; it's easier if it's frozen" (Graham 1992), observing in respect to incremental development that "it is easier to freeze a pond than an ocean."

Various strategies are possible for deciding which increments to develop in which order. For example, critical tasks can be implemented first to reduce development risk, or one may possibly develop interface components to allow testing, or possibly important functional features to support incremental product delivery. Graham recommends three guidelines: think small, think useful, and think complete. Think small refers to developing as minimal an increment as possible to produce a partial product. Think useful refers to the need to remember a key motivation behind incremental development—that is, rapidly providing a benefit to the user. Think complete refers to the intention that each incremental phase should be treated as a small, self-contained life cycle.

Similar to the incremental development discussed by Graham, Basili and Turner (1975) very early defined what they called *iterative enhancement* as a practical way to achieve step-wise refinement. A paradoxical or systemic problem with step-wise refinement is that it side steps the dilemma that it is difficult to identify a good design for a solution to a problem at the beginning because the difficulties with a design only show up as the implementation proceeds. As a response to this, Basili and Turner proposed to develop the system through a series of subsystems; the emerging system would be understood more thoroughly as the process proceeded—just like what happens in a learning process. This learning process can be used to improve the design as the system is iteratively extended through a sequence of partial systems, ultimately converging to the complete solution. The outcome at each iterative step is a simple extension of the functionality of the system or a redesign of the preceding implementation "motivated by a better understanding of the problem, obtained through the development process" (Basili & Turner 1975).

The developer begins with an implementation of a skeletal subproblem and maintains a *project control list* identifying the remaining tasks needed to complete the project. At any point in time, the control list "acts as a measure of the distance between the current and the final implementation" (Basili & Turner 1975). A good skeletal system should have several characteristics. It should contain a good sample of the key desired system functions. It should be "simple to understand and implement easily" and the initial system should produce a "usable and useful product" for the user. The implementation extension at each successive step should be straightforward so as to be modified easily and thereby allow redesign when difficulties or flaws are recognized. The project control list is dynamically revised as the "successive implementations" are analyzed. The idea is that the repeated analysis and redesign of an increasingly well-understood system tends to lead to a reliable product. Thus, iterative enhancement is not like the more familiar iterative refinement of an entire problem solution, but iterative extension of the functionality of partial systems as is done in incremental development.

Advantages of incremental development include:

- Improved development team morale
- Early solution of implementation problems
- Reduced risk of the disasters that occur because a system cannot be developed as proposed or because of late integration of components
- Improved maintenance
- Improved control of overengineering or gold-plating
- Measurement of productivity
- Estimation feedback
- Smoother staffing requirements

Table 1.3   Profiles of Incremental and Iterative Development Models

Category	Specifics
Evolution of goals	Reduce risk and improve user satisfaction
Methodology	Iterative or incremental
Technology	Can accelerate the process
Critical factors	User feedback
Interdisciplinary effects	Cognition
Behavioral considerations	User expectations
Problem nature	Smaller systems
Application domain	General

It exploits the advantage of the partial systems developed to fix unanticipated problems quickly and train users in parallel with software improvement. This strategy can partition development work more efficiently because each of the self-contained incremental stages requires a similar mix of personnel because it constitutes a mini-life cycle (Graham 1992). It increases the ability to measure productivity more effectively by doing so with respect to the release of meaningful partial products rather than in terms of metrics such as the amount of code developed (Pfleeger 1998).

Difficulties with incremental and iterative development (see Table 1.3) include hardware-related problems, life-cycle problems, management problems, financial and contractual problems, and user–developer relationship problems (Graham 1992). For example, the hardware chosen for the initial system will be based on specifications that have not yet been finalized, with a corresponding increased risk to system development. The response time of the initial simplified system may also be significantly faster than the fully developed system, generating high initial expectations from users, which may be subsequently disappointed as the system extends and performance deteriorates under further development complexity. Graham suggests circumventing this difficulty by using the artifice of including "slowing-down system code" initially. The slowing code is removed when the system is later performance tuned. Generally speaking, incremental approaches require dealing with a great deal of uncertainty, issues of configuration management, and organizational culture change.

The iterative approach serves as the strategic framework for the Unified Process Model proposed by the UML object-oriented group at Rational Rose and for many other software process improvement models such as the Spiral Model. Because of their piecemeal character, the Iterative and

Incremental process models are often used by the Spiral Model, with project risk reduced as each new increment or iteration is reviewed and enhanced. Prototyping can play a significant role in Incremental and Iterative development. These methods also overlap the Rapid Application Development (RAD) approach because the latter shares the same goal of reducing process cycle times. Applied in combination with CASE tools, RAD and prototyping can be used to improve the efficiency of Incremental and Iterative process models.

1.4 Risk-Reduction Models

Building a bridge or investing in a business involves a risk, as does developing a software product. Just as with other enterprises, the product may turn out to be harder to construct than expected—or even infeasible—or the market for the product may disappear. This section reviews various models that address the issue of risk in software development.

1.4.1 The Prototyping Model

Prototypes are used in many engineering disciplines. Although what constitutes a software or information systems prototype cannot be uniquely defined, there are three readily identifiable characteristics. The *prototype* should be able to (Alavi 1984; Lichter, Schneider–Hufschmidt, & Zullighoven 1994):

- Be a temporary system
- Be designed rapidly
- Provide a tangible or visual expression of a proposed system

Prototyping (see Table 1.4) has been adopted in almost every process model since the Waterfall Model and was even thought of as an extension to the bidirectional, feedback-control feature of that model (Boehm 1988). The prototyping approach usually involves building a small version of the intended system prior to building the proposed complete system. This allows developers an opportunity to work out the kinks in the specification and design of the system before its full-scale development is attempted; the expectation is that this will significantly reduce the risk of development. The need for such risk reduction may derive from the novelty of the application or because the user interface design requires user experience and feedback based on the user's live interaction with a tangible approximation of the desired product (Graham 1992).

Table 1.4   Profile of Prototyping Development Model

Category	Specifics
Evolution of goals	Overcoming the risks of late implementation in long development cycles
Methodology	Iterative
Technology	Programming tools and languages to facilitate prototyping
Critical factors	User feedback
Interdisciplinary effects	Psychological; learning processes
Behavioral considerations	Interactions with users; effects on user expectations
Problem nature	Small-scale projects, but can be integrated with other large-scale oriented models
Application domain	General

Prototyping can be accomplished in various ways and (be forewarned) they are not necessarily mutually exclusive. The terminology *rapid prototyping* usually refers to the rapid development of a primitive system based on the use of tools such as code generators or 4GL languages. So-called "quick and dirty" or *throwaway prototyping* refers to situations in which the prototype is discarded once development of the actual system begins (Graham 1992). Alternatively, the prototype might sometimes be used by a customer until the full system becomes available. Throwaway prototypes do not have to be developed according to the same strict process standards as those for an actual system. A throwaway prototype is thus like an experimental system that is later replaced by an actual production system (Alavi 1984). In terms of waterfall phases, throwaway prototypes are most commonly used during the analysis or requirements and design phases of development.

The term *incorporated prototype* refers to a prototype intended to be included eventually in a real product in some fashion. In such a case, the prototype development should follow normal development standards, including the maintenance of appropriate documentation, testing, and so on. If a sequence of prototypes is developed, then the development process becomes similar to that used in incremental development as described previously. One classification distinguishes five categories of prototypes:

- *Exploratory prototyping* refers to the use of prototyping as a technique for gathering and clarifying requirements (Floyd 1984). This approach gives the developer a better understanding of the user's work problems and needs and helps the users clarify their requirements as well.

- *Experimental prototyping* is used as a testing or evaluation technique to verify whether the proposed system will meet user or customer expectations, to determine system feasibility, or to explore alternative solutions.

- *Evolutionary prototyping* is used to explore changing requirements incrementally and adapt a system to them.

- *Embedded prototyping* refers to prototyping as a component of another software development strategy. A convenient dichotomy is between horizontal and vertical prototyping.

- In *horizontal prototyping*, most of the system functions are at least nominally accessible, but only a few are actually operational. In *vertical prototyping*, a narrow vertical slice of the system functions is implemented.

Another dichotomy is between low-fidelity and high-fidelity prototyping. *Low-fidelity prototyping* simulates the proposed product in some very rudimentary way—even by pencil and paper, or by slides (Nielsen 1990). *High-fidelity prototyping* is intended to closely mimic the look and feel and the responsiveness of the system, including its temporal delay characteristics. However, it is generally not straightforward to mimic the nonfunctional requirements of a system in a prototype (such as speed of response) precisely because the prototype is only a draft implementation of the system. Thus, its performance characteristics may not be at all representative of the actual system; they may be possibly slower or faster in terms of response.

Lichter et al. (1994) comment on the usefulness of a variety of other kinds of prototypes such as presentation prototypes, breadboards, mockups, and pilot systems for successful development. For example, a *presentation prototype* can serve a marketing purpose by illustrating to potential users the expected system behavior. It provides users a concrete, first look at a real version of the intended system. *Breadboards* help the developers determine whether proposed technical characteristics of the system will work. *Mockups* can determine whether the system will be usable, for example, by tricking up an interface shell to give the user a feel for the span of system functions and their accessibility. *Pilot systems* provide essential system functions and, after a few evolutionary iterations, can develop into the complete system.

Prototypes can be coded in any language, but some special, high-level languages are particularly relevant. Prolog is one example. Prolog allows one to program the first-order predicate calculus and can be used to help test the correctness of formal specifications. CASE, 4GL, user interface generators, and visual programming tools such as Visual Basic are other examples of enabling technologies. The use of reusable components glued together to implement a prototype is another approach. Shell scripts in UNIX, which allow the programmer to define interacting collections of commands, are also powerful programming tools for rapid prototyping.

Lichter et al. (1994) observed that prototyping reflects an evolutionary view of software development. It is closely related to incremental development except that, in prototyping, the development phase turn-around time is reduced by the quick development of a primitive version of the product. In contrast, in incremental approaches, the successive development steps are kept short in time by restricting the augmented work product of a given cycle to simple increments of system function.

Prototyping has been proposed for several purposes in process modeling (Pfleeger 1998; Alavi 1984; Lichter et al. 1994). Thus, it can be used as a generic tool in the development process. Pfleeger (1998) argued that it could form the basis of a complete process model and proposed a comprehensive prototyping model beginning with system requirements and ending with a complete delivered system, with iterative revisions implemented during the process. On the other hand, other studies have contended that prototyping does not offer effective support for structuring the software development process and is most appropriately used only as an integrated part of the conventional software development life cycle (Lichter et al. 1994).

Aside from being integrated with other process models, prototyping is obviously especially helpful in model phases like requirements or in assessing the feasibility of the entire development cycle for which it can be used as an experimental tool. Minimally, prototyping is an option in the case in which developers are dealing with "undecided users and clarifying fuzzy requirements" or when there is a "need for experimentation and learning before commitment of resources to development of a full-scale system" (Alavi 1984). The Operational Specification Model of Zave (1982, 1984) is a variation of prototyping based on the use of so-called *executable specifications*, which allow testing incomplete, executable formal specifications that can be dynamically extended by step-wise refinement.

Some of the major benefits of prototyping (Lichter et al. 1994) include the ability to:

- Gain important feedback from users early in the development process
- Provide a common baseline for users and developers to identify problems and opportunities
- Motivate user involvement
- Help prevent misunderstanding between users and developers
- Strengthen working relationships between the users and developers

Prototyping represents an experimental method for obtaining an understanding of a proposed system for the user and the developer. Timely prototype development greatly increases project visibility in the user organization by quickly providing a working system; helps the project gain credibility with the prospective users; and gives the users a greater sense of ownership or buy-in into the project because it allows their immediate impact on the system design (Alavi 1984). The availability of a tangible system cognitively facilitates user feedback because they can critique and evaluate a tangible, existing system, rather than speculatively describe what they need in a potential system. Early exposure to the prototype system also tends to increase user utilization of the system (Alavi, 1984).

The prototype provides a common baseline in the sense of a "reference point for both users and designers by which to identify problems and opportunities early in the development process" (Alavi 1984). The interaction between developers and users that occurs as a result of discussions of the prototype also tends to lead to "better communication and rapport, and a better appreciation of each other's jobs," thereby enhancing the working relationship between the two groups (Alavi 1984). These improvements in user–developer dynamics are significant advantages, given the recurrent behavioral problems between developers and users in systems development. Furthermore, although prototyping is commonly perceived to be more expensive, it addresses some of the limitations of the Waterfall Model, such as an ability to deal with semistructured or nonstructured requirements (Khalifa & Verner 2000).

Prototyping has been criticized for a variety of shortcomings (Alavi 1984), including:

- Leading users to overestimate the capabilities of a software product
- Difficulties in project management and control
- Difficulty in applying the technique to large systems design
- Potential difficulties in maintaining necessary user interest

The management difficulties arise partly from the difference between the prototyping approach and the more well-defined life-cycle approaches: system specifications evolve over the course of the project; users are more involved; and changes are more frequent. Management is consequently complicated by the uncertainty of the development; the revisions to the prototype or versions of the prototype; and the associated potential for reduced development discipline, which is required in order to maintain proper managerial control. Ironically, although the quick availability of a responsive prototype can stimulate user interest, heightened interest may decline precisely because "high priority user requirements" may have been satisfied by the prototype (Alavi 1984).

1.4.2 The Spiral Model

In terms of software development, the term *risk* may be defined as the state or property of a development project that, if ignored or left unresolved, will increase the likelihood of project failure (Ropponen & Lyytinen 2000). Alternatively, Boehm (1991) defined risk as "potential loss times the probability of loss." Perhaps one should call risk neither necessarily a clear nor a present danger, but a threat nonetheless. Even a straightforward risk analysis of a basic problem may be quite complex. As an illustration, consider the case of the risk involved if a firewall has a security hole. A certain probability is that the hole will be detected by a potential intruder and used for exploitation. Another probability is that the perpetrator or the intrusion will be detected. There is an estimated cost to the intruder if detected as well as an estimated damage to the organization if the perpetrator is successful (Walnau, Hissam, & Seacord 2002).

It is easy to see that, for a full-scale development project, a risk analysis can be daunting. Risk is information dependent because the more certain information is available about a project and its global context, the lower the expectation of risk will be. Some recent investigators have considered a more nuanced understanding of risk, differentiating among risk, uncertainty, danger, and chance. Thus, Stahl, Lichtenstein, and Mangan (2003) identify *uncertainty* as referring to the lack of knowledge of the future, *danger* to factors beyond the control of the participants, and *chance* to the possibility that future events may produce unforeseen opportunities that can lead to a positive or negative reevaluation of the current project. However, these terms do not have a uniformly agreed on meaning. Any software development incurs a risk of failure because the system is large or novel, or because resources may prove inadequate.

Addressing risk in software development has been an important driving factor in the evolution of process models. Boehm (1984) seems to have been the first to emphasize explicitly the importance of the concept of risk factors in development, although previous models addressed risk implicitly. In any case, the introduction of risk-driven models was a major advance over the existing document-driven or code-driven models.

Table 1.5 Profile of Spiral Development Model

Category	Specifics
Evolution of goals	Addressing risk assessment (inadequately handled in previous process models)
Methodology	Iterative, with risk metrics and collaborative reevaluation
Technology	Recent automated tools can facilitate model generation
Critical factors	Risk management and collaboration
Interdisciplinary effects	Economics, psychology, sociology
Behavioral considerations	High level of user interaction especially in the win–win version
Problem nature	Mainly large-scale projects with a high degree of uncertainty
Application domain	General

In Boehm's risk-focused *Spiral Model* (see Table 1.5), project development consists of a series of Waterfall-like cycles. Each cycle addresses the development of the software product at a further level of elaboration; the cycle begins with an initial concept and progresses to the coding of individual components. The Spiral Model is usually depicted as an expanding spiral curve in contrast to the linear diagram of the classic Waterfall Model. The Spiral embodies the idea that the model repeatedly circles back again to a go or no-go decision on the project, based on repeatedly revised understandings of the risk of the development.

The *radial dimension* of the Spiral reflects the project development cost to date, increasing as the project progresses. The *angular aspect* of the Spiral reflects the extent of completion of a particular cycle. Each cycle consists of four phases: analysis; design; code; and test—just as the entire Waterfall Model does. In each successive cycle, the developers identify the objective of "the portion of the product being elaborated" (Boehm 1988), as well as alternative implementations and constraints under which the alternatives must operate. The developers then reevaluate the alternatives with respect to the project's objectives and constraints; they identify potential sources of development risk or uncertainty for the project and promising means for resolving or alleviating these risks.

The Spiral Model relies heavily on prototyping (Yamamichi et al. 1996) and on concepts from software engineering economics to understand and minimize development risk (Boehm, 1984). For example, the risk analysis and resolution may entail prototyping or risk-resolution techniques such as benchmarking and simulation. If the performance characteristics of the proposed system are decisive, then prototyping may be used to resolve outstanding risk issues with the expectation that the prototype can exhibit a solution that is "operationally useful and robust enough to serve as a low-risk base for future product evolution" with subsequent phases also evolving through a series of prototypes. If the performance risks are decided to be acceptable or resolved and program development risks come to predominate, then the next cycle of the spiral may follow a waterfall approach. Yamamichi et al. (1996) describe the Spiral Model as similar to a prototyping approach in which an initial software core or kernel is repeatedly confirmed through testing as functions are added. This makes the model quite effective in evaluating and verifying quality and performance as development proceeds.

The model is highly flexible and designed for customization (Boehm 1988). It allows one to incorporate other process models (such as the Waterfall, Evolutionary, Incremental, or Transform models) in an inclusive framework driven by project requirements and the dual objective of maximizing user satisfaction while minimizing development uncertainty. As an example of the flexible choice of methodology at each phase, the developers may choose to use simulation rather than prototyping to test the feasibility of the project.

Alternative development models can be used as tools on an as-needed basis rather than being adopted in their entirety. The Spiral Model illustrates how process models can be combined with one another to good effect, such as by integrating prototyping (or, say, simulation) in order to reduce risk. Additionally, formal methods can be combined with prototyping to further improve the quality of the process (Liu et al. 1998). In fact, the Spiral Model can be used as a process-model generator by combining it with a model decision table that automates guided decisions on process selection (Boehm & Belz 1988).

The spiral model's structure enforces close attention to user satisfaction and approval as it iterates through the succession of cycles of validation and verification. Each cycle closes with a review by the stakeholders of the system being developed that has the objective of ensuring a consensus that "all concerned parties are mutually committed to the approach for the next phase" (Boehm 1988). The consensus points act as anchors or project milestones. Furthermore, the stakeholder consensus entails agreement not only on the plan for the following phase, but also on the resources required to carry out the plan. These spiral risk-reduction reviews can be as simple as a programmer walk-through or, at the other extreme, may involve all classes of stakeholders from customers and users to developers and maintainers. Boehm proposes a hypothesis-testing view of the entire development process.

The Spiral gets started with the hypothesis that a "particular operational mission (or set of missions)" can be improved by a proposed software effort. This hypothesis is then recurrently tested and perhaps modified as the spiral develops, with termination of the development process if, at any point, the hypothesis is shown to fail the test. The failure may well be for exogenous reasons, such as because a window of opportunity for the product passes or because a better product becomes available. Terminologically, Boehm describes the model as comprising a succession of different types of *rounds* in the spiral.

The startup round 0 consists of a preliminary feasibility study. The following round 1 is the concept-of-operation round. Round 2 is a top-level requirements specifications round. Succeeding rounds vary depending on the project. Eventually a finished system or product is produced; however, because of the compromises and revisions made along the way, it may vary considerably from the initial intention.

The Spiral Model inherits the advantages of the existing process models that it incorporates, but tries to overcome their limitations by its persistent focus on development risk management. Boehm (1988) claimed on the basis of empirical experience at TRW that projects that used the system increased productivity by 50 percent. Some difficulties are associated with application of the model, however. For example, complications occur when it is used in the context of contract-based software acquisition; in which system specifications are agreed upon up front and consequently the highly fixed specification-oriented Waterfall Model is favored. The spiral approach also relies on experience with risk assessment and the need for "explicit process guidance in determining [the] objectives, constraints, and alternatives" required for the next cycle of elaboration (Boehm 1996).

Boehm (1988) claimed that the spiral approach was adaptable to the full range of software projects and flexible enough to dynamically accommodate a range of technical alternatives and user objectives. However, the model's risk classification needs further calibration to be more broadly applicable. Boehm's proposed list of risk-related factors in software development was popular and widely adopted. However, Ropponen and Lyytinen (2000) contend that these risk factors were excessively oriented towards very large software systems and also lacked an adequate theoretical foundation in the sense that they were inductively derived. Boehm's list included factors that needed further resolution or decomposition; some of the risks were not distinct from one another and thus covaried. Overall, the risks had a preponderantly project management flavor. The connotation of risk has been generally negative, but, more recently, so-called opportunistic interpretations of risk have been considered (Smith, McKeen, & Staples 2001). Stahl et al. (2003) examine the socially constructed nature

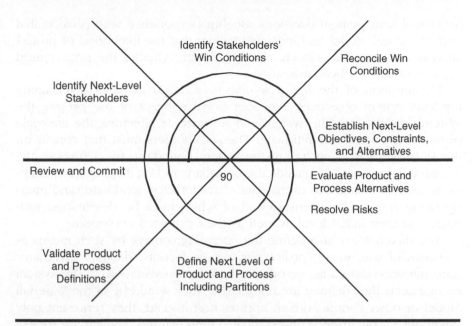

Figure 1.2 Win–Win Spiral Model. (Adopted from Boehm, B., *IEEE Computer*, 21(5), 61–72, 1988.)

of risk, its strong dependence on the perceptions of different classes of stakeholders, and even the risk of overlooking risks.

In the course of several papers (Boehm & Bose 1994; Boehm 1988; Boehm & Port 1999), Boehm and his colleagues extended the spiral model to a variant called the *Win–Win Spiral Model*; this was intended to "converge on a system's next level objectives, constraints, and alternatives" (Boehm 1988) using a so-called *win–win stakeholder approach* to determine the objectives–constraints–alternatives for each cycle of the spiral. This approach entailed identifying the stakeholders of the system, determining their (win) conditions, and negotiating an agreed upon set of objectives–constraints–alternatives. Figure 1.2 illustrates the process elements, including "identify next level stakeholders," "identify stakeholders' win conditions," and "reconcile win conditions" (Boehm 1988). In a sense, these steps define a "collaborative foundation for the model." The modified approach fills a critical gap in the original Spiral Model by providing a means for resolving such fundamental questions as, "Where do the next-level objectives and constraints come from?" and "How do you know they're the right ones?" (Boehm 1996).

Boehm's (1996) win–win stakeholder approach is used to determine three critical project milestones that together anchor the development of the project: namely, life-cycle objectives, life-cycle architectures, and initial operational capability. These milestones act as a set of reference points for critical management decisions. Boehm's experience with projects that used the Spiral Model had indicated to him that the likelihood of project success or failure was closely connected with whether the project used the equivalents of these milestones.

Identification of the *life-cycle objectives* (LCO) includes determining top-level system objectives; the operational concept of the project; the system requirements; the system and software architecture; the life-cycle plan; and the feasibility rationale. The stakeholders must first concur on the *system objectives*, including the system boundary. By definition, the system environment lies outside the boundary and establishes key parameters; assumptions about users; data characteristics; workload; and inter-operating system characteristics—all of which must be determined with respect to their initial level as well as their expected evolution.

The stakeholders also define the *operating concept* by such means as scenarios of use, using "prototypes, screen layouts, dataflow diagrams, state transition diagrams, or other relevant representations." The system requirements thus defined are not fixed as they would be in the Waterfall Model or other contract-driven approaches; instead, they represent only stakeholder "concurrence on essential system features," which are subject to subsequent collaborative modification as opportunities or difficulties arise. At least one feasible *architectural definition* must be identified to demonstrate the ability of the plan to support system objectives. Consistent with the Spiral Model's risk-driven philosophy, if a viable architectural option cannot be identified at this point, then the project should be cancelled or its scope reworked. As a part of the *life-cycle plan*, stakeholders are identified, including any organizations that supply major systems with which the proposed system must interoperate. A simple organizing principle that scales to small projects is the *WWWWWHH principle*, which addresses:

- Why is the system being developed (objectives)?
- What is supposed to be done?
- When (milestones and schedules) is it supposed to be done?
- Who is responsible for a particular function?
- Where are they organizationally (responsibilities)?
- How will the work be done (approach)?
- How much of each kind of resource will be needed to do the work (resources)? (Refer to Boehm, 1996.)

The *life-cycle architecture* (LCA) milestone primarily elaborates on the LCO elements, including the system and software components, mediators between these components, and constraints. It specifies, as necessary, off-the-shelf or reusable software components, as well as performance attributes such as response time and reliability, and likely architectural trends over time. This milestone should lead to stakeholder agreement on the feasibility of the architecture and its compatibility with the stakeholder life-cycle objectives. The life-cycle architecture should conclude with "all the system's major risks resolved or at least covered by an element of the system's risk management plan" (Boehm 1996). If the life-cycle architecture milestone is considered unsatisfactory, this once again indicates that the stakeholders must reconvene to work out a plan that meets the milestone criteria.

Unlike the usual software project milestones, the LCO and LCA milestones explicitly emphasize how specifications can meet system evolution, i.e., they are not intended to be mere point-in-time snapshots. The specifications are far more flexible in terms of how they can be defined; for example, they can be prototypes or off-the-shelf products. *The emphasis is consistently on the risk attached to the specifications rather than their completeness.* For example, critical interfaces should be completely defined, but user interfaces are "less risky to define as prototypes" and thus represent a less urgent consideration. The (cycle) process model used is flexible: it may be Spiral or it may be the Waterfall or another method. Most importantly, stakeholder concurrence on the milestones "establish[es] mutual stakeholder buy-in to the plans and specifications, and enables a collaborative, team approach to unanticipated setbacks rather than the adversarial approach in most contract models" (Boehm 1996).

The *initial operational capability* (IOC) milestone occurs at the end of the development cycle. This includes software preparation (software support, documentation, licensing, etc.); site preparation (off-the-shelf vendor arrangements); and user and maintainer preparation. The progression from LCA to IOC can be done using any suitable mix of models. Boehm (1996) describes the successful application of the Win–Win Spiral Model to a DoD (Department of Defense) project called STARS. The project used a custom mix of software process models (Waterfall, Evolutionary, Incremental, Spiral, and COTS) to suit different project needs.

1.4.3 The Cleanroom Model

The *Cleanroom* approach (see Table 1.6) to software engineering was developed at IBM by Harlan Mills around 1982. It uses a team-oriented model that focuses on enforcing the use of theoretically sound engineering processes and practices. It has three foundations: incremental development under statistical quality control; software development based on mathematical principles; and software testing based on statistical principles. Its quality-control-driven philosophy is intended to improve the manageability

Table 1.6 Profile of Cleanroom Development Model

Category	Specifics
Evolution of goals	Focus on accuracy, reliability, reducing ambiguity, incompleteness, inconsistency
Methodology	Mathematical transformation and statistical testing of usage profiles
Technology	Facilitated by software automation
Critical factors	Specification language
Interdisciplinary effects	Mathematical specification, statistical sampling, project management
Behavioral considerations	Peer-review teams
Problem nature	Complex systems
Application domain	General

and predictability of the development process. Its formal mathematical and correctness techniques are intended to ensure its validity.

The idea of the Cleanroom Model is that by developing software under statistical guaranteed levels of quality control, one can produce a certifiably reliable product that "exhibits zero failures in the field" (Oshana & Linger 1999). The approach puts an intense premium on "defect prevention, effectively eliminating costly error removal phases (i.e., debugging)" in order to produce "verifiably correct software parts" (Oshana & Linger 1999). Each incremental component is "measured and compared with preestablished standards to determine whether or not the process is in control" (Oshana & Linger 1999) before developers move onto the next increment.

Rigorous intellectual control of the process is achieved by using ongoing reviews by a small, highly qualified team and applying formal methods at every incremental phase (Trammell, Binder, & Snyder 1992). This leads to what is tantamount to an inductively established level of correctness based on mathematical and statistical "certification of code increments as they accumulate into a system" (Trammell et al. 1992). A central theme is to develop modules correctly the first time and verify their correctness even *before* (that's right, *before!*) execution and testing; the idea is to eliminate the need for expensive defect-treatment processes. Linger and Trammell (1996) cite remarkable improvements in reliability for Cleanroom-designed systems. Oshana and Coyle (1997) describe a highly successful application of Cleanroom techniques to a large-scale, real-time system and claim that the intense emphasis on defining unambiguous and complete requirements led to a significant reduction of risk. The approach is applicable not only to newly developed systems, but also to legacy environments by appropriately reengineering existing legacy components.

The testing process in Cleanroom is intended to demonstrate the validity of the system under expected usage, rather than to detect and remove defects. First, a highly detailed *usage profile* or specification is defined; this serves as the basis for thorough random testing of the intermediate products, with the final product therefore expected to represent a scientific level of quality certification. In fact, the performance of the software on the tests is viewed as defining a statistical experiment in which a thorough set of "test cases [is] randomly generated from the usage model" (Oshana & Linger 1999). The test cases are selected to be a statistically representative sample of the system's expected usage, so the testing is arguably as reliable as any statistical sampling process. This kind of sampling is a realistic approach, given that exhaustive testing is almost always computationally impossible because of the vast number of potential test cases.

The software components are viewed as defining mathematical functions in which the function domain is the set of possible input histories and the function range is the set of all correct outputs. The functions are described using different kinds of *box structures*. In an object-oriented context, a so-called *black box* would correspond purely to the behavior of an object; a *state box* would correspond to the object's encapsulated state data; and a *clear box* would correspond to the object's methods. The specifications of system functions and their design decompositions are required to satisfy *referential integrity*, which means that the design and the specification correspond to the same mathematical function. If referential integrity is satisfied, then the design is a provably correct implementation of the specification (Linger & Trammell 1996). The correctness is verified by the review teams by checking the correctness of the effects of individual control structures, an approach that turns out to be "remarkably effective in eliminating defects, and is a major factor in the quality improvements achieved" (Linger & Trammell 1996).

The Cleanroom Development Architecture comprises 14 processes and 20 work products that, in combination, implement the development technology (Mills, Dyer, & Linger 1987). Just to give a sense of what is involved in the development process these processes will be briefly mentioned.

- The Management Processes involve project planning; project management; performance improvement; and engineering change.
- The Specification Processes comprise requirements analysis; function specification; usage specification; architecture specification; and increment planning.

- The Development Processes consist of software reengineering; increment design; and correctness verification.
- The Certification Processes are the usage modeling and test planning process and the statistical testing or certification process.

Linger and Trammell (1996) offer a detailed discussion of each Cleanroom process and process element. Some highlights will be discussed briefly here.

- The performance improvement process is a reflection of the fact that the Cleanroom process structure is not static, but explicitly subjected to review and adjustment.
- In contrast, the engineering change process addresses modifications with regard to the work product rather than the process. In collaboration with the customer, the requirements analysis process creates a software requirements document, which defines the system function, usage, and environment and obtains customer agreement.
- The function specification process transforms the requirements into a mathematically precise form and completely specifies possible customer usages.
- The usage specification process identifies users and their usage scenarios and environments, as well as probability distributions for software usage. This can help prioritize development and facilitate scheduling and resource planning.
- The architectural specification process defines the conceptual model for the architecture and spans the entire life cycle.
- Increment planning is a process that supervises a revisable strategy for incremental development.
- The reengineering process adapts the system to reusable components possibly developed *outside* the Cleanroom framework. In such a case, the components are redesigned to Cleanroom standards or the Cleanroom software is protected from the preexisting components through what amount to "firewalls."
- As part of the increment design process, the development team develops an increment, although the certification team first executes the process.
- Using mathematical techniques, the development team performs correctness verification during team reviews to ensure that the software is a correct implementation of the specifications.
- The usage and test planning process refines the usage models, defines the test plans, and statistically generates the test cases. In principle, the usage model allows an unlimited number of test

cases, but only a finite sample is derived from the usage model on the basis of the usage probability distribution.

■ The statistical testing and certification process then statistically establishes the software's "fitness for use." Depending on the certification results, testing can, for example, be continued, terminated, or stopped to make engineering changes.

Like the Cleanroom Model, the Capability Maturity Model (CMM) represents a carefully disciplined approach to software development. However, CMM focuses on management of the entire development environment or process in a team or organizational context, emphasizing "process management and the principles and practices associated with software process maturity." In contrast, the Cleanroom Model focuses on "rigorous engineering" and "enforces the mathematical basis of software development and the statistical basis of software testing" (Oshana & Linger 1999). In fact, these are issues from which the CMM prescinds precisely because it is intentionally "silent on the merits of various methods."

Nonetheless, although differently oriented, the Cleanroom and Capability Maturity models are compatible and even complementary. Oshana and Linger observe that the *key process areas* of the CMM can be largely mapped to the activities in a Cleanroom environment. Thus, three of the six level-2 CMM key process areas (software project tracking and oversight, software project planning, and requirements management) are highly consistent with Cleanroom processes. Five of the eight CMM level-3 process areas (peer reviews, intergroup communication, software product engineering, integrated software management, and training program) are closely consistent with Cleanroom activities. Finally, the level-4 KPAs (software quality management and quantitative process management) and the CMM level-5 KPA of defect prevention are consistent with Cleanroom requirements.

References

Abdel-Hamid, T. & Madnick, S.E. (1989). Lessons learned from modeling the dynamics of software development. *Commun. ACM*, 32(12), 14–26.

Alavi, M. (1984). An assessment of the prototyping approach to information systems development. *Commun. ACM*, 27(6), 556–563.

Basili, V.R. & Turner, A.J. (1975). Iterative enhancement: a practical technique for software development, *IEEE Trans. Software Eng.*, 1(4), 390–396

Bennington, H.D. (1956). Production of large computer programs, *Proc. Symp. Adv. Computer Programs Digital Computers*, ONR 1956. Republished in *Ann. Hist. Comput.*, October, 1983, 350–361.

Blank, G. (2004). Lecture notes for object oriented development. Retrieved on July 15, 2004 from http://www-ec.njit.edu/~gblank.

Boehm, B. (1976). Software engineering, *IEEE Trans. Computers*, 1226–1241.

Boehm, B. (1981). *Software Engineering Economics*, Englewood Cliffs, NJ: Prentice Hall.

Boehm, B. (1984). Software engineering economics, *IEEE Trans. Software Eng.*, 10(1), 4–21.

Boehm, B. (1988). A Spiral Model of software development and enhancement, *IEEE Computer,* 21(5), 61–72.

Boehm, B. (1991). Software risk management, principles and practices, *IEEE Software,* 8(1), 32–41.

Boehm, B. (1996). Anchoring the software process. *IEEE Software,* 13(4), 73–82.

Boehm, B. & Belz, F.C. (1988). Applying process programming to the Spiral Model: lessons learned. *Proc. IEEE 4th Software Process Workshop,* Devon, U.K.

Boehm, B. & Bose, P. (1994). A collaborative Spiral Software Process Model based on theory W. *Proceeding of ICSP,* 3. New York: IEEE Press.

Boehm, B. & Port, D. (1999). Escaping the software tar pit: model clashes and how to avoid them. *Software Eng. Notes* 24(1), 36–48.

Chase, J.D., Schulman, R.S., Hartson, H.R., & Hix, D. (1994). Development and evaluation of a taxonomical model of behavioral representation techniques. *Proceedings on Human Factors in Computing Systems: Celebrating Interdependence,* Boston. New York: ACM Press, 159–165.

Daft, R.L. & Lengel, R.H. (1986). Organizational information requirements, media richness and structural design. *Manage. Sci.,* 32(5), 556–557.

DeRemer, F. & Kron, H.K. (1976). Programming in the large versus programming in the small. *IEEE Trans. Software Eng.,* 2(2), 80–86.

Floyd, C. (1984). A systematic look at prototyping, in: Budde, R., Kuhlenkamp, K., Mathiassen, L., & Zullighoven, H. (Eds.), *Approaches to Prototyping,* Heidelberg: Springer–Verlag, 1–17.

Gamma, E., Helm, R., Johnson, R., & Vlissides, J. (1995). *Design Patterns Elements of Reusable Software.* Reading, MA: Addison–Wesley.

Gilb, T. (1988). *Principles of Software Engineering Management,* Reading, MA: Addison–Wesley.

Graham, D. (1992). Incremental development and delivery for large software systems, *IEEE Computer,* 25(11), 1–9.

Hamlet, D. & Maybee, J. (2001). *The Engineering of Software.* Reading, MA: Addison–Wesley.

Humphrey,W.S. & Kellner, M.I. (1989). Software process modeling: principles of entity process models, in *Proceedings of the 1989 International Conference on Software Engineering,* Pittsburgh, PA. New York: ACM Press, 331–342.

IEEE 610.12-1990, *IEEE Standard Glossary of Software Engineering Terminology,* Institute of Electrical and Electronics Engineers, Inc.

Keen, P.G.W. (1981). Information systems and organizational change. *Commun. ACM,* 24(1), 24–33.

Khalifa, M. & Verner, J.M. (2000). Drivers for software development method usage. *IEEE Trans. Eng. Manage.,* 47(3), 360–369.

Leveson, N.G. (2000). Intent specifications: an approach to building human-centered specifications. *IEEE Trans. Software Eng.,* 26(1), 15–35.

Lichter, H., Schneider–Hufschmidt, M., & Zullighoven, H. (1994). Prototyping in industrial software projects, *IEEE Trans. Software Eng.,* 20(11), 825–832.

Linger, R.C. & Trammell, C.J. (1996). Cleanroom Software Engineering Reference Model, technical Report, CMU/SEI-96-TR-022, ESC-TR-96-022, version 1.0.

Liu, L. & Horowitz, E. (1989). A formal model for software project management. *IEEE Trans. Software Eng.,* 15(10), 1280–1293.

Liu, S., Offutt, A.J., Ho–Stuart, C., Sun, Y., & Ohba, M. (1998). SOFL: a formal engineering methodology for industrial applications. *IEEE Trans. Software Eng.,* 24(1), 24–45.

Lott, C. (1997). Breathing new life into the Waterfall Model. *IEEE Software,* 14(5), 103–105.

Madhavji, N.H., Hoeltje, D., Hong, W., & Bruckhaus, T. (1994). Elicit: a method for eliciting process models. *Proc. 3rd Int. Conf. Software Process,* Reston, Virginia, October, 111–122.

McCracken, D.D. & Jackson, M.A. (1982). Life-cycle concept considered harmful. *ACM Software Eng. Notes,* April, 29–32.

Mills, H.D., Dyer, M., & Linger, R.C. (1987). Cleanroom software engineering. *IEEE Software,* September, 19–25.

Nielsen, J. (1990). Paper versus computer implementations as mockup scenarios for heuristic evaluation, in *Human–Computer Interaction–Interact '90,* D. Diaper et. al. (Eds.) Amsterdam: Elsevier Science Publishers B.V. (North Holland), 315–320.

Oshana, R. & Coyle, F.P. (1997). Implementing Cleanroom software engineering into CMM-based software organization. *Proceedings of the International Conference on Software Engineering,* ICSE 97, Boston MA. New York: ACM, 572–573,.

Oshana, R. & Linger, R. (1999). Capability Maturity Model software development using Cleanroom software engineering principles—results of an industry project. *Proceedings of the 32nd Hawaii International Conference on System Sciences.* Washington, D.C.: IEEE, 1–10.

Pfleeger, S.L. (1998). *Software Engineering: Theory and Practice.* Englewood Cliffs, NJ: Prentice Hall.

Pressman, R.S. (1996). *Software Engineering: a Practitioner's Approach,* 4th ed. New York: McGraw–Hill.

Ropponen, J. & K. Lyytinen. (2000). Components of software development risk: how to address them? A project manager survey. *IEEE Trans. Software Eng.,* 26(2), 98–112.

Smith, H.A., McKeen, J.D., & Staples, D.S. (2001). Risk management in information systems: problems and potentials. *Commun. Assoc. Inf. Syst.,* 7(13), 5–36.

Stahl, B.C., Lichtenstein, Y., & Mangan, A. (2003). The Limits of risk management—a social construction approach. *Communications of the IIMA,* vol. 3, (Ed., Stahl, B.C.) International Information Management Association, Las Vegas, 15–22.

Trammell, C.J., Binder, L.H., & Snyder, C.E. (1992). The automated production control documentation system: a case study in Cleanroom software engineering. *ACM Trans. Software Eng. Methodol.,* 1(1), 81–94.

Walnau, K.C., Hissam, S.A., & Seacord, R.C. (2002). *Building Systems from Commercial Components*. Reading, MA: Addison–Wesley.

Yamamichi, N. et al. (1996). The evaluation of new software developing process based on a spiral modeling. *Proc. IEEE Global Telecommun. Conf.*, Westminster, London, 3, 2007–2012.

Zave, P. (1982). An operational approach to requirements specification for embedded systems. *IEEE Trans. Software Eng.*, SE-8(3), 250–269.

Zave, P. (1984). The operational versus the conventional approach to software development. *Commun. ACM*, 27(2), 104–118.

Chapter 2

Software Development Strategies: Tools, Objects, and Reuse

2.1 Introduction

This chapter examines computer support tools for software development and models that emphasize reusability. The computer support tools are called CASE tools and are particularly prominent in the Rational Unified Process (RUP) Model considered. The concept of reusability is highly compatible with object-based development models and is realized in a different manner but at a much higher scale of functionality in the application of commercial off-the-shelf components. The Reengineering Model represents a different aspect of reusability in which entire systems are effectively recycled by modification or adaptation.

2.2 CASE Tools

Fields such as mechanical and computer engineering or architecture use computer-aided design (CAD) tools extensively to automate many parts of the design processes in their fields. These tools can automate routine tasks, check for consistencies, provide templates for design, etc. The analogous tools in software development are called *CASE tools*, which stands for computer-aided software engineering (see Table 2.1). These

Table 2.1 Profile of CASE Tools-Based Development Models

Category	Specifics (CASE tools-based models or automated development models)
Evolution of goals	Supportive to many other process models, especially the Rational Unified Process
Methodology	Can use with any methodology
Technology	Dependent on CASE tools
Critical factors	Significantly improved if seated on top of a formal language such as UML
Interdisciplinary effects	AI
Behavioral considerations	None
Problem nature	General
Application domain	General

tools can assist developers throughout the development life cycle, although they are more beneficial at some stages than at others. Tools used in the early phases of the life cycle (analysis of requirements, specifications, and design) are called *upper* CASE tools or front-end CASE tools; those used during implementation and maintenance are called *lower* CASE tools or back-end tools. CASE tools are currently available for every stage of the development cycle, including:

- Project management tools for budgeting, scheduling, and metrics
- Tools for configuration management
- Various tools for analysis and design, such as data modeling and interface development
- Tools that assist object orientation (OO) development
- Tools for testing, for formal methods, and for reengineering

CASE tools not only can speed up the development process, but they also can provide machine-readable representations for process information that can then be shared with other tools.

The earliest CASE tools facilitated the graphical structured analysis and design techniques developed during the 1970s and originally implemented in a cumbersome, manual manner. Automated tools for creating data flow diagrams were developed during the early 1980s and they were soon integrated with data dictionaries, thereby providing tools that could automatically ensure that dictionaries and DFDs remained consistent. Soon so-called synthesizers became available that further facilitated the DFD design process by supporting the development of hierarchically related DFDs. CASE tools were also developed that supported transforming data flow diagrams into structure charts (high-level module architecture hierarchies) by assisting in the customary process of identifying the central transform in the data flow diagram; demarcating system boundaries; and tracing input and output streams to their highest levels of abstraction (see Hamlet & Maybee, 2001, for a good overview of the process).

By the late 1980s automatic code generators and fourth-generation languages (4GLs) that greatly simplified mapping design specifications into code were developed (Barclay & Padusenko 1999). In particular, the UNIX shell environment, combined with the UNIX pipe, also obviously constituted a powerful fourth-generation language-like capability that had the additional benefit of complete compatibility with the UNIX environment. Similar capabilities are available in DOS. Strictly speaking, fourth-generation languages are not CASE tools because the user must specify algorithms and data types; for CASE tools the user need only specify the task. On the other hand, the domain of applicability of the CASE tool will be much more limited than the 4GL.

CASE tools are also helpful for mocking up interfaces during the design stage (Schaffer & Wolf 1991). Test scripting tools and test description languages were developed to facilitate testing. Another important benefit of CASE tools was their applicability to change management because they could allow tracing the rippling effect of changes through a variety of interrelated artifacts such as structure charts, DFDs, data dictionaries, and process specifications. CASE tools also represent an important technology for developing and maintaining Web sites (Jung & Winter 1998).

Part of the reason for the success of the CAD (computer-aided design) tools that have been used so effectively in engineering fields is that they were built on top of formal description languages. For example, in computer engineering, standardized high-level hardware description languages (HDL) are available that can be used to describe the low-level design of hardware systems. The descriptions are then used as input to the CAD tool that automatically generates the corresponding circuit model, even adapting the model to a particular technological realization like a VLSI environment, and allowing simulated execution of the CAD produced model. In the situation of CASE tools, the formal languages that underpinned the tool environment did not actually model the "semantics of a design" as they did in engineering (Hamlet & Maybee 2001).

However, an important step in this direction has been the introduction of the standardized universal modeling language (UML) in object-oriented design. UML uses *class diagrams* to describe the relations between the objects or classes in a problem. This language also has a version of usage scenarios called *use cases* that represent "functional test cases of an important sequence of operations" intended to clarify what is happening at the requirements level rather than at the code testing level (Hamlet & Maybee 2001). A use case represents a sequence of acts or steps that occur between a user (or *actor*) and the system when the user is trying to enact one of the functionalities of the system. Use cases are not the same as atomic actions provided by the system, but represent the enactment of a sequence of steps that together comprise the elaboration of a coherent user goal. UML *sequence diagrams* describe how objects implement a use case. CASE tools are also available that support the kinds of role-playing by actors that occur in a use case.

Technology-enabled models include those based on automation using CASE tools. Although traditional environments have been supported by loosely coupled CASE tools that independently assisted in each phase of the life cycle, later more sophisticated architectures have been introduced that provide mechanisms for ensuring that tools are properly used and that the user interface can support monitoring the actions of team members as well as coordinating their activities in an integrated manner (Ramanathan & Soumitra 1988). Their architecture uses a rule-based AI (artificial intelligence) approach. The TAME process modeling approach represented an outstanding advance in integrating process modeling with product metrics and the computer-supported capabilities of CASE tools in a comprehensive framework (Basili & Rombach 1988).

It is very significant that CASE tools can facilitate the analysis and improvement of the software development process. For example, the goal of so-called *empirical software engineering* is to improve the software development process by empirically monitoring process artifacts that have been created in an experimental development venue. Torii et al. (1999) describe a system, GINGER2, that collects real-time process development behavior in an experimental development context. The idea is that, by collecting data and building a knowledge base during a test development process, one can more accurately identify behavior patterns that can ultimately help make process models better. Obviously, if the process life cycle is extensively supported by CASE tools, many of the process artifacts will be automated and so data about them can be collected more readily.

The kinds of experimental data that can be collected include data about the CASE tools such as the average load on the tool program; data about the tools' artifacts like progressive frequent snapshots of source code development; data sent back and forth between the developers and the CASE tools; and even (remarkably) physiological data about the developers such as eye-tracking, skin resistance, and three-dimensional motion data. The idea is that the data can be used, for example, to identify patterns that might be correlated with deleterious development behavior such as bug creation so that programmers can be automatically warned if they are exhibiting a tell-tale pattern. This type of live empirical analysis of the software process using CASE tools to capture experimental data for the purpose of process analysis and improvement is called *computer-aided empirical software engineering* (CAESE). It is reminiscent of the early Taylorian approach to analyzing industrial work that led to the emergence of the field of industrial engineering (Hamlet & Maybee 2001).

2.3 Object-Oriented and Reuse Models

The central motivation underlying the use of objects is that they represent a natural way to model phenomena and correspond to the most funda-mental of cognitive elements: the concept. The conceptual nature of objects also underlies their ability to be designed for reuse. Reuse is a decisively important idea in software engineering because it reduces risk and development costs. This section describes process models that capi-talize on the idea of reuse. At one level, it examines how objects can be systemically used throughout the development process. An overview of the Rational Unified Process and its comprehensive suite of tools for object-oriented development is presented. Commercially available reusable system components or commercial off-the-shelf (COTS) components rep-resent reuse at a different scale. Finally, even when objects or COTS components are not applicable, for a huge number of systems the issue of reuse presents itself as the reengineering of existing systems that would be totally prohibitive to develop *ab initio.*

Before proceeding, another important instance of reuse is briefly addressed: the reuse of patterns of solutions to problems. Patterns for problem solutions frequently repeat themselves. What have come to be called *design patterns* represent abstractions or generic types of proven, successful, standard software architectures for solving regularly recurring problem types. Thus, design patterns represent a kind of reusable design template. In the seminal book on the subject, Gamma et al. (1995), the so-called "Gang of Four," compiled over 20 standard design patterns for software applications that had been developed and proven useful in software engineering over the years. The book can be thought of as a handbook of architectural patterns. The idea for this approach was partly motivated by work done on the architectural design of buildings by Christopher Alexander. The Gang of Four's standard design patterns can keep developers from "reinventing the wheel." Perhaps equally signifi-cantly, they can also serve as a standardized means of communication among developers, enabling them to convey the nature of their solutions accurately and succinctly to others.

The design patterns developed by Gamma et al. (1995) fall into three broad categories: creational patterns; structural patterns; and behavioral

Table 2.2   Profile of Object-Oriented Development Models

Category	Specifics
Evolution of goals	Promotes reusability through encapsulation and inheritance
Methodology	Objects and components
Technology	Computer-supported environments such as Rational Unified Process and automated tools such as DRAGOON are available; UML notation and tools
Critical factors	Defining model objects and their interaction
Interdisciplinary effects	None
Behavioral considerations	None
Problem nature	General
Application domain	General

patterns. Creational patterns include the *abstract factory* for building related objects. Structural patterns include *adapters*, which adapt one class to another class with which it might not be compatible by using a type of *wrapper* and *bridges* for binding implementations. Behavioral patterns include the *chain of responsibility* pattern in which requests are delegated to appropriate services providers. The design patterns are like tried-and-true templates for solving problems. They represent a significant advance in facilitating and standardizing the architectural or system design phase of software development.

2.3.1 Object-Oriented Models

Object-oriented techniques (see Table 2.2) can be used at different points in the software life cycle, from problem analysis and requirements specification to programming. At analysis, the result of an object-driven approach is an object-oriented model of the application domain. At requirements, the outcome is a description of the system to be designed in an object-oriented manner. At implementation, the source programming is done using an object-oriented programming language (Coad & Yourdon 1991).

Using a traditional software process model in conjunction with object-oriented programming has little impact on the overall process structure because the object-oriented aspects are subordinated to the classic development framework. A typical example of this would be to develop a system using the Waterfall Model with implementation done in an object-oriented language such as C++, Java, or Smalltalk. When an object-oriented design strategy is used, the system modules become classes or objects that are defined, analyzed, associated, and aggregated using object-oriented analysis, design, and implementation techniques and notations. Examples of this approach include component-based process models, COTS development, and the UML-based Rational Unified Process. These strategies have gained considerable attention in rapid application development because they can significantly improve productivity due to the reusability of the objects or components. Furthermore, these approaches can be extensively supported by CASE tools.

Consider an object-oriented approach to requirements and specification. Requirements engineering entails identifying the requirements that the user expects of a system and specifying those requirements in an appropriate manner. The process involves the elicitation, specification, and validation of stakeholder objectives for an application in a problem domain. The requirements document tells what is acceptable to the user. The correct requirements are critical because, without correctly identified requirements, the project is doomed to failure and irrelevance. The specifications, on the other hand, must also accurately reflect what the user wants, but they are primarily for the benefit of the developer.

Social or collaborative factors are involved in requirements gathering because the elicitation of requirements is based on a cooperative social interaction between the developers and users. The requirements can be defined via use cases, with subsequent development iterations planned around the use cases. The specifications can be represented by various means: formal, informal, or based on natural language. Nonfunctional requirements must also be addressed, including quality, reliability, usability, and performance.

Typically, the specification aspect of requirements engineering has been done using a structured approach based on data flow diagrams and structure charts. However, this can also be done using an object-oriented approach (Dawson & Swatman 1999). An object-oriented problem analysis is first performed to understand the real-world problem domain. A *domain model* is created to give a visual description of the partitioning of the application domain into conceptual objects, which can be determined, for example, from use cases. The emphasis on objects as opposed to functions distinguishes object-oriented analysis from structured analysis; the focus of the latter is on the identification of system functions rather than domain objects. The purpose of the object analysis is to discover the objects in the application domain and the information and behaviors needed by the objects to meet the requirements. Blank (2004) observes that object-oriented analysis and design depend critically on correctly "assigning responsibilities to objects."

The system design phase involves creating a conceptual solution to the problem that meets the requirements. This includes architectural, database, and object design. Object-oriented design involves identifying the software objects needed to fulfill the requirements analysis, including their properties, methods, and how they interact or collaborate with one another. Such objects are anticipated to be relatively stable throughout development.

UML diagrammatic models or tools are widely used for describing objects and their interactions. Static UML models are used to define the objects, their properties, and relations. Dynamic UML models are used to define the states of the objects, their state transitions, event handling, and message passing. The interaction between the objects reflects the system flow of control. UML *collaboration diagrams* are used to illustrate the interactions between objects visually. UML *sequence diagrams* are used to illustrate the interactions between objects arranged in a time sequence (the sequence of messages between objects) and to clarify the logic of use cases. These are examples of so-called interaction diagrams.

System sequence diagrams show the system events that the so-called actors generate (see the RUP discussion for further details), their order during a scenario, and the system responses to the events and their order. A system sequence diagram is a visual illustration for the system responses in the use case for a scenario; it describes the system operations triggered by a use case (Blank 2004). UML *activity diagrams* are used to understand the logic of use cases and business processes. Traditional *state machine diagrams* illustrate the behavior of an object in response to events and as a function of its internal state. For a further discussion of UML modeling, refer to the section on the Rational Unified Process. Larman (2001) provides an important treatment of UML and object-oriented analysis and design. Incidentally, Liu et al. (1998) describe the application of SOFL (Structured Object-Oriented Formal Language) for integrating structured and object-oriented methodologies. SOFL combines static and dynamic modeling and may potentially overcome some of the problems with formal methods that have limited their use.

One can also model the entire development process in an object-oriented way for such purposes as to apply automation for process improvement (Riley 1994). In this perspective, the development process is what is captured and formulated in an object-oriented manner. Riley observed that current process descriptions are often "imprecise, ambiguous, incomprehensible, or unusable," and there is also frequently "a lack of fidelity between actual behavior and a [development] organization's stated process." To address this, he proposed an object-oriented approach for modeling software processes based on a language called DRAGOON, which is also object oriented.

DRAGOON is used as a metamodeling language to represent the process model. This type of process representation is intended to facilitate improving process quality via automation. Riley claimed that his approach avoided some of the drawbacks associated with process modeling techniques based on functional approaches—such as structured analysis and design for defining system data flows and control. The idea is that his approach can be used to develop a theoretical model of software process, including formalization, as well as support simulation and automated enactment of processes.

Models like this are needed to develop life-cycle support environments that can partially automate process enactment. Automation could help ensure that processes were enacted in a standard manner by the individuals and teams using the processes. This could allow "enforcement and verification of the process and the unobtrusive collection of metrics," which could then be used to improve the process (Riley 1994). Riley's metamethod is based on a four-step approach:

1. Define an object-oriented process model
2. Specify the DRAGOON syntax for each model object
3. Develop object behavior models for DRAGOON
4. Develop object interaction models for the overall process

2.3.2 Rational Unified Process Model (RUP)

UML has become a widely accepted, standard notation for object-oriented architecture and design. The widespread acceptance of UML allows developers to perform system design and provide design documentation in a consistent and familiar manner. The standardization reduces the need for developers to learn new notational techniques and improves communication among the development team and stakeholders. The *Rational Rose* software suite is a GUI or visual modeling tool available from Rational Software that lets developers model a problem, its design, implementation, and indeed the entire development process, all the way through testing and configuration management, using the UML notation. The Rational suite is arguably one of the most important demonstrations of an approach that reflects Osterweil's famous aphorism that "software processes are software, too" (Osterweil 1987).

Myriad sources of information about the Rational approach are available in books and on the Internet. This development product is widely used, especially for e-business applications. Krutchen (2003) provides an excellent overview of the approach and its software engineering motivations. Jacobson, Booch, and Rambaugh (1999) give a detailed description of the

Rational Rose product and its associated development process. Tool mentors are provided with the actual product that can be used as a sort of "electronic coach on software engineering" (Krutchen 2003). For a simple but useful introductory tutorial about how to use at least a part of the Rational Rose CASE tool, with detailed discussions and illustrations of the Rose tools and windows for use case diagrams and class diagrams, see cse.dmu.ac.uk/Modules. Refer to Booch, Jacobson, and Rumbaugh (1998) for UML and Larman (2001) for UML object-based design and analysis. The Web site, http://www.agilemodeling.com, provides useful guidelines on UML diagramming tools.

The *rational unified process* (RUP) is built around visual software support for what its designers believe are the essential *best practices* for effective software development, namely:

- *Iterative development.* The iterative, Boehm-style, spiral approach is intended to mitigate development risk by using a combination of early implementation and requirements testing and modification in order to expose requirements errors early.
- *So-called requirements management.* The management requirements objective specifically addresses evaluating and tracking the effect of changes to the requirements.
- *Use of component-based software architectures.* Component-based development allows the use (or reuse) of commercially available system components and ultimately continuous (re)development, but involves the complexities of gluing the components together. This is also highly consistent with the fundamental principle of separation of concerns.
- *Use of tools that support visual design of the system, continuous verification, and change management.* Intelligently designed visual modeling tools help manage and share development artifacts, allow differing levels of design resolution, and support classic UML artifacts such as cases and scenarios. Computer-supported testing tools simplify verification. Automated coordination tools organize the workflow of system requirements, a coordination that involves a complex network of development activities and artifacts executed by multiple development teams at possibly many sites, and coordinate the process iterations and product releases.

The RUP constitutes a complete framework for software development. The elements of the RUP (not of the problem being modeled) are the *workers* who implement the development, each working on some cohesive set of development *activities* and responsible for creating specific development *artifacts*. A worker is like a role a member plays and the worker can play many roles (wear many hats) during the development. For example, a designer is a worker and the artifact that the designer creates may be a class definition. An artifact supplied to a customer as part of the product is a deliverable. The artifacts are maintained in the Rational Rose tools, not as separate paper documents. A *workflow* is defined as a "meaningful sequence of activities that produce some valuable result" (Krutchen 2003). The development process has nine core workflows: business modeling; requirements; analysis and design; implementation; test; deployment; configuration and change management; project management; and environment. Other RUP elements, such as tool mentors, simplify training in the use of the Rational Rose system. These core workflows are spread out over the four phases of development:

- The *inception* phase defines the vision of the actual user end-product and the scope of the project.
- The *elaboration* phase plans activities and specifies the architecture.
- The *construction* phase builds the product, modifying the vision and the plan as it proceeds.
- The *transition* phase transitions the product to the user (delivery, training, support, maintenance).

In a typical two-year project, the inception and transition might take a total of five months, with a year required for the construction phase and the rest of the time for elaboration. It is important to remember that the development process is iterative, so the core workflows are repeatedly executed during each iterative visitation to a phase. Although particular workflows will predominate during a particular type of phase (such as the planning and requirements workflows during inception), they will also be executed during the other phases. For example, the implementation workflow will peak during construction, but it is also a workflow during elaboration and transition. The goals and activities for each phase will be examined in some detail.

The purpose of the inception phase is achieving "concurrence among all stakeholders" on the objectives for the project (Krutchen 2003). This includes the project boundary and its acceptance criteria. Especially important is identifying the essential *use cases* of the system, which are defined as the "primary scenarios of behavior that will drive the system's functionality." Based on the usual spiral model expectation, the developers must also identify a candidate or potential architecture as well as demonstrate its feasibility on the most important use cases. Finally, cost estimation, planning, and risk estimation must be done. Artifacts produced during this phase include the vision statement for the product; the business case for development; a preliminary description of the basic use cases; business criteria for success such as revenues expected from the product; the plan; and an overall risk assessment with risks rated by likelihood and impact. A throw-away prototype may be developed for demonstration purposes but not for architectural purposes.

The following elaboration phase "ensures that the architecture, requirements, and plans are stable enough, and the risks are sufficiently mitigated, that [one] can reliably determine the costs and schedule" for the project. The outcomes for this phase include an 80 percent complete use case model, nonfunctional performance requirements, and an executable architectural prototype. The components of the architecture must be understood in sufficient detail to allow a decision to make, buy, or reuse components, and to estimate the schedule and costs with a reasonable degree of confidence. Krutchen (2003) observes that "a robust architecture and an understandable plan are highly correlated…[so] one of the critical qualities of the architecture is its ease of construction." Prototyping entails integrating the selected architectural components and testing them against the primary use case scenarios.

The construction phase leads to a product that is ready to be deployed to the users. The transition phase deploys a usable subset of the system at an acceptable quality to the users, including beta testing of the product, possible parallel operation with a legacy system that is being replaced, and software staff and user training.

Software architecture is concerned with the major elements of the design, including their structure, organization, and interfaces. The representation of architecture traditionally uses multiple views—for example, in the architectural plans for a building: floor plans, electrical layout, plumbing, elevations, etc. (Krutchen 2003). The same holds for RUP architectural plans, which include the logical view of the system, an organized view of the system functionality, and concurrency issues.

RUP recommends a so-called 4 + 1 view of architecture. The logical view addresses functional requirements. The implementation view addresses the software module organization and issues such as reuse and off-the-shelf components. The process view addresses concurrency, response time, scalability, etc. The deployment view maps the components to the platforms. The use-case view is initially used to define and design the architecture, then subsequently to validate the other views. Finally, the architecture is demonstrated by building it. This prototype is the most important architectural artifact; the final system evolves from this prototype.

The RUP is driven by use cases that are used to understand a problem in a way accessible to developers and users. A *use case* may be defined as a "sequence of actions a system performs that yields an observable result that is of value to a particular actor" (Krutchen 2003); an *actor* is any person or external system that interacts with the proposed system. Put another way, a use case accomplishes an actor's goal (Cockburn 1997). The requirement that the action be useful to the end-user establishes an appropriate level of granularity for the requirements so that they are understandable and meaningful to the users.

Just as it is important to identify use cases by recognizing interactions that create value for an actor, it is also important to define the cases from the actor's viewpoint and in the actor's vocabulary—not from the system's viewpoint (Blank 2004). The flow of events that occurs during a use case is defined using a natural language description of the actions that occur between the system and the user. The situation in which the use case pattern follows a normal, unexceptional flow of events is called the *Happy Path* as the basic focus of attention. For example, consider a case (described in Krutchen, 2003) in which the user is a client of a bank and is using an automated teller machine (ATM). The flow of events that transpires might be as follows:

1. (User): insert the bank card for the ATM to read and validate
2. (System): prompt user for personal PIN number, which the user enters and the system validates
3. (System): prompt user for requested services, such as withdrawal
4. (System): request amount to withdraw, user enters amount
5. (System): request account type, user selects a type such as checking
6. (System): perform validation of request for ID, PIN, amount, and type through the ATM network
7. (System): query user for receipt
8. (System): tell user to remove card, verify removal
9. (System): dispense cash requested
10. (System): optionally print receipt

Another name for such use cases is scenarios. Successful concurrent use case execution is initially ignored, but addressed later when nonfunctional requirements are handled. The role of use cases in the process workflows can be summarized as follows: use cases are an outcome of the requirements workflow. Appropriate objects can be defined during design by tracing through the use cases, and these cases then become the basis for implementation. They are also obviously precisely what is needed to define test cases.

2.3.3 Commercial Off-the-Shelf Model (COTS)

The component-based approach to development such as that represented by the use of *commercial off-the-shelf* (COTS) products (see Table 2.3) is

Table 2.3 Profile of Commercial Off-the-Shelf (COTS) Development Models

Category	Specifics
Evolution of goals	Utilizing ready-made software solutions
Methodology	Outsourcing and reusability to build cost-effective systems
Technology	Can be useful
Critical factors	Ready-made reused applications and their properties
Interdisciplinary effects	Economics; marketplace dependence
Behavioral considerations	None
Problem nature	Might be difficult to manage change in complex environments because of ongoing product evolution
Application domain	Dependent on availability

a good example of how object-oriented methodologies have dramatically affected development strategies. COTS development reflects a radically expanded concept of reuse in which proposed systems are configured out of prebuilt components or subsystems. The software economics of COTS components is very unlike that of custom-built components. Cost estimates call for components that must be reused at least two or three times to recoup the development expense (Walnau, Hissam, and Seacord 2002); however, commercial components can be reused thousands of times by different developers.

The term *COTS* typically refers to a "software product, supplied by a vendor, that has specific functionality as part of a system—a piece of prebuilt software that is *integrated* into the system and must be *delivered* with the system to provide operational functionality or to sustain maintenance efforts" (Morisio et al. 2000). The COTS component is delivered in binary form and has an interface that allows the product to be integrated with other components. The packages used in COTS development permit the rapid configuration of composite systems. However, the new paradigm places a stiff premium on developers' understanding the characteristics, incompatibilities, and performance quality of these preexisting products. Integrating the COTS approach into the different phases of the process life-cycle model creates a new kind of development framework (Fox, Lantner, and Marcom 1997) or life-cycle model (Braun 1999). However, in many respects, the classic Boehm Spiral Model provides a good skeletal architecture for the approach, although with a new emphasis on technology competence and the just-in-time learning and exploration of COTS components by the developers (Walnau et al. 2002).

Studies by Forrester Research estimate that most European software development will soon be component or COTS based. The same phenomenon is occurring among U.S. defense contractors who, until relatively recently, spent only a small portion (about 10 percent) of their budgets on outsourcing component and subsystem requirements. Indeed, the percentage of DoD outsourcing on COTS has increased to the point at which it represents a substantial majority of development. The corresponding success of COTS suppliers has been at least partially due to this paradigm shift in the defense community. Other factors driving COTS development are the increased pressure for shorter development times and the expanding supply of standardized COTS products that facilitate system integration (Fröberg 2002).

Carney (1997) identified several levels of COTS usage. The simplest is the *turnkey* level in which a single COTS product is used and left unaltered. The next is the *intermediate* level, in which a single COTS product is integrated with other system components. The most advanced level occurs when multiple peer COTS products are integrated in a single system. The role of a software developer in a COTS development project is one of identifying and acquiring appropriate prepackaged software components and assembling those components to build or synthesize the desired system. COTS software is offered in an increasing variety of types, ranging from component-based software libraries to stand-alone applications.

The components come in many forms: complete applications (such as Web browsers or servers); generic services (such as databases or geographic information systems); libraries of subroutines or abstract data types; application generators; problem-oriented language processors; and frameworks with plug-in classes or for which specific applications can be addressed via parameterized choices (Gentleman 1997). The components can be classified using the notions of a technology versus a product. A *component technology* refers to all available COTS components, regardless of vendor, that provide similar functionality (for example, the relational database technology). A *component product* refers to all the functionally similar COTS components offered by a particular vendor (Walnau et al. 2002).

Component-based efforts in which the developer can define the interface differ fundamentally from development in which the component is a given, as in the COTS approach. Although COTS is a component-based approach, the key characteristic distinguishing COTS from other component-based strategies is that COTS components are usually outsourced as ready-to-use components developed by third parties rather than internally developed. The developer typically does not have access to the COTS

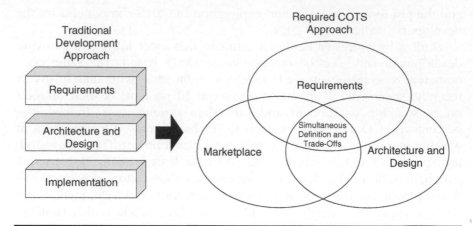

Figure 2.1 Traditional versus COTS approaches. (Adopted from Brownsword, Oberndorf, and Sledge, *IEEE Software*, Software Engineering Institute, 2000.)

source code, is only one of many users of the COTS component, and exercises little control over the subsequent version evolution or maintenance of the COTS components. On the positive side, the vendor or supplier is likely to be an expert in the implemented functionality, which is relatively immediately available (Fröberg 2002). Refer to Figure 2.1 for a schematic comparison of the traditional and the COTS approaches.

Morisio et al. (2000) analyzed the impact of COTS on traditional software development in an empirical study of COTS usage in NASA projects. They note that the requirements-gathering phase in COTS is similar to the usual approach but includes an added step in which candidate COTS products are identified and preliminarily evaluated—after which some potential selections are designated. The evaluation involves "prototyping, vendor demonstrations, and in-depth review of literature such as manuals and user guides." There is a certain which-comes-first-the-chicken-or-the-egg aspect to the requirements analysis in COTS development. Walnau et al. (2002) remark that predefining component interfaces "practically guarantees that no components will be found." The requirements objective changes from the traditional one of getting the requirements right (in collaboration with the stakeholders) to getting the right requirements (in collaboration with the stakeholders and depending on the available pool of vendor products). In other words, the commercial components "condition the requirements."

Realism compels the requirements engineer and the stakeholders to distinguish carefully between what is absolutely needed for the proposed system versus what is only preferential. To a real extent, the requirements are discovered (or certainly) adapted during the COTS exploration process. This is one reason why the spiral model supplies an appropriate framework for COTS development. It recognized that stakeholders often do not initially understand what they want out of a system, but only clarify their requirements through a revelatory process of iterative prototype development. In the COTS model, an ongoing dynamic exists between what the users want (or think they want) and the characteristics of the available COTS components (Walnau et al. 2002). Ironically, although the role of the requirements engineer is more expansive than previously, the engineer now has less control over the requirements because they are predetermined by the characteristics of the available products. Procurement issues are also far more prominent than in traditional environments, with new issues such as "development fees for added requirements, licensing and maintenance fees, and [for] sustaining engineering support."

COTS development naturally places a far greater emphasis on integration efforts with a prominent role played by "glueware and interfaces as dictated by the system architecture, operating system and hardware" (Morisio et al. 2000). The integration of the COTS components obliges developers to focus on properties of the components that are likely to affect integration including "operational limitations, temporal behavior, preconditions, robustness, and many forms of underlying assumptions on the intended environment" (Fröberg 2002).

The determination of these component characteristics can be formidable. The integration and testing phases generally must view the COTS products as black boxes and put their primary focus on the interface glueware. The common lack of access to the source code of the COTS components that makes them black boxes means that they lack appropriate means of introspection, "so determining their behavioral properties, which is necessary for reliability, predictability, security, and integration, requires extensive testing" (Fröberg 2002). Ordinarily tangential support issues such as the "availability of the vendor technical staff or Help Desk" become far more critical than in traditional development (Morisio et al. 2000). Indeed, this strong vendor dependence and interaction persist throughout even the long-term maintenance stage of the life cycle.

Furthermore, in a system consisting of multiple COTS components, maintenance integration will occur very frequently because new product releases continually arrive for some component. Although traditional development activities such as "coding, debugging, unit testing, and code inspections" decline in magnitude and importance, new COTS-related activities such as "product evaluations, product familiarization, vendor interaction (of technical, administrative, and commercial kinds)" become correspondingly prominent. Indeed, questions of project schedule and cost are now driven by the vendor, who represents "the ultimate decision maker on the functionalities available, the schedule for releases, the architecture, the reliability level, the documentation, and the service level."

To implement COTS-based projects successfully, developers must be willing to buy off on the restrictions imposed by the preexisting functionalities of the available COTS products. Thus, a trade-off occurs between the reductions in cost, development effort, and shortened schedule that are derived from using COTS versus the resulting restrictions on functionality and heavy dependence on the vendor. Strategies that have been used to reduce the risk in COTS development range from establishing a close relationship with vendors to identifying contingency plans, such as having an alternative choice of COTS or alternate plans for internal development, if the first COTS alternative fails (Morisio et al. 2000). Other risks include the impact of future vendor upgrades, backward compatibility of downstream releases, and even the long-term economic viability of the vendor (Fröberg 2002).

Once COTS components have been integrated into the intended system, there is a risk and also a likelihood of *vendor lock*. This refers to the situation in which the cost of changing vendors is prohibitive because of the risk of disruption that would occur if components from alternative vendors were used as replacements as the vendor product lines evolve. The risk is minimized when the substituted component is only a new release of the product from the same vendor (Walnau et al. 2002). A noteworthy disadvantage from a mission-critical viewpoint is the inability of the developer to see into the COTS black box; this means that the developer has only an opaque understanding of the COTS component. On the other hand, if the product was produced by a reliable vendor, its level of reliability may well significantly exceed that of an internally developed component. Previous experience with the vendor and in-house familiarity with the particular COTS product selected thus become important factors in the process.

The decision to employ COTS as opposed to developing a system internally involves technical and managerial issues. Morisio et al. (2000) observe that "selecting a COTS approach means selecting a [set of] requirement(s) and assuming it to be available cheaper and faster"; however, they claim that the decision to use COTS, as opposed to making a product from scratch, is "often made implicitly" and may not be formalized or rigorously analyzed from the viewpoint of cost and risks. A preliminary first pass at the decision to use COTS may focus on nontechnical matters such as the acceptability of the vendor and the flexibility of the developer's system requirements. Once a few potential COTS have been identified and a deeper look taken at them, a more detailed feasibility study can be made of the risks, effort, and architectures associated with each candidate versus an internally built alternative.

The number of candidates examined for actual use must be kept small because the cost of the in-depth examination required for the candidates is significant. Ideally, ongoing in-house technical expertise should maintain an up-to-date understanding of what is available in the COTS marketplace. There is a much stronger reliance than otherwise on in-house *technology competence*. Achieving this competence is easier said than done, however, because expertise on one vendor's products is not portable to others and new product releases can quickly date the expertise (Walnau et al. 2002). Thus, a concomitant need exists for training or sustaining in-house personnel in technology competence.

Indeed, because completely current technology competence is a prohibitive endeavor, COTS-based design involves not only ongoing learning but also real-time exploration of component features and just-in-time learning during development. The exploration must be deep and tangible. The component should be installed in an appropriate test bed, configuration options investigated, and documentation reviewed; even case studies that describe applications that used the component should be examined and a toy application of the component implemented that illustrates the kind of underlying capabilities or features in which one is interested (Walnau et al. 2002). Technology competence is decisive to defining requirements appropriately and to reducing the risks of design. Once candidates have been examined, the preliminary *make-versus-buy* decision can then be reexamined at a technically more informed level. However, the design risks remain considerable and inevitable because the features and behavior of the products may be misunderstood (Walnau et al. 2002).

The final requirements review is substantially more important than in the traditional life cycle because of the abbreviated or accelerated analysis of requirements typical of the beginning of a COTS development. A main activity at the design stage is integrating the COTS products with internally developed software. The subsequent design review may even lead to the conclusion that it is problematic to integrate the selected COTS component effectively, thus forcing a return to an earlier phase in which an alternative COTS is examined. Software project management is strongly affected by the introduction of these new tasks as well as by the common lack of experience with estimating the scheduling requirements of these new activities.

In comparing COTS-based development with proprietary in-house development, one must keep in mind that a key advantage of the latter is the latitude it provides for precise system specification in contrast with the off-the-shelf acquisition of a component that, although it saves time in development, "may require substantial effort in integration and perhaps negotiation of the requirements" (Fröberg 2002). The available COTS component interfaces may be restrictive and limited (Walnau et al. 2002). They are typically non-negotiable as far as the vendors are concerned. The interfaces may also be poorly described with important component properties obscured not only by the complexity of the component but also by the fact that "we often do not discover which property is important until the lack (or excess) of such a property becomes apparent" (Walnau et al. 2002). The properties may be changed by the vendor without notice, invalidating design assumptions and introducing almost random disruptions into the development.

Indeed, market pressures exacerbate the need for COTS product change and tend to compel vendors to differentiate their products, thus artificially complicating integration and design complexity (Walnau et al. 2002). The products may be easy to integrate with products from the same vendor but hard to integrate with products from other vendors; this is a likely complication because the best functional choices are likely to be spread over different vendors. Vendor support for integration complications may be unsatisfactory because the vendor may pass the buck to the COTS product of another vendor with which integration is taking place. These points demonstrate that, although the COTS component-based approach does indeed nicely demonstrate the principle of separation of concerns, it also seems to cede engineering design control over key concerns—such as partitioning the system and defining interfaces—to marketplace forces (Walnau et al. 2002). Furthermore, vendor control largely supplants engineering control, and the scope of that dependency is massive and includes whether support for features or even the product will continue. Under this new regime, the old software development factory model is no longer preeminent; rather, the marketplace rules.

2.3.4 The Reengineering Model

The Reengineering Process Model (see Table 2.4) originally emerged in a business or organizational context as a response to the customary business metrics of time, cost, and risk reduction. Reengineering is especially attractive in situations in which significant advances in existing technologies have been made that may enable breakthroughs in the performance or functionality of an existing system. Although reengineering has influenced the software process modeling literature and some reengineering models have been introduced, it has nonetheless been a somewhat overlooked approach. This status is perhaps attributable to its relatively recent introduction or to its categorization as a technique that usually appears integrated with other process modeling approaches.

Somerville (2000) identifies three main phases in software reengineering: defining the existing system; understanding and transformation; and reengineering the system. The process entails "taking existing legacy systems and reimplementing them to make them more maintainable. As part of this reengineering process, the system may be redocumented or

Table 2.4   Profile of Reengineering Development Models

Category	Specifics
Evolution of goals	Cost-effective adaptation of pre-existing systems
Methodology	Reverse engineering techniques to uncover original design
Technology	Reengineering tools very useful
Critical factors	Altering mission-critical service without shutdown
Interdisciplinary effects	Modern business process engineering
Behavioral considerations	Business constraints
Problem nature	Complex legacy systems
Application domain	General but more likely with legacy systems with maintenance and interface issues

restructured or even retranslated to a more modern programming language." The system may be implemented on a different architectural platform and data may be "migrated to a different database management system." Pressman (1996) introduced a six-phase software reengineering process model in which the phases worked together in a cyclical, iterative fashion: inventory analysis; document restructuring; reverse engineering; code and data restructuring; and forward engineering.

The Somerville and Pressman approaches emphasize the importance of automatic techniques to make the development cost effective.

■ An *inventory analysis* makes a detailed review of all existing business applications with respect to their longevity, size, maintainability, and criticality.

■ *Reverse engineering* refers to the attempt to extract and abstract design information from the existing system's source code; in other words, it attempts to recover the design implemented in the code. Reverse engineering uses the information about the system's scope and functionality provided by the inventory analysis.

■ *Forward engineering* refers to the use of the process results or products from the reverse engineering phase to develop the new system. Obviously, one of the most common adaptations is the development of new interactive interfaces. These may not precisely match the characteristics of the old interface but may use new styles of interaction instead.

- *Data reengineering* refers to translation of the current model to the target data model—for example, converting from flat tables or a hierarchical organization to a relational data model.
- *Redocumentation* creates new system documentation from legacy documentation according to an appropriate documentation standard.
- *Restructuring* transforms the structure and source code for the system while "preserving the system's external functional behavior" (Olsem 1995).

Reengineered components can be constructed through the application of an externally provided reengineering service, through reengineering tools, or through COTS software if there is a fit between the available COTS software and the reengineered need.

Olsem (1995) cites some of the reasons for reengineering an existing system as: expediting the transition of legacy software to changing organizational requirements or standards; converting an existing system to newer software technologies or paradigms (such as object oriented) and platforms; and improving the maintainability of the software. Reduction in the cost of maintenance is a major consideration because maintenance costs are like the tail that wags the proverbial dog. For example, an estimated 70 percent of the costs of DoD software activities is consumed by maintenance (Olsem 1995). An interesting methodological observation can be made here. Thus, if only 20 to 30 percent of software costs are for development, even a radical increase in the efficiency of development has only at most a 10 to 15 percent impact on costs. In contrast, given the dominance of the maintenance cost, if a comparable improvement were made in maintenance, an equivalent impact would yield an effect on the order of 35 to 40 percent of overall expenditures.

Granted the aforementioned considerations, one may wonder why not just redevelop the existing system, rather than trying to reengineer it? Once again, Olsem (1995) reviews some of the key elements of the rationale. First, legacy systems embody "critical corporate knowledge" and it may be difficult or impossible to understand adequately the rationale underlying the original system and its modifications because of insufficient documentation and because the original developers of the system have long since departed. Second, the *sunk cost* represented by the legacy developments is also a critical factor; some estimates indicate that legacy COBOL code alone reflects an investment on the order of a trillion dollars (Olsem 1995). One does not just trash this magnitude of investment any more than one would demolish Hoover dam. Finally and conversely, the cost to develop reengineered code is recognized to be significantly less than for newly developed code. Reengineering is also far more effective in terms of return on investment than another alternative of *continuous* (system) *improvement* in which the maintenance operation is sharpened by the use of improved tools and processes. As a demonstration of this, consider that the National Institute of Standards and Technology's famed Baldridge Quality Awards for systems in which continuous improvement was applied achieved an average savings of only about 5 to 12 percent, as opposed to the impressive 150 to 200 percent savings reported for reengineered applications.

The term *business process reengineering* (BPR) is derived from the business management literature and should not be confused with software process reengineering. Software reengineering refers to the reengineering of components of an existing software system. Business process reengineering, on the other hand, refers to the "fundamental rethinking and radical redesign of business processes to achieve dramatic improvements in critical, contemporary measures of performance, such as cost, quality, service, and speed" (Hammer & Champy 1993). The two areas are obviously related in certain aspects of their objectives, but BPR addresses a reorganization of business organizational structure, and software reengineering addresses the redesign of a software system.

On the other hand, a causative relation exists between the two because the need or desire to reengineer a business process will likely require a redesign of that business's software systems. However, the redesign may be accomplished in other ways than by reengineering. For example, it could be done by new development or redevelopment. Nonetheless, reengineering is a very plausible alternative in such a scenario. The reorganization of a business may involve its transformation from a conventional vertically organized structure in a top-down fashion to a more responsive, flatter organization. Software reengineering techniques can be used to "capture the software design information" and break it up into "functionally cohesive chunks" that can subsequently be "analyzed and regrouped around the newly identified key business processes" (Olsem 1995), a technique called *reaggregation*.

Bianchi, Caivano, and Visaggio (2000) describe in detail the application of a systematic reengineering methodology to a legacy system whose performance had degraded. They define a legacy system as a system that is still "operative and constitutes a useful and essential factor in the organization's business function" (Bianchi et al. 2000). As has been previously indicated, the importance of such legacy systems is well known. Typically, because these systems evolve over the course of many years under repeated maintenance modifications, their maintenance becomes costly and system performance and quality tend to deteriorate over time. These degenerative characteristics have sometimes been referred to as *aging symptoms* (Visaggio 2001).

One of the advantages of reengineering is that it can reverse aging symptoms. Aging systems exhibit characteristic symptoms. One of these is *pollution*, which refers to the presence of code or system features that are no longer required for the present business purpose of the system. Another interesting symptom is *embedded knowledge*, which refers to the fact that the understanding of the application behavior has become embedded in the system rather than available through the system documentation. Another classic symptom is the significantly increased *coupling* between system software components due to repeated long-term maintenance changes.

Because a legacy system is very often a mission-critical system, the system cannot be shut down for any length of time while the newly redesigned and implemented system is developed. In response to this development constraint, Bianchi et al. (2000) propose that the reengineering process be iterative and gradual—done in such a way that the reengineering required is handled in stages, with each stage applied to only a narrow subsystem and the reengineering increment done as quickly as possible. A consequence of this strategy is that legacy components and reengineered components will coexist and must interoperate while the system continues to be operational. The same restriction applies to any newly introduced component or functions. One principle that guides the reengineering process is that the legacy components should be reused to the extent feasible because it is likely that "the maintenance team that operated on the legacy system is also likely to operate on the reengineered system and...it is therefore desirable to preserve such familiarity with the system as is compatible with the updating process" (Bianchi et al. 2000). Naturally, the revised documentation about the design of the system is done as the system is reengineered.

References

Barclay, S. & Padusenko, S. (1999). Notes on system development tools and techniques. Retrieved on July 15, 2004 from http://educ.queensu.ca/~compsci/units/casetools.html.

Basili, V.R. & Rombach, H.D. (1988). The TAME project: towards improvement-oriented software environments, *IEEE Trans. Software Eng.*, 14(6), 752–772.

Bianchi, A., Caivano, D., & Visaggio, G. (2003). Iterative reengineering of legacy systems, *IEEE Trans. Software Eng.*, 29(3), 225–241.

Blank, G. (2004). Lecture notes for object-oriented development. Retrieved on July 15, 2004 from http://www-ec.njit.edu/~gblank.

Booch, G., Jacobson, I., & Rumbaugh, J. (1998). *The Unified Modeling Language User Guide*. Reading, MA: Addison–Wesley.

Braun, C.L. (1999). A lifecycle process for the effective reuse of commercial off-the-shelf (COTS) software. *Proceedings of the Fifth Symposium on Software Reusability*, Los Angeles, CA, New York: ACM Press, 29–36.

Brownsword, L., Oberndorf, T., & Sledge, C.A., (2000). *IEEE Software*, Software Engineering Institute, Pittsburgh, PA.

Carney, D. (1997). Assembling large systems from cots components: opportunities, cautions, and complexities. SEI monographs on use of commercial software in government systems, Software Engineering Institute, Pittsburgh, PA.

Coad, P. & Yourdon, E. (1991). *Objected-Oriented Analysis*. Englewood Cliffs, NJ: Prentice Hall.

Cockburn, A. (1997). Structuring use cases with goals. *J. Object-Oriented Programming*, Sept. and Nov., 10, 35–40.

Dawson, L. & Swatman, P. (1999). The use of object-oriented models in requirements engineering: a field study. *20th International Conference on Information Systems*, Charlotte, NC: ICIS—Omnipress, 260–273.

Fox, G., Lantner, K., & Marcom, S. (1997). A software development process for COTS-based information system infrastructure: part 1. *Proceedings of the Fifth International Symposium on Assessment of Software Tools and Technologies,* June 3–5, Pittsburgh, PA. IEEE Computer Society Press, Piscataway, NJ, 133–142.

Fröberg, J. (2002). Software components and COTS in software system development, in *Building Reliable Component-Based Systems*, Crnkovic, I. and Larsson, M. (Eds.), Artech House, London, U.K., Chapter 15, 59–67.

Gamma, E., Helm, R., Johnson, R., & Vlissides, J. (1995). *Design Patterns—Elements of Reusable Software*. Reading, MA: Addison–Wesley.

Gentleman, W.M. (1997). Effective use of COTS (commercial-off-the-shelf) software components in long-lived systems (tutorial). *Proceedings of the 1997 International Conference on Software Engineering*, Boston, MA, New York: ACM Press, 635–636.

Hamlet, D. & Maybee, J. (2001). *The Engineering of Software*. Reading, MA: Addison–Wesley.

Hammer, M. & Champy, J. (1993) *Reengineering the Corporation: A Manifesto for Business Revolution*, New York: Harper Business.

Jacobson, I., Booch, G., & Rambaugh, J. (1999). *The Unified Software Development Process*, Reading, MA: Addison–Wesley.

Jung, R. & Winter, R. (1998). CASE for Web sites—towards an integration of traditional CASE concepts and novel development tools for Internet-based systems. *Proceedings of the 1998 ACM Symposium on Applied Computing*, Atlanta, GA (USA). New York: ACM Press, 726–731.

Krutchen, P. (2003). *The Rational Unified Process: An Introduction*. Reading, MA: Addison–Wesley.

Larman, C. (2001). *Applying UML and Patterns: An Introduction to Object-Oriented Analysis and Design and the Unified Process*, 2nd ed., Upper Saddle River, NJ: Prentice Hall.

Liu, S., Offutt, A.J., Ho–Stuart, C., Sun, Y., & Ohba, M. (1998). SOFL: a formal engineering methodology for industrial applications. *IEEE Trans. Software Eng.*, 24(1), 24–45.

Morisio, M., Seaman, C.B., Parra, A.T., Basili, V.R., Kraft, S.E., & Condon, S.E. (2000). Investigating and improving a COTS-based software development process. *Proc. 22nd Int. Conf. Software Eng.*, ICSE 2000, Limerick, Ireland, 31–40.

Olsem, M. (1995). Reengineering technology report. Document No: TRF-RE-9510-000.04, Software Technology Support Center, Ogden ALC/TISE, Hill AFB, UT.

Osterweil, L. (1987). Software processes are software too. *Proc. 9th Int. Conf. Software Eng.*, Monterey, CA, 2–13.

Pressman, R.S. (1996). *Software Engineering: A Practitioner's Approach*, 4th ed. New York: McGraw–Hill.

Ramanathan, J. & Soumitra, S. (1988). Providing customized assistance for software lifecycle approaches. *IEEE Trans. Software Eng.*, 14(6), 749–757.

Riley, J.D. (1994). An object-oriented approach to software process modeling and definition. *Proceedings of the 1994 conference on TRI-Ada '94*, Baltimore, MD (USA). New York: ACM Press, 16–22.

Schaffer, E. & Wolf, M. (1991). The Unix shell as a fourth-generation language. Retrieved on Aug 15, 2004 from www.rdb.com/lib/4gl.pdf.

Somerville, I. (2000). *Software Engineering*. 6th ed. Reading, MA: Addison–Wesley.

Torii, K., Matsumoto, K., Nakakoji, K., Takada, Y., Takada, S., & Shima, K. (1999). Ginger2: an environment for computer-aided empirical software engineering. *IEEE Trans. Software Eng.*, 25(4), 474–491.

Visaggio, G. (2001). Aging of a data-intensive legacy system: symptoms and remedies. *J. Software Maint. Evol.*, 13(5), 281–308.

Walnau, K.C., Hissam, S.A., & Seacord, R.C. (2002). *Building Systems from Commercial Components*. Reading, MA: Addison–Wesley.

Chapter 3

Software Development Strategies: Process Improvement

3.1 Introduction

The theme of process improvement is to take a proactive role in creating better software development models. One approach to achieving this is to use simulation models to better understand the internal dynamics of process models, such as how changes in one process parameter can affect other process parameters. Another approach is to address more explicitly and carefully the human factors involved in development, including cognitive, psychological, and social factors that come into play at different stages of development. The establishment of explicit standards for software development and for related organizational and managerial practices, as is done in the Capability Maturity Model, is a further tactic that has been taken to improve the overall excellence with which software best practices are applied and improved. Software development excellence can also be promoted by improving the professional and technical abilities of the individual developers, as typified by Personal Software Process, and the teams to which they belong. Each of these approaches is considered in this chapter.

3.2 Productivity-Driven Dynamic Process Modeling

Abdel–Hamid and Madnick described a simulated approach to process modeling in a series of papers in 1983, 1989, and 1991. Their research represented an attempt to understand the impact of project management and economic effects on software development by using simulation. They examined the effect of management and process structure on team effectiveness by designing a computer model of software project management based on a systems dynamics methodology. The work was motivated by a perceived fundamental shortcoming in previous research on software project management: its "inability to integrate our knowledge of the microcomponents of the software development process such as scheduling, productivity, and staffing to derive implications about the behavior of the total sociotechnical system" (Abdel–Hamid & Madnick 1989).

The 1989 article includes an intentionally simplified but nonetheless instructive flow diagram of project management. In this model, people and resources are first allocated, then simulated work is done and its progress is monitored. A revised simulated estimate of the project completion date is made on the basis of progress so far, and resource allocation is revised depending on the business requirements and the available budget. The computer model allows one to address certain obvious management concerns in an automated scenario-like fashion. For example, suppose a project is behind schedule. Should the completion date be revised, should new staff be added, or should existing staff work overtime? Scenarios like this can be automatically implemented for each alternative. Consider the perennial problem concerning the trade-off among quality assurance, project completion time, and cost versus the "impact of different effort distributions among project phases" (Abdel–Hamid & Madnick 1989). The simple flow model can address these what-if's too.

A more complete model incorporates additional organizational subsystems, including human resource management, software production, process control, and planning and allows one to test scenarios experimentally via the simulation and a built-in COCOMO style framework for cost estimation. Modeling the impact of quality assurance procedures is also an important ability of the model. The purpose of this work was to understand how to improve productivity in software development by understanding the dynamic inter-relations among key project elements such as task management, team effectiveness, and quality control.

The system dynamics model can be used to examine the so-called *productivity paradox*, which refers to the often disappointing lack of improvement in software development productivity despite the application of powerful new development techniques and automated support like CASE tools. Abdel–Hamid (1996) observes that, although laboratory-scale experiments on the effect of using CASE tools often report dramatic improvements in development productivity, actual results in field studies of real development environments appear to reflect modest or no improvement. The explanation for this phenomenon suggested by the systems dynamics model is that the shortfall in performance improvement does not reflect a failure in management implementation of design strategies, but rather inherent complexities in the social system in which the development is implemented.

Abdel–Hamid (1996) argues that predictably modeling the behavior of the complex organizational systems underlying software development requires using computer-based systems dynamics models to create microworlds that are digital replicas of the organizations. The details of these models must, of course, be defined or specified on the basis of close empirical review and analysis of existing project management environments and statistical studies. In the absence of such simulation techniques, the observed behavior of development environments may seem counterintuitive or puzzling and may exhibit unintended side effects.

The model applies Steiner's (1972) theory of group productivity, which computes actual productivity as potential productivity minus process defects. The simulation models factors such as human resource management, turnover rate, error rates, learning, development rate, workforce level, schedule pressure, project task control, etc., with cost estimates done using COCOMO—although simulation-driven variations of the COCOMO estimation strategy and data are also used.

According to the Steiner theory, faulty processes are a key element in explaining why group problem-solving processes fall short of their potential. The faulty processes that may detract from the potential productivity of a system include so-called dynamic motivation factors and communication overhead. The dynamic motivation factors include things such as the impact of schedule pressures on work and the effect of budget slack (excess) on the temptation to gold-plate features or underwork. The communication overhead is related to the requirements of intrateam communications. The consequences of faulty processes are not always clear. For example, schedule pressure can make personnel work harder; however, more rapid work can also increase the likelihood of errors, which can affect product quality or entail inefficient rework later in the project.

The results of the simulated development indicated significant shortfalls in productivity over what had been forecast on the basis of the standard COCOMO model. One of the factors causing this was the result of a classic staffing mistake: an initial underestimation of needed project resources was followed (in the simulation) by a reactive, quick increase of resources when the (simulated) project began to fall behind schedule. This generated (in the simulation) an equally classic disruptive effect. Namely, the added personnel required learning to become familiar with the development project and the correlated instruction had to be supplied by the current project staff, thereby slowing down the development rather than expediting it. Communication costs also escalated as a result of the increased staffing in the simulated developments.

Significantly, managerial productivity estimates could also affect the outcomes by affecting how personnel spend their time. For example, when there is "fat in the estimate, Parkinson's law indicates that people will use the extra time for training, personal activities...slack components that can make up more than 20 percent of a person's time on the job" (Abdel–Hamid 1996). It is noteworthy that such overestimates can easily become hardwired into the prediction process because the prediction model is based on empirical data about productivity from past projects, which can easily reify past development problems. This kind of misestimate based on misunderstood prior experience represents a type of failure to learn from the past. In a sense, a variant of the Heisenberg Uncertainty Principle is at work here because of "the difficulty in separating the quality of estimates from the effect of actions based on those estimates!" Additionally, cognitive errors like the saliency with which distinctive past events stand out in memory also affect the interpretation of experience from previous projects.

A major advantage of the system dynamics model is that it permits computerized, simulated controlled experiments to test the impact of different development strategies—that is, hypothesis-testing. With respect to the productivity paradox, Abdel–Hamid suggests that a possible explanation for the failure of productivity to increase adequately in response in new technologies and methods may be what is referred to in engineering as *compensating feedback*. This refers to a phenomenon in complex systems in which potentially beneficial exogenous effects such as new technologies produce "natural feedback effects within the intended system that counteract the intended effect" of the external intervention.

3.3 Human Factors in Development Models

The role of human factors in models of the development process deserves greater attention because technological considerations alone do not provide a comprehensive, deep model for software processes. Human factors enter the picture in many ways. Thus, some software process models address the impact of personal competence and behavior on software development, such as discussed in Section 3.5. Other models, such as the Capability Maturity Model (in Section 3.4), closely and formally address the team and organizational context in which a development process is embedded. However, no comprehensive models systemically address the development process from the viewpoint of the human actors engaged in and implementing the process and its artifacts. Actually, this book tries to fill this gap, at least partially, by broadly considering the impact on the development process of cognitive problem-solving factors, stakeholder roles and concerns, organizational context, and marketplace forces.

This section offers a brief overview of some of the human-centered issues that affect the software process. For example, cognitive phenomena affect how individuals (team members or stakeholders) think about a problem and its solution. A cognitive perspective on development would address how the people involved perceive, understand, and solve problems. At the group level, social and psychological factors affect group behavior, such as how developers interact with one another as individuals or as a team, but group cognition affects the collective analysis of problems and group communication.

Human factors also have a role in the development process. The structure and artifacts of a software process affect how the process is enacted by developers and may, for example, affect their motivation. Most familiar is the role of human factors as understood in Human–Computer Interface (HCI) design, in which the concern is the human effectiveness of the interface of a software product. The HCI perspective considers the myriad cognitive and physiological factors that affect the successful design of an interactive interface. Regardless of whether one approaches the issue from a systems dynamics and managerial perspective (Abdel–Hamid & Madnick 1989) or cognitive or psychological and sociological perspective (Leveson 2000), the human element is important to appreciate.

Vennix (1999) describes some of the cognitive affects that affect the development process, including the role of selective perception; cognitive tendencies that incline one to oversimplify problems; the cognitive predisposition *not* to learn from failures by inaccurately attributing them to external forces rather than to acts of one's own; and the existence of unsurfaced or unspoken multiple interpretations in group cognition. The cognitive accessibility of system specifications has an ongoing impact on development. To simplify solving the kinds of problems that arise during development, specifications should reflect a correct understanding of human cognitive requirements.

Leveson (2000) adopts a cognitive engineering approach that defines cognitive-friendly specifications called intent specifications, which are based on "psychological principles of how people use specifications to solve problems." Although they combine mathematical and nonmathematical characteristics, they are intended to be easily readable, understandable, and useable by developers. In motivating the introduction of intent specifications,

Leveson makes an interesting analogy between the role of control panels in an industrial plant and software specifications. Control panels serve as the interface between a computer operator and the plant's system. Similarly, "software requirements and design specifications are the interface between the system designers and builders or builders and maintainers." These software specifications are intended to help the developers at different stages of development (building, testing, debugging, maintaining, etc.) "understand the system well enough to...find problems," just as the control panels are intended to help the plant operator understand the plant well enough to identify and solve plant problems.

System specifications should be designed so as to make it easy for the users of the specification to "extract and focus on the important information for the specific task at hand" (Leveson 2000) without forcing the users of the specification to adapt a particular, restricted mental model or problem-solving strategy. *Intent specifications* are system specifications based on so-called means–end abstractions in which, at each point in a hierarchical view of the system, the "information at one level acts as the goals (the ends) with respect to the model at the next lower level (the means)." In this kind of hierarchy, the "current level specifies *what*, the level below *how*, and the level above *why*" (Leveson, 2000; see also Rasmussen, 1986). Intent specifications are intended to simplify the task of finding specific, needed information; tracing relations between different instances of system information; understanding the rational for the system design; and allowing the user to shift attention to differing levels of detail at each intent level.

These specifications can facilitate the kind of zooming-in behavior characteristic of expert problem solvers known to "spend a great deal of their time analyzing the functional structure of a problem at a high level of abstraction before narrowing in on more concrete details" (Leveson 2000). These higher, abstract states of the system are needed as a point of reference for understanding erroneous behavior of the system because higher level states describe how the system *should* be functioning—issues relevant, for example, during debugging. Intent specification can support a rational design philosophy with a smooth progression from system requirements to component requirements, and all the way down to implementation.

Visualization plays a key role in defining and understanding the artifacts produced during development. Larkin and Simon (1987) did seminal work on the relation between visualization and cognition. Effective visualizations are known to improve learning and understanding; however, the research on visualization has tended to focus on its use in data visualization. Dulac et al. (2002) describe cognitively based interactive methods for helping developers, domain experts, and other stakeholders navigate through complex, visually presented software system specifications. The techniques are illustrated for a highly complex flight management system whose formal specification was over 500 pages in length.

It is known that a variety of cognitively based cues can facilitate effective visual representations. For example, the use of simple so-called secondary perceptual cues such as indenting or layout conventions can facilitate readability or clarify syntactic and semantic information. It may also be useful to present the same information redundantly, using different representations, with each representation simplifying some cognitive task. Dulac et al. (2002) introduce a list of factors that characterize visualizations. These include:

- Scope (focus on structure or focus on behavior of the system)
- Content (the entire model or the model with temporarily elided or hidden parts)
- Selection strategy (based on dependencies between model elements or by eliding model elements)
- Annotation support (optional domain information added)
- Flexibility (allow different kinds of search strategies)
- Static or dynamic (a snapshot in time or dynamic visualizations that illustrate behavior over time)

These characteristics can be used to categorize a particular visualization. This in turn can help a visualization designer create alternative visualizations of a process—suggesting, for example, the recoding of an artifact so that it focuses in one case on the structure of the system and, in another, on the behavior of the system.

The study by Dulac et al. presents a number of relevant and interesting visualizations, including question-based decision trees; inverse transition diagrams that display the *impossible* transitions in a system; and sliced diagrams that also allow selective dependency relations. These researchers summarize a number of principles that can be used to evaluate and formulate visualization aids. For example, they emphasize the importance of minimizing the so-called *semantic distance* between "the model in the system specification and the mental model of the system in the mind of the users." This increases not only the readability and reviewability of specifications, but also the acceptance and usability of formal specifications by stakeholders.

The structure of requirements visualizations should match as closely as possible the structure of the problem. This is related to the notion of cognitive fit (Vessey & Conger 1991), which emphasizes the impact of a problem representation on how well problem tasks can be carried out. The visualizations should support the most difficult tasks performed by the users; therefore, this entails a task analysis of potential uses. Visualizations highlight some dependencies and suppress others; if the hidden dependencies may be relevant, a visual way of surfacing their existence should be available. Overall or gestalt views are needed to clarify global structures and relations. It should also be possible to adapt the representation of information to facilitate different kinds of reasoning, thus reflecting the cognitive principle that "the reasoning paradigm is distinct from the representation paradigm" (Dulac et al. 2002).

Alertness to different "roles" may provide significant help in simplifying representations. For example, in navigational control systems, the amount of relevant behavior that must be considered can be greatly reduced by using modes to partition the system into disjoint behaviors that are more manageable cognitively. For example, in a flight system, the partitioning modes could be landing mode versus cruising mode. Redundant encodings, as mentioned previously, facilitate different kinds of information access. For example, consider the elementary case of a table about classes, times taught, and instructors. Ordered by class, the table simplifies identifying the different instructors for a class; ordered by instructor, it facilitates identifying what classes a given instructor is teaching. Finally, it is very useful to design visualizations to be able to show the impact of changes and the indirect side effects of changes.

The interface to a system is how people gain access to the system's functionality, so effective interface design can make all the difference in the success of a product. System design is not merely a question of implementing needed functionality; it is equally about effectively implementing user access to that functionality. Ineffective user interaction may be the result of interface designs that impede users from developing simple, accurate mental models for the interaction. Cognitive psychology emphasizes the significance of cognitive models for explaining how people interact with systems; users develop mental models of system behavior and these guide their interaction with the system (Rushby 2001). Indeed, so-called *automation surprises* occur when a cognitive mismatch is present between system behavior and the user's mental model of the system.

Interestingly, although mental models of physical objects like buildings are kinematic three-dimensional visualizations, the format of mental models for logical systems is not clearly understood—for example whether they are akin to state transition diagrams or to "goal-oriented representations, e.g., chains of actions for satisfying specific goals" (Rushby 2001). The mental models of users evolve over time as they gain greater familiarity with the system. Cognitive processes involved in this evolution include frequential and inferential simplification. *Frequential simplification* refers to the process by which infrequently taken interactions are forgotten; *inferential simplification* refers to the process in which similar interactions are merged into prototypical rules where differences are blurred.

Behavioral approaches have also been applied to enhance software usability in the area of user interface design. Chase et al. (1994) apply a technique based on a *User Action Notation* (UAN) to describe the cooperative behavior manifested by a user and an interface during an interaction. The UAN descriptions can utilize scenarios, screen displays, and state transition diagrams to characterize the interaction. The authors claim that developing a model or representation of the user behavior exhibited in an interface environment requires addressing the scope of interface activities, the content of the interface, and certain performance requirements.

In this case, *scope* refers to activities within the interface development process such as task analysis and design. *Content* refers to the interaction components being represented, including user definition; cognitive processes; interface state; screen pictures; temporal relations; feedback display; etc. *Requirements* refer to the qualities of the representation, including facility attributes such as readability and learnability, extensibility, and expressiveness. The conclusions of an empirical analysis suggest that Chase and colleagues' method provides useful support for the interaction development process. This work is generalized and applied to development process artifacts in the previously cited work by Dulac et al. (2002).

Curtis, Krasner, and Iscoe (1988) defined a social-context model of a software development process based on five "environmental" layers that envelop a project. An initial tecadmin layer comprises the familiar software process artifacts, constituencies, and the roles of the various players in the development process. An individual layer concerns the attitudes, opinions, and knowledge of the individuals involved in the project. A team layer focuses on group dynamics. A company layer addresses organizational context such as political affects, organizational culture, structure, and power. Finally, the business milieu layer addresses the organization's broader business environment or context. The contention is that the impact of each layer is correlated to the size of the project.

McGrath (1997) applies the layered framework of Curtis et al. (1988) to understanding various organizational affects that can (for example) hinder the success of a software project, such as resistance to the changes caused by a project. In terms of the company layer, for example, a project is by no means a neutral entity. Thus, a project outcome may lead to a "redistribution of power sources" (McGrath 1997) in which winners and losers are found, the latter threatened with a real or perceived loss of resources or control. On the other hand, with respect to the business milieu layer, factors from competitive threats to market opportunities affect the business case for the project, which in turn affects its resources, staffing, deadlines, priority, etc.

The McGrath model formalizes these factors and concerns using a rule-based Prolog-like entity relationship description that is intended to help predict likely sources of resistance to proposed changes. Formalisms are also given that characterize the effect of system dynamics factors such as deadlines and schedule pressures on productivity. This model is related to the system-dynamics, project management model of Abdel–Hamid and Madnick (1989) described in the previous section.

Following the social context model described in Curtis et al. (1988), Curtis (1989) presents a rather cogent critique of the relation between project stages and the behavior of individual developers. He observes that, regardless of whether the model is the Sequential Waterfall, Iterative Exploratory Prototyping, or the Spiral, these management abstractions, although providing a way of "ordering, monitoring, and accounting for what is happening in the project," do not explain the design behavior of individuals, which phenomenologically "is better characterized as opportunistic." This opportunistic pattern of behavior is exactly what is to be expected from cognitive research on planning, which indicates that "designers move back and forth across levels of abstraction ranging from application domain issues to detailed design and even coding issues." These variations in the behavior of developers are not triggered by timeline events, such as crossing project stage boundaries, but are recognized when problems are identified, regardless of the level of abstraction.

Thus, from a behavioral and cognitive view, the software tools that designers use should be designed to be compatible with how designers and developers actually behave, as opposed to managerial templates for how the process is supposed to work. The implication is that software tools should allow designers to "rapidly switch levels of abstraction in the artifact and support the opportunistic exploration of design concepts" (Curtis 1989). This is similar to what is described in the recommendations by Leveson (2000). In particular, problems related to the "thin spread of application domain knowledge, fluctuating and conflicting requirements, and communication and coordination breakdown" must be analyzed in behavioral terms rather than in terms of software life-cycle artifacts.

The demands of dòmain knowledge strongly affect the developers, who may require considerable learning time and effort to become adequately familiar with the application domain—an expenditure that can be easily ignored in planning. The customer is similarly subject to the same learning requirements, which also perturb the process through specification changes and their impacts. Collaboration among the designers entails extensive communication to ensure design issues are understood in a consistent manner by different individuals; tools that support this communication and coordination are at least as essential as tools that support transformation of artifacts.

Other behavioral factors such as the competence and training of the developers are well known to be critical to successful development; they depend on processes that reside outside the normal life-cycle purview, like recruiting and continual growth in technical competency. In other words, the development of people is an ongoing part of a continuous, nonterminating, global software process in an organization.

3.4 The Capability Maturity Model

A set of quality assurance standards was originally developed by the International Standards Organization (ISO) under the designation ISO 9000 in 1987 and revised subsequently in 1994 and 2000. The purpose of these standards was to define the quality system that a business or industrial organization would need to follow to ensure the consistency and quality of its products. A procedure for certifying that a business met these standards was also established so that potential customers would have some confidence in the organization's processes and products. The Capability Maturity Model developed by the Software Engineering Institute (SEI) at Carnegie–Mellon University is a model for identifying the organizational processes required to ensure software process quality.

The *Capability Maturity Model* (CMM) (see Table 3.1) is a multistaged, process definition model intended to characterize and guide the engineering excellence or maturity of an organization's software development processes. The *Capability Maturity Model: Guidelines for Improving the Software Process* (1995) contains an authoritative description. See also Paulk et al. (1993) and Curtis, Hefley, and Miller (1995) and, for general

Table 3.1 Profile of Capability Maturity Model

Category	Specifics
Evolution of goals	Evaluating and improving an organization's software development process quality
Methodology	Capability Maturity Model standards and organizational levels
Technology	Automated software development tools
Critical factors	Predictability in software development
Interdisciplinary effects	Project management
Behavioral considerations	Organizational behavior
Problem nature	Midrange to large-scale problems
Application domain	General

Table 3.2 Profile of Process Improvement Models

Category	Specifics
Evolution of goals	Assessing and improving software product quality
Methodology	Mainly CMM and ISO standards
Technology	Becoming strongly correlated with software automation
Critical factors	Customer satisfaction
Interdisciplinary effects	Industrial engineering and marketing
Behavioral considerations	Play important role
Problem nature	Large systems
Application domain	General

remarks on continuous process improvement, Somerville, Sawyer, and Viller (1999) (see Table 3.2). The model prescribes practices for "planning, engineering, and managing software development and maintenance" and addresses the usual goals of organizational system engineering processes: namely, "quality improvement, risk reduction, cost reduction, predictable process, and statistical quality control" (Oshana & Linger 1999).

However, the model is not merely a program for how to develop software in a professional, engineering-based manner; it prescribes an "evolutionary improvement path from an ad hoc, immature process to a mature, disciplined process" (Oshana & Linger 1999). Walnau, Hissam, and Seacord (2002) observe that the ISO and CMM process standards "established the context for improving the practice of software development" by identifying roles and behaviors that define a software factory.

The CMM identifies five levels of software development maturity in an organization:

- At *level 1*, the organization's software development follows no formal development process.
- The process maturity is said to be at *level 2* if software management controls have been introduced and some software process is followed. A decisive feature of this level is that the organization's process is supposed to be such that it can *repeat* the level of performance that it achieved on similar successful past projects. This is related to a central purpose of the CMM: namely, to improve the *predictability* of the development process significantly. The

major technical requirement at level 2 is incorporation of config-uration management into the process. *Configuration management* (or *change management*, as it is sometimes called) refers to the processes used to keep track of the changes made to the development product (including all the intermediate deliverables) and the multifarious impacts of these changes. These impacts range from the recognition of development problems; identification of the need for changes; alteration of previous work; verification that agreed upon modifications have corrected the problem and that corrections have not had a negative impact on other parts of the system; etc.

■ An organization is said to be at *level 3* if the development process is *standard and consistent*. The project management practices of the organization are supposed to have been formally agreed on, *defined*, and codified at this stage of process maturity.

■ Organizations at *level 4* are presumed to have put into place qualitative and quantitative measures of organizational process. These process *metrics* are intended to monitor development and to signal trouble and indicate where and how a development is going wrong when problems occur.

■ Organizations at maturity *level 5* are assumed to have established mechanisms designed to ensure continuous process improvement and optimization. The metric feedbacks at this stage are not just applied to recognize and control problems with the current project as they were in level-4 organizations. They are intended to identify possible root causes in the process that have allowed the problems to occur and to guide the evolution of the process so as to prevent the recurrence of such problems in future projects, such as through the introduction of appropriate new technologies and tools.

The higher the CMM maturity level is, the more disciplined, stable, and well-defined the development process is expected to be and the environment is assumed to make more use of "automated tools and the experience gained from many past successes" (Zhiying 2003). The staged character of the model lets organizations progress up the maturity ladder by setting process targets for the organization. Each advance reflects a further degree of stabilization of an organization's development process, with each level "institutionaliz[ing] a different aspect" of the process (Oshana & Linger 1999).

Each CMM level has associated *key process areas* (KPA) that correspond to activities that must be formalized to attain that level. For example, the KPAs at level 2 include configuration management, quality assurance, project planning and tracking, and effective management of subcontracted software. The KPAs at level 3 include intergroup communication, training, process definition, product engineering, and integrated software management. Quantitative process management and development quality define the required KPAs at level 4. Level 5 institutionalizes process and technology change management and optimizes defect prevention.

The CMM model is not without its critics. For example, Hamlet and Maybee (2001) object to its overemphasis on managerial supervision as opposed to technical focus. They observe that agreement on the relation between the goodness of a process and the goodness of the product is by no means universal. They present an interesting critique of CMM from the point of view of the so-called *process* versus product controversy. The issue is to what extent software engineers should focus their efforts on the design of the software product being developed as opposed to the characteristics of the software process used to develop that product.

The usual engineering approach has been to focus on the product, using relatively straightforward processes, such as the standard practice embodied in the Waterfall Model, adapted to help organize the work on developing the product. A key point of dispute is that no one has really demonstrated whether a good process leads to a good product. Indeed, good products have been developed with little process used, and poor products have been developed under the guidance of a lot of purportedly good processes. Furthermore, adopting complex managerial processes to oversee development may distract from the underlying objective of developing a superior product.

Hamlet and Maybee (2001) agree that, at the extremes of project size, there is no particular argument about the planning process to follow. They observe that for small-scale projects, the cost of a heavy process management structure far outweighs the benefits; however, for very large-scale projects that will develop multimillion-lines systems with long lifetimes, significant project management is clearly a necessity. However, in the midrange of projects with a few hundred thousand lines of code, the trade-offs between the "managed model" of development and the "technical model" in which the management hierarchy is kept to an absolute minimum are less obvious; indeed, the technical model may possibly be the superior and more creative approach.

Bamberger (1997), one of the authors of the Capability Maturity Model, addresses what she believes are some misconceptions about the model. For example, she observes that the motivation for the second level, in which the organization must have a "repeatable software process," arises as a direct response to the historical experience of developers when their software development is "out of control" (Bamberger 1997). Often this is for reasons having to do with configuration management—or mismanagement! Among the many symptoms of configuration mismanagement are:

confusion over which version of a file is the current official one; inadvertent side effects when repairs by one developer obliterate the changes of another developer; inconsistencies among the efforts of different developers; etc.

A key appropriate response to such actual or potential disorder is to get control of the product and the "product pieces under development" (configuration management) by (Bamberger 1997):

- Controlling the feature set of the product so that the "impact[s] of changes are more fully understood" (requirements management)
- Using the feature set to estimate the budget and schedule while "leveraging as much past knowledge as possible" (project planning)
- Ensuring schedules and plans are visible to all the stakeholders (project tracking)
- Ensuring that the team follows its own plan and standards and "corrects discrepancies when they occur" (quality assurance)

Bamberger contends that this kind of process establishes the "basic stability and visibility" that are the essence of the CMM repeatable level.

3.5 Personal and Team Software Development Models

Process improvement models such as the Capability Maturity Model usually address development at the team or organizational level, but the quality and delay problems associated with software development often reflect and derive from the competence and behavior of individual developers. Researchers like Boehm have long emphasized the decisive impact of the capabilities of the individuals implementing a project. However, in addition to attempting to staff a project with the most capable people available, how does one optimize the people associated with a project? Obviously, the answer is that it is essential to improve the competence and discipline of individuals at the level of their personal development behavior.

The *Personal Software Process* model (PSP) (see Table 3.3) developed by Watts Humphrey (1995, 1997) of the Software Engineering Institute is an important step in this direction. It attempts to guide individual developers in sharpening the discipline with which they approach software development. Just like the Capability Maturity Model at the organizational level (in which Humphrey was also a major influence), the PSP model uses a stage-wise approach aimed at gradually improving individual behavior by progressing through a multilevel set of standards. In fact, the PSP model was developed to support the CMM because the latter ultimately depends on the competence and professionalism of the practitioners to

Table 3.3 Profile of Personal and Team Development Models

Category	Specifics
Evolution of goals	Improving personal ability and discipline in software processes
Methodology	Monitoring personal and organizational people processes
Technology	Maturity model approach
Critical factors	Human assets
Interdisciplinary effects	Human resources management, workforce development, and cognitive psychology
Behavioral considerations	Personal practice
Problem nature	General
Application domain	General

be effective (Humphrey 1996). The PSP approach represents a continuation of the quality assurance work of Deming (1982) and, ultimately, Taylor's original time and motion studies that established scientific management. Although Taylor's work addressed the efficiency with which manual tasks could be done, intellectual tasks such as those done in programming also lend themselves to measurement, analysis, and optimization (Drucker 1999).

The idea of the Personal Software Process is to allow software engineers to plan and track the quality of their work so that they can produce better quality products (Ferguson et al. 1997). It requires developers to plan their work beforehand, monitor their time and effort, and log the errors that they make. An essential benefit of the process is the relatively prompt feedback that the developers get from the data that they collect on their performance. At the initial level 0.1, developers record the time that a particular activity takes and log errors. These are used to set a baseline benchmark for improvement. At level 1, individuals record process problems that they face and learn to use historically based regression estimates for work size. At level 1.1, developers address personal schedule estimation. At level 2, individuals develop their "personal design and code review checklists" (Ferguson et al. 1997). At level 2.1, they learn "design specification techniques and ways to prevent defects." Finally, at level 3, developers become conversant with verification techniques.

Defect monitoring and removal is a key element in the process. Indeed, a central belief is that "defect management is a software engineer's personal responsibility. If you introduce a defect, it is your responsibility to find and fix it" (Humphrey 1996). People learn to keep track of the phases in which defects were introduced or "injected" and removed; how long it took to fix them; and descriptions of the type of defect. The types can range from documentation errors, instruction syntax errors, change management errors, etc.

The fundamental measure of quality is the "yield," defined as "the percentage of defects found and fixed before the engineer starts to compile and test the program" (Humphrey 1996). Evidence suggests a high correlation between the number of defects found at compilation and the number of errors detected during system test. Similarly, it appears that a significant correlation exists between the number of errors at test and the number of defects subsequently found by users. Empirical studies at the SEI suggest a 30 to 40 percent improvement in the ability of developers to estimate the size of a prospective effort and the time required. Even better results have been reported for improvements in testing, with a 60 to 70 percent reduction in testing time and defects.

The clerical form-filling demands imposed by the PSP requirement for developers to monitor their work in order to create benchmarks for gauging improvement have met with some criticism (Johnson & Disney 1998). However, despite concerns, the authors concluded that the PSP model more than compensated for the extra overhead incurred in terms of improvements in design quality, defect removal, and the ability to estimate project size and time. Furthermore, the availability of automated applications to support the data gathering mitigates the clerical demands. Johnson and Disney (1998) also suggest that external measures of improvement, such as the acceptance test defect density, are more accurate measures of the impact of the PSP model. The actual PSP metrics may not always be calculated accurately, even in an automated framework; nonetheless, the external test metrics demonstrate the effect of the approach.

Zhong, Madhavji, and Emam (2000) try to identify and test the impact of specific aspects of personal processes in order to understand how one can systematically improve these processes. They examine productivity factors that underlie global factors such as defect density (Dd), defect removal rate (Drr), and productivity in terms of lines of code per hour (LOC/h). Their objective is to get beyond viewing the PSP model as a black box by addressing "detailed factors underlying personal processes and affecting product quality and productivity." The primitive factors that they consider include measures such as the average number of development phases (Abtk) that must be backtracked to detect a defect. A backtracking activity might range from an extensive effort starting at the first compile and going back through code review, code, design review, design, and planning in order to identify the source of a problem, or it might involve a more local backup of a few steps.

Zhong and colleagues (2000) claim that it is important to study the "low-level details of a personal software process...because they give a deeper insight into what drives process improvement." For example, the smaller the backtracking depth Abtk is to the development phase where errors were injected into the product, the more quickly and easily errors can be detected, resulting in better productivity.

Another metric that these researchers examine is the appraisal-to-failure Ratio (A/FR), defined as the "time spent in design review and code review as a percentage of the time spent in compile and test." A high A/FR ratio may reflect an excessive level of review or merely reflect quick repairs identified early in the project. Their small-scale study found that Drr increases with A/FR. They conclude that a high value of Drr suggests that "defects are fixed closer to their source, implying that software is high in quality at release time." However, the two metrics should be kept in balance because, beyond a certain point, higher values of A/FR will not positively affect Drr.

The metric Dds (number of defects removed per thousand lines of code developed) appeared closely related to "yield" (the percentage of defects removed before the first compile). It appears that a low Dds value in the context of a low yield value may reflect poor code quality combined with poor defect detection. This provides a certain kind of guidance for developers in interpreting how to allocate their time. The tentative conclusion is that although further study is required to see what the typical A/FR ratio should be, this ratio is a "useful guide for personal practice" and provides a relevant metric to evaluate one's development behavior.

Furthermore, Abtk and A/FR are inversely related, so a "decrease in Abtk might contribute to an increase in Drr and LOC/h." The rationale is that Abtk tends to be small when the defects detected are related to the current or recent development phases; thus, they can be removed more readily, leading to an improvement in other cost-related metrics like LOC/h.

The development of human resources is increasingly recognized as an essential element in improving the outcomes of software development processes. For example, the Japanese version of continuous process improvement, called *Kaizen*, uses a strategy for quality enhancement based on viewing human resources as an organization's most important asset (Bandinelli et al. 1995). The idea of designing Human Resource Management Systems (HRMS) that systematically enhance the performance of teams and that place special emphasis on the human assets of an organization is related to the people concerns underlying the Personal Software Process Model.

Türetken and Demirörs (2002) review such an approach implemented in application software called Oracle and derived from the *People Capability*

Maturity Model (Curtis et al. 1995). This approach views an organization as having five possible levels of process maturity with respect to its people management processes; each level is associated with a set of workforce practices called key process areas. These levels mimic those used in the Capability Maturity Model with level 1 representing no or minimal attention to HR processes. In a level-2 process (repeatable) the objective is to establish practices that can be continually improved. The associated key process areas include the work environment, communication, staffing, performance management, and training. The objectives of the communication process include ensuring that the social environment of an organization fosters interaction and improves the ability of the workers to share information and coordinate activities. The performance management process sets suitable metrics or criteria for team and individual performance, thus allowing feedback and continuous performance improvement.

In a level-3 process (defined level), the objective is for the organization to identify its "core competencies and plans, and tailor and execute its defined workforce practices to enhance its capabilities in the core competencies required by its business environment. The organization tailors its workforce activities for developing and rewarding these core competencies" (Türetken & Demirörs 2002). At this level, the Competency Development Process persistently seeks to improve the workforce's ability to perform its required tasks. The organization also seeks to establish a "participatory culture…to ensure a flow of information within the organization, to incorporate the knowledge of individuals into decision-making processes, and to gain their support for commitments. Establishing such a participatory culture lays the foundation for building high-performance teams." Human resource or team development models such as the People Capability Maturity Model and personal professional improvement models such as the Personal Software Process can be combined to address the requirements and opportunities for effectively applying process modeling concepts at the individual and group or organizational levels.

References

Abdel–Hamid, T. (1996). The slippery path to productivity improvement. *IEEE Software*, 13(4), 43–52.

Abdel–Hamid, T. & Madnick, S.E. (1983). The dynamics of software project scheduling. *Commun. ACM*, 26(5), 340–346.

Abdel–Hamid, T. & Madnick, S.E. (1989). Lessons learned from modeling the dynamics of software development. *Commun. ACM*, 32(12), 14–26.

Abdel–Hamid, T. & Madnick, S.E. (1991). *Software Project Dynamics: An Integrated Approach*. Englewood Cliffs, NJ: Prentice Hall.

Bamberger, J. (1997). Essence of the Capability Maturity Model, *IEEE Computer*, 30(6), 112–114.

Bandinelli, S., Fuggetta, A., Lavazza, L., Loi, M., & Picco, G.P. (1995). Modeling and improving an industrial software process, *IEEE Trans. Software Eng.*, 21(5), 440–454.

Capability Maturity Model: Guidelines for Improving the Software Process. (1995). Pittsburgh, PA: Carnegie–Mellon University.

Chase, J.D., Schulman, R.S., Hartson, H.R., & Hix, D. (1994). Development and evaluation of a taxonomical model of behavioral representation techniques. *Proceedings on Human Factors in Computing Systems: Celebrating Interdependence*, Boston. New York: ACM Press, 159–165.

Curtis, B. (1989). Three problems overcome with behavioral models of the software development process. ACM 0270-5257/89/0500/0398, 398–399.

Curtis, W., Hefley, W.E., & Miller, S. (1995). People Capability Maturity Model, Ver. 1.0. Software Engineering Institute, Carnegie–Mellon University, CMU/SEI-95-MM-02, September.

Curtis, B., Krasner, H., & Iscoe, N. (1988). A field study of the software design process for large systems. *Commun. ACM*, 3(11), 1268–1287.

Deming, W.E. (1982) *Out of the Crisis.* MIT Center for Advanced Engineering Study. 1982.

Drucker, P.F. (1999). *Management Challenges for the 21st Century.* New York: Harper–Collins.

Dulac, N., Viguier, T., Leveson, N., & Storey, M.A. (2002). On the use of visualization in formal requirements specification. *Int. Conf. Requirements Eng.*, Essen, Sept., 10 pages.

Ferguson, P., Humphrey, W.S., Khajenoorl, S., & Matvya, A. (1997). Introducing the Personal Software Process: three industry case studies. *IEEE Computer*, 30(5), 24–31.

Hamlet, D., & Maybee, J., (2001). *The Engineering of Software.* Reading, MA: Addison–Wesley.

Humphrey, W.S. (1995). *A Discipline for Software Engineering*, Reading, MA: Addison–Wesley.

Humphrey, W.S. (1996). Using a defined and measured software process. *IEEE Software*, 13(3), 77–88.

Humphrey, W.S. (1997). *Introduction to the Personal Software Process.* Reading, MA: Addison–Wesley.

Johnson, P.M. & Disney, A.M. (1998). The Personal Software Process: a cautionary case study. *IEEE Software*, 15(6), 85–88.

Larkin, J.H. & Simon, H.A. (1987). Why a diagram is (sometimes) worth ten thousand words. *Cognit. Sci.*, 11(1), 65–99.

Leveson, N.G. (2000). Intent specifications: an approach to building human-centered specifications. *IEEE Trans. Software Eng.*, 26(1), 15–35.

McGrath, G. (1997). A process modeling framework: capturing key aspects of organizational behavior. *Proc. Aust. Software Eng. Conf. (ASWEC '97)*, 118, September 28–October 02, 1997.

Oshana, R. & Linger, R. (1999). Capability Maturity Model software development using Cleanroom software engineering principles—results of an industry project. *Proc. 32nd Hawaii Int. Conf. Syst. Sci., IEEE,* 3(6), 1–10.

Paulk, M.C., Curtis, B., Chrissis, M.B., & Weber, C.V. (1993). *Capability Maturity Model for Software.* Pittsburgh, PA: Software Engineering Institute, 1993. (Technical report CMU/SEI-93-TR-024).

Somerville, I. Sawyer, I.P., & Viller, S. (1999). Managing process inconsistency using viewpoints. *IEEE Trans. Software Eng.,* 25(6), 784–799.

Steiner, I. (1972). *Group Process and Productivity.* New York: Academic Press.

Rasmussen, J. (1986). *Information Processing and Human–Machine Interaction: An Approach to Cognitive Engineering.* Amsterdam: North–Holland.

Rushby, J. (2001). Modeling the human in human factors. Safecomp, Budapest, Hungary, *Springer–Verlag LNCS,* 2197, 86–91.

Türetken, O. & Demirörs, O. (2002). Using human resource management suites to exploit team process improvement models. *Proc. 28th Euromicro Conf. (EUROMICRO'02), IEEE.*

Vennix, J.A.M. (1996). *Group Model Building: Facilitating Team Learning Using System Dynamics.* Chichester, U.K.: Wiley & Sons.

Vessey, I. & Conger, S. (1991). Cognitive fit: a theory-based analysis of the graphs versus tables literature. *Decision Sci.,* 22(2), 219–240.

Walnau, K.C., Hissam, S.A., & Seacord, R.C. (2002). *Building Systems from Commercial Components.* Reading, MA: Addison–Wesley.

Zhiying, Z., (2003). CMM in uncertain environments. *Commun. ACM,* 46(8), 115–119.

Zhong, X., Madhavji, N., & Emam, K. El. (2000). Critical factors affecting personal software processes. *IEEE Software,* 17(6), 76–83.

Chapter 4

Software Development Strategies: Reinventing How It Is Done

4.1 Introduction

This chapter examines a number of more recent trends in software process models. Especially remarkable is the open source movement, which represents a paradigm shift in how software is developed and even has some of the characteristics of a disruptive technology. Agile development is not quite as radical but reflects a new order of lightweight process models intended to reduce what some perceive as the unwieldy process overhead in other approaches. Rapid Application Development has a similar objective of expediting the return time on product delivery. Workflow models, akin to the production line models common in manufacturing, view business environments as networks of collaborating agents in which information is transformed as it moves between agents. They attempt to automate the enactment of these processes. Aspect-oriented models address difficulties with object orientation that arise because phenomena such as concurrency and scheduling tend to straddle objects, making the application of the central principle of separation of concerns problematic. Each model is part of a continuing exploration into how to develop software systems effectively.

Table 4.1   Profile of Open Source Development Models

Category	Specifics
Evolution of goals	Need for high-quality, reliable code, faster development, and open standards
Methodology	Asynchronous computer-supported collaboration on incremental releases over the Internet
Technology	Internet communication and distribution
Critical factors	Experienced professional developers
Interdisciplinary effects	Business model impact and legal restrictions
Behavioral considerations	Enthusiasm and need
Problem nature	Large system applications
Application domain	System infrastructure and development tools

4.2 Open Source Model

Open source software (see Table 4.1) is software with a source code available to users under the conditions provided for in a license with terms specified in a standard contract by the *Open Source Initiative*. Under an open source license, the user of the software is free to modify the software and redistribute the modified version. This license cannot discriminate against any class of users. Any derivative modified software must also be recursively redistributable and subsequent derivative works must also be allowed. The open source licensing arrangement is called the *Gnu General Public License.*

The idea of open source should not be confused with *shareware*, which does not require open source code and ultimately expects the user to purchase it. Open source is also different from *freeware*, which is released as binary executables and is not readily modifiable. It is also not like use-restricted software such as Netscape, which although free, can only be redistributed free to nonprofit organizations. The open source movement offers significant potential for addressing certain elements of the perennial software crisis, especially in those quintessential problem areas in which the speed and cost of software development and the quality of the software produced are critical. Refer to the Web site, www.opensource.org, as a basic source for information on the open source movement.

Classic examples of open source software include Linux, the Apache Web server, BIND (the software that underlies the domain name service for the Web), and the scripting language Perl. Another phenomenally successful instance of open source is the Mozilla source code underlying the Netscape browser. In fact, its open source character was instrumental in enabling Netscape to maintain and increase the market share for its browser. As Feller and Fitzgerald (2000) observe in their review article on the open source paradigm, some of the technological drivers behind open source development include "the need for more robust code, faster development cycles, higher standards of quality, reliability and stability, and more open standards/platforms," all of which are core issues in the software crisis.

The power of the "methodology" underlying open source development is based on the opportunities for massive parallel development made possible by computer-supported collaboration over the Internet. In a sense, the massive parallel development represented by open source overturns Brooks' classic warning that "adding manpower to a late software project makes it later." Instead, it is precisely the application of an enormous number of developers that gives the method its potency. For example, Feller and Fitzgerald (2000) observe that the Linux kernel, which is one of the best known results of open source development, was built using over 1000 developers working in a globally distributed, asynchronous environment.

At least as important, open source developers or contributors like those involved in Linux tend to be highly experienced professional programmers. In terms of the product niche that they serve, open source products "are typically development tools, back-office services and applications, and infrastructural and networking utilities" in which "performance and reliability are critical factors." Furthermore, the products selected for development are "chosen by technically aware IT personnel" (Feller & Fitzgerald 2000) who are driven by issues of reliability and robustness and are far less attracted to software as a result of mere marketing appeals or fads.

Despite its revolutionary attitude to development cost and proprietary or intellectual property rights, the business model implications of open source indicate that it arguably exhibits a far more rational correlation between the costs of development versus the cost of maintenance. Feller and Fitzgerald (2000) observe that between 70 to 80 percent of software costs are traditionally associated with the postdevelopment, maintenance phase of the software life cycle. However, the traditional model for development cost allocation, which places a premium price on proprietary software, "does not reflect the reality of the cost distribution in practice" (Feller & Fitzgerald 2000).

In terms of how open source works as a viable business model, the thing to keep in mind is that "even if the software is free, customers are willing to pay for convenience and a brand they can trust." The practice in successful open source companies like Red Hat is adapted to this asymmetric or skewed cost phenomenon. The software distribution costs imposed by such companies are free or nominal, but users pay for the quality of the subsequent maintenance. Furthermore, it is possible for businesses to exploit the capabilities provided by free software by, for example, "develop[ing] and sell[ing] software that runs 'on top of' free software" (Hamlet & Maybee 2001).

Interestingly, the benefits of open source are especially strong when the project is large, and might, in a traditional environment, incur substantial management overhead and when the specifications or requirements for the application are emergent—a likely circumstance in current corporate environments. Indeed, open source development has an almost magical power. Its "modus operandi of frequent, incremental releases encourages adaptation and mutation, and the asynchronous collaboration of developers means that OSS projects achieve an agility of which corporations often only dream. Geographically, OSS is characterized by massive distribution, with teams, community, and peer groups defined by virtual, rather than physical, boundaries" (Feller & Fitzgerald 2000).

As Hamlet and Maybee (2001) observe, "businesses can muster only small teams to develop and test their code, [but] the entire world of [computer] enthusiasts and developers is available to write and test free software." Open source software may represent a so-called *disruptive technology* (Clayton 2000)—that is, a technological development that emerges from outside the mainstream of scientific development and radically challenges the existing technological paradigm. In this case, that paradigm is the traditional proprietary approach to software development. Disruptive technologies tend to shatter the conventional wisdom because they require businesses dominant under the old technology to change dramatically what they do. In other words, the entire development paradigm must be rethought.

4.3 Agile Software Development

The "Agile Manifesto" of Beck et al. (2001) and the seminal book by Kent Beck (2000), *Extreme Programming Explained*, express some of the defining characteristics of *agile development* (see Table 4.2). These include an emphasis on people and their interactions—as opposed to formal development processes and development tools; an emphasis on ongoing interactions and collaboration with customers—as opposed to more legalistic contract-driven negotiations; and an emphasis on the ability to make dynamic responses to change—as opposed to following frozen plans rigidly. Cockburn and Highsmith (2001) observe that agile development

Table 4.2   Profile of Agile Development Models

Category	Specifics
Evolution of goals	Improve responsiveness and reduce turnaround time on development decisions
Methodology	Incremental development of working software; pair programming
Technology	UML tools
Critical factors	Individual competency and mutual trust
Interdisciplinary effects	Human relations and management practices
Behavioral considerations	Intense and close people interaction required
Problem nature	General
Application domain	Smaller projects

is dominated by the twin objectives of making software development teams more effective by reducing "the cost of moving information between people" and reducing "the elapsed time between making a decision" and "seeing the consequences of that decision."

Many of the ways for simplifying communication are straightforward and traditional. For example, a standard tactic is to co-locate team members as much as possible, preferably using old-fashioned, face-to-face communication as opposed to electronic collaborative exchanges. In the extreme programming version of agile development, a core practice is to use a technique called *pair programming* in which a pair of programmers actually shares the same computer and collaborates in real time (Williams & Kessler 2003). Under such circumstances, it is essential for the human relations among team members to be as amicable as possible. The "social lubricant" of amicability helps foster a sense of community, which greatly enhances the likelihood that members will feel comfortable and mutually trusting enough to exchange vital project-related information freely.

Another principle of agile programming is its strong emphasis on the importance of the individual and team talents (Cockburn & Highsmith 2001). Agile development places a high premium on "individual competency as a critical factor in project success." This reflects Boehm's (2002) principle of emphasizing the pivotal role of superior expertise: use better and fewer people. This principle is applied regardless of the variant of agile development used; whether that is Scrum, Adaptive Software Development (ASD), or Feature-Driven Development, the emphasis tends to be "on people and their talent, skill, and knowledge." The operative phrase is that "people trump politics" (Cockburn & Highsmith 2001).

The characteristics that help make a development model more agile include techniques to reduce risk; interaction with customers; using people-oriented management practices; a certain style of iterative development; adaptive teams; and a thoroughgoing emphasis on developing working software (Dagnino 2002). In particular, plans and designs are refined as work progresses and the problem requirements become better understood. Techniques such as continuous testing and the already mentioned pair-programming reduce the amount of testing needed. The generation of planning artifacts is kept to a minimum and working software is delivered incrementally and frequently from the beginning. As Dagnino strikingly observes, in an agile environment, "working software is the primary measure of progress. A working system at the end of each cycle is the primary measure of progress in the project." Beck (2000) makes a related point: "code is the one artifact that development absolutely cannot live without."

As indicated, plans and requirements emerge as the work progresses. Team members are chosen for their skills and versatility. User experts are considered as core members of an effective agile team. The user works with the team to hone the product over time, through intimate, ongoing, daily interaction with the development team. Cohn and Ford (2003) observe that "agile processes do not have separate coding and testing phases; rather, code written during an iteration must be tested and debugged during that iteration. Testers and programmers work more closely and earlier in an agile process than in other processes."

Evolutionary development models are compatible with an agile approach, but they are certainly not identical to agile models as they stand. First of all, the evolutionary models place a substantially greater emphasis on continuously updating documentation throughout the process. For example, in evolutionary models, considerable effort is expended documenting changing requirements. Furthermore, evolutionary testing tends to occur at the end of the development life cycle, with the result that "the time and effort devoted to testing the software become very limited" (Dagnino 2002). Such practices would need to be revised to make the evolutionary model more agile.

Dagnino (2002) observes that the "most obvious difference between plan-driven life-cycle models and agile development is that agile models are less document oriented and place more emphasis on code development." This researcher describes the degree of planning, defined as the "amount of documentation, schedules, specification of roles and responsibilities, work breakdowns, procedures, reporting," and so on, as a continuum. At one end lies the practice of undisciplined hacking, which in a sense corresponds to an extreme version of agile development in which almost no planning is used. This naturally presents unacceptable development risks and is known from long experience to generate systems that are typically not maintainable.

The amount of planning done progresses from this kind of undisciplined hacking at one end of the spectrum through the more disciplined approaches represented by Extreme Programming and Scrum. These latter approaches generate code from the very start, but in contrast to unprofessional hacking, they exhibit a significant degree of planning. Towards the increased planning end of the spectrum are plan-driven methodologies such as milestone and risk-driven models, and then milestone plan-driven models which subject projects to increasing levels of control.

Agile development is based on iterative, incremental delivery "as a response to changing and emergent requirements" (Dagnino 2002). In order to keep development risk under control, the emphasis is on frequent inspection of the work product to ensure that the product meets user expectations as well as to be able to respond quickly and adaptively to better understood requirements or changing conditions. One of the techniques for reducing risk is the use of ongoing risk mitigation meetings, which are usually on a weekly basis. The testing is also persistent and ongoing as code is developed. Acceptance tests are designed in collaboration with the customer. As the user experts observe the evolving development and system, they can identify which of their requests or requirements do not work as well as expected. They can also rapidly identify where the developers have misunderstood the user requirements.

In the Scrum model of agile development, the work is broken into a series of steps called *sprints*. Prior to each sprint, developers meet with the customer to identify and prioritize the work to be done in the upcoming sprint. Within the time period of a sprint, teams meet daily. Upon completion of a sprint, the development team "delivers a potentially shippable product increment" (Cohn & Ford 2003). Incidentally, the term *scrum* comes from the sport of rugby where it refers to a group that cooperatively pushes the "football" down the field. The initial phase of development is based on meetings with users during which the desired system characteristics or so-called *features* are identified. These features are then reviewed to estimate the scope, risk, and resource characteristics of the project. Acceptance tests are developed for each feature requirement prior to initiating coding and the tests are jointly reviewed with the customer, who prioritizes the features. The outcome of the first feature development phase is a preliminary prototype that is reviewed, evaluated, commented on, and modified or accepted by the user.

The agile models are relatively *lightweight* in terms of their learning requirements. This simplicity has important psychological and cognitive advantages because it reduces "potentially demotivating work and overhead" (Dagnino 2002). From a managerial perspective, organizational practices in an agile development environment tend to emphasize a collaborative style rather than the more traditional command-and-control approach. In terms of scale, agile practices are usually applied in smaller projects in which work can be accomplished by teams of ten or fewer people. The agile model, as the name implies, is not intended to be predictive so much as adaptive and more focused on the people involved in the development than on the development process. Expedited decision-making, shared objectives, and a high degree of mutual trust (Dagnino 2002) are a sine qua non of the process.

The dynamic manner in which product requirements emerge is another distinctive aspect. The agile approach facilitates early release of products to market. This gives a competitive advantage in terms of market impact and also, perhaps even more critically in development terms, allows real feedback from real users, reflecting what might be called "continuous *emerging* of requirements" (Dagnino 2002). In fact, the objective is to attain "short release cycles with fully functioning code." The agile team structure reflects this dynamic environment in the teams' self-organizing behaviors. They self-adapt to the emerging product requirements, guided by the objective of finding the "best way to convert requirements and technology into product increments" (Dagnino 2002).

4.4 Rapid Application Development (RAD) Models

Rapid Application Development (see Table 4.3), a term introduced by Martin (1991), is intended to improve the productivity of development and delivery times for applications. Agarwal et al. (2000) claim that "growing evidence supports RAD as an order of magnitude improvement in the speed of software construction." Of course, such improvements would be meaningful only if the applications also exhibited "reusability and maintainability so that total life-cycle costs are reduced" (Agarwal et al. 2000).

RAD bears a superficial resemblance to open source development. In both approaches, users play a more prominent role and product versions are released more frequently. However, the differences are even more notable. Most obviously, the open source availability of program code is not an issue in the RAD environment, but is a defining feature of the open source environment. The scale of the projects to which the approaches are applied also differs significantly. Open source applications are often mission critical; typically involve a large number of developers; and expect a large audience of users. Open source applications tend to revolve around infrastructure software; in contrast, RAD applications tend to be for single-user, stand-alone products (Feller & Fitzgerald 2000). Users

Table 4.3   Profile of Rapid Application Development Model

Category	Specifics
Evolution of goals	High-speed adaptation of the Waterfall Model
Methodology	Rapid linear sequential development and reuse
Technology	Important influence
Critical factors	Cycle time reduction and reusable program components
Interdisciplinary effects	None
Behavioral considerations	None
Problem nature	Good for small systems but need sufficient human resources for large scalable systems
Application domain	May not be appropriate for high-performance systems, for high technical risks, or when a system cannot be properly modularized

play a major role in each of these approaches; however, users are involved even in coding in the case of OSS, but this is not so for RAD.

The development tools are also very different; RAD tools emphasize the user interface, in contrast to the frequently algorithmically complex problems addressed in open source development. The attitude towards requirements is substantially different too. In open source, the requirements are under continual development, but in RAD the intended system ultimately has a stable set of requirements, which may have been finalized relatively early at the initial prototype stage. As Feller and Fitzgerald (2000) observe, in RAD prototypes are used to pin down the specification of requirements and "become part of the final project."

The RAD methodology is similar to the iterative and spiral models of software development, but it emphasizes development tools that facilitate "speedy object development [and building] graphical user interfaces and reusable code for client/server applications" (Agarwal et al. 2000). RAD tools include support for multitier architectures, visual programming, and object-oriented design, and emphasize reusability and the object- or message-passing model. The three broad classes of RAD tools are roughly correlated with project management issues, development issues, and modeling. The project management tools assist in problems such as configuration and development team management. The development tools support screen organization, GUI development, and software to support testing and debugging. The modeling tools support data and business process modeling.

A key issue in RAD development is "how to incorporate RAD tools into an IS shop's tool kit" (Agarwal et al. 2000), an issue with strong managerial and personnel aspects. This is a nontrivial matter because the successful application of RAD technologies requires buy-in from the developers that cannot be coerced or mandated. A number of cognitive factors affect the likelihood that tools such as those required in RAD will in fact be used by the developers for whom they are intended. First of all, a developer must be convinced that the cost-benefit analysis balance favors the new tool's ability to make a real impact on development. The perceived gain must be enough to overcome the initial hurdles represented by the adoption and learning barriers. This perception or belief is in turn critically affected by the "perceived cognitive effort necessary to effectively utilize the new tool." This belief is affected by the actual or "perceived congruence of [the] new technology with preferred methods of accomplishing tasks."

Thus, the three key criteria influencing prospective adopters correspond to the relative advantage of the new methodology; its ease of use; and its cognitive compatibility. These criteria are decisive determinants of cognitive perceptions and useful predictors of adoptive success. A developer's prior personal experience affects how difficult it will be for the individual to adapt to the new methodology. One implication of this, according to Agarwal et al. (2000), is that senior developers, who are presumably more experienced and comfortable with existing methodologies, may be more likely to "have more difficulty accepting new development paradigms" such as RAD. These researchers observe that, although programmers with mainframe programming experience may tend to have a negative perception about the benefits of RAD methodology, this has not been found to be true of those with experience in client and server environments. The attitudinal characteristics of early adapters can also be brought to bear. It is known that "early adapters" of technologies tend to be positive with regard to RAD methods. Such individuals are typically personally innovative and can act as "change agents" whose adaptiveness can help diffuse the RAD technology through an organization.

A common shortcoming in how developers utilize RAD tools is selective preference for which tool features are emphasized. Agarwal et al. (2000) claim that "systems developers appear to be utilizing the features of the tool that allow them to deliver systems in a speedy manner, but are not fully utilizing the features that contribute to longer term quality and maintainability of systems." This observation is consistent with the most common managerial motivation for introducing RAD technology: the increasing pressure for rapid application deployment, combined with industry-wide interest in applying these tools. For example, RAD methodology and tools allow system developers to provide demo systems to users very rapidly, with a consequent disincentive for developers to hone the system and business model design more carefully. An ironic reason for this tendency is the shared expectation that design and specification errors can be caught later and addressed at that point, which seems (to quote Casey Stengle) like "déjà vu all over again"; design practice has been retrojected to the early days of on-the-fly design and implementation.

Overall, the negative behaviors associated with RAD include a proclivity to focus on the RAD development tools while underemphasizing the RAD modeling tools and generally exhibiting a decreased level of systems analysis, specification, and planning. Agarwal et al. (2000) observe that this tends to "subvert good development practices" ranging from placing an undue major "emphasis on system construction, [to] not enough on domain analysis." RAD also appears to predispose developers to avoid seeking out "errors and misspecifications early in the development cycle." Obviously, managers must be on guard against such pitfalls.

4.5 Workflow Application Models

Traditional business organizations structure work around functions, but the relationship between those work functions is typically not adequately taken into account (Weske 2000). This omission leads to process inefficiencies for reasons ranging from waiting time delays to redundant work. In contrast, in a process-oriented view of business operations, the focus is on the entire production process rather than merely the separate, individual functions performed during the process. This perspective is a familiar one in manufacturing environments in which the production line model is the central point of reference, rather than in an organization based around individual functions.

The process orientation is dominant in the case of *information processes*, which include, for example, the systems for processing insurance claims in a business context or for enrolling students in a university in an academic context. In a business environment, information processes are of fundamental importance, often involving the "mission-critical processes of an organization" (Weske 2000). Information (business) processes may be partially or fully automated and manage the processing and flow of information in an organization. The actual formulation and establishment of these business processes is done by domain experts. Workflow models of information systems view enterprises as a network of collaborating agents (Jeusfeld & deMoor 2001) in which informational transactions or tasks are "passed from one participant to another according to a set of procedural rules" (Allen 2001).

A workflow may be defined as a set of "basic work steps called activities which are carried out by processing entities that are either humans or software systems" (Kradolfer 2000). Kradolfer classifies workflows as ad hoc, collaborative, administrative, or production workflows depending on their characteristics.

- *Ad hoc* and *collaborative workflows* involve human actors collaborating on a goal, but with few if any defined procedures for interaction. These workflows differ in the level of business value that they produce. Ad hoc workflows typically handle low business value activities such as scheduling an interview. Collaborative workflows typically handle high business value activities like preparing product documentation. These workflows can be supported by groupware such as conferencing systems, email, calendaring tools, etc.
- *Administrative workflows* refer to low business value administrative domain chains of activities such as purchase-order processing.
- *Production workflows*, on the other hand, refer to high value core business processes, such as insurance claims handling or loan processing in the case of a bank. These workflows correspond to the central, value-producing activities of the business.

Another category is that of transactional workflows, which are required to operate correctly even when concurrency effects and failures are present, such as travel reservation systems involving timed resources such as flight and hotel reservations. If the workflow activities are carried out by humans, the workflow is said to be *human oriented*; in *system-oriented* workflows, the activities are carried out by computers.

Workflow processes can be computer supported by *workflow management systems*. Kradolfer (2000) observes that the "basic idea in workflow management is to capture formal descriptions of business processes and to support the automatic enactment of the processes based on these formal descriptions." Workflow management systems can be used to implement business processes more effectively and flexibly than approaches that hard-code the business processes in the component systems. The development of such workflow management applications may be considered as a special, but widely applicable, class of software engineering applications. The basic steps involved in developing workflow applications are information gathering; business process modeling; and workflow modeling.

The underlying business processes are first modeled using business process modeling tools in order to understand and possibly reengineer the business process. The business tools are not intended to create a model that supports automation of the workflow process. Rather, the business models focus on the "application-oriented point of view, whereas workflow modeling focuses on the technological aspects of the application process and its organizational and technical environment" (Weske 2000). The *workflow model* of the business process formally specifies the process and contains sufficiently detailed information to allow the business process to be automated. The workflow model enhances the business model to incorporate any additional information needed to permit the business process to be controlled automatically by a workflow management system. Furthermore, any application-specific information irrelevant to workflow management is pruned from the model. The workflow model is defined using a *workflow language* and is then implemented in a workflow management system and, finally, deployed (Weske 2000).

Weske (2000) describes the workflow application development in terms of a six-phased development cycle. It begins with a survey phase of the existing process, which generates an *as-is business process* model. A design phase follows that refines the as-is model to reflect the updated business goals in order to create a *to-be business model.* This model is then enhanced with the technical information needed to support the workflow management system producing a *to-be workflow model.* At this point, if the problem is judged amenable to workflow technology, a workflow language is selected to define the workflow. During the next phase, a workflow management system is selected based on constraints that involve integration, interaction, development, and run-time criteria. Then, the workflow model is implemented according to the rules of the selected workflow management system. Subsequently, laboratory and field tests are done on the system.

The development of workflow applications differs from typical software development in a number of significant ways. For example, the constraints imposed by existing legacy systems and the granularity of such systems must be addressed at an early stage. Their integration into the workflow is critical to the success of a workflow project (Weske 2000). Selection of a workflow management system is also tricky because it may be nontrivial to fit available systems to the application requirements (Weske 2000). Prototyping is an important technique in developing workflow environments because, as usual, it increases the likelihood of user acceptance; allows early detection of technical problems; and helps determine the feasibility of the workflow approach to the application.

Workflow system development tends to be susceptible to performance problems that are not recognized until field tests, when they are finally identified under the stress of heavy case loads. This is unsurprising because workflow systems typically have extremely intense performance requirements such as very high reliability demands (such as 24/7 availability) and extensive fault tolerance requirements. An important area of recent workflow management research is how to modify running workflow environments dynamically (Weske 2000) and, in particular, how to integrate legacy systems (which are usually the oldest, most reliable, and mission-critical components of the software environment). One integration technique uses so-called wrappers. A *wrapper* is defined as a software layer that "hides the particularities of the legacy system and presents a clean interface" to an external system like a workflow management system (Weske 2000).

The workflow model can be defined using concepts derived from a *workflow metamodel*, of which there are two kinds. The first type focuses on the network of communications that occur between the actors in the workflow. An example is the model proposed by Winograd and Flores (1987), which viewed the activities as initiated by customer requests whose satisfaction requirements were then negotiated with the actor that performed the request. However, *activity-based models* are the more common workflow metamodel. These provide a number of capabilities (Kradolfer 2000), including:

- Detailed modeling of the worksteps executed by the processors or actors
- Hierarchically nesting workflows for top-down refinement
- Identifying the agents that perform the activities
- Representing workflow control and data flow
- Assigning activities to agents

The metamodels follow a variety of different paradigms. Those that emphasize the flow of control include models based on rules, states, logic, events, or scripting language; Petri nets; etc. (Kradolfer 2000). The objective of a workflow metamodel is to support *workflow enactment*—that is, actual coordinated execution of the workflow activities. In schedule-based metamodels, requests for execution of different types of workflow activities are submitted to a *workflow engine*, which interprets the requests and then "interacts with the processing entities [to ensure] that the activities are executed as prescribed by the workflow type" (Kradolfer 2000). The Workflow Management System must be able to address the distribution of workload to processors; availability of processors; rework requirements when activities are implemented incorrectly; etc.

Weske and colleagues (1999) provide reference models for software engineering and business process reengineering and describe a reference model for workflow application development processes (WADP). This generic model is intended to avoid or minimize difficulties that arise in workflow projects, but the authors underscore that, with respect to effective implementation, there is no substitute for knowledgeable managers, skilled developers, and efficient users. Furthermore, tailoring the reference model to individual projects requires additional overhead. The objective of standardization of workflow management is addressed by the *Workflow Management Coalition*, established in 1993, whose goal is "to establish standards to enable interoperability among different workflow management systems" (Kradolfer 2000).

4.6 Aspect-Oriented Development

Object-oriented programming is best adapted to applications in which the interfaces between the objects are relatively simple. However, in the case of distributed and concurrent systems such as "scheduling, synchronization, fault tolerance, security, testing and verification, [phenomena] are all expressed in such a way that they tend to cut across different objects." This lack of locality tends to undermine the preconditions necessary for the object-oriented paradigm to be successful, so its potential benefits are reduced. Critically, although the key issue of "separation of concerns is at the heart of software development," how to accomplish this separation under such circumstances has not yet been resolved at a methodological level.

The traditional approach to designing software systems has been to focus on partitioning the systems along functional lines and identifying maximally independent functions that can then be implemented with a minimum of cross-dependence. This functional approach is now widely supported by existing programming environments and design paradigms, which provide for modular units for functionality and components using mechanisms such as procedures for functions and objects or classes for components. In many cases, important system properties do not align naturally with the natural functional components in systems (Constantinides et al. 2000). This can occur for objects in object-oriented programming whenever important system properties are not naturally localized to objects. Other system phenomena that exhibit nonlocal characteristics include resource allocation; exception handling; persistence; communication; replication; coordination; memory management; and real-time constraints (Constantinides et al. 2000).

Kiczales et al. (1997) defined *aspects* as "system properties that cut across functional components, increasing their interdependencies." This cross-functional behavior leads to implementation difficulties such as the so-called *code-tangling problem*. Code tangling undermines the originally intended modularity of the system design and degrades the quality of the resulting software. *Aspect-Oriented Software Architecture* (see Table 4.4) is a design strategy that tries to address the design and implementation complications associated with such interdependencies by explicitly introducing aspects as system characteristics. These characteristics straddle the functional divisions of a system and of OO components.

Table 4.4   Profile of Aspect-Oriented Development Model

Category	Specifics
Evolution of goals	How to design effectively when system functions are not localized in objects
Methodology	Aspect-Oriented Software Architecture
Technology	Development tools such as aspect weavers
Critical factors	Identify properties or functions that cross-cut objects or components
Interdisciplinary effects	None
Behavioral considerations	None
Problem nature	Synchronization, coordination, communication, real-time constraints, etc.
Application domain	Distributed and concurrent systems

For example, in an object-oriented environment, the source code that provides the ability to distribute a system across multiple hosts may straddle multiple object-oriented classes and methods. Murphy, Walker, and Baniassad (1999) observed how the design decisions required in such environments may "cross-cut the structure chosen to provide a system's functionality." The purpose of aspect-oriented programming is to facilitate a modular expression of these design decisions in the actual code. The general idea of such a programming approach is as follows. One begins by using a "component language to describe the basic functionality of the system." Then, an aspect language is used "to describe the different cross-cutting properties." The partial products that result from this preliminary separation of concerns are then combined using a so-called *aspect weaver*, which combines the components and the aspects into a cohesive system.

One of the issues that arise during this integration process is whether the weaving should be done in a static or dynamic manner. Under *static weaving,* the system's source code is modified "by inserting aspect-specific statements at join points" (Constantinides et al. 2000) in an inline manner. Murphy and colleagues (1999) conducted a preliminary empirical study to determine the benefits of aspect-oriented programming and its impact on the design process. Their tentative conclusion was that, at least for some small-scale studies, in cases when "an aspect language matched a design concern, such as concurrency, the language provided a vocabulary for expressing and reasoning about that concern." However, when there was a poor match between the expressiveness of the aspect language and the aspect concerns that arose in the project, the aspect language could even exacerbate the complexity of the design.

Constantinides et al. (2000) specifically considered the case of a concurrently shared object. From the point of view of software abstraction, such an object exhibits some type of functional behavior, but the object also requires synchronization and scheduling because it is concurrently shared. The synchronization and scheduling characteristics or phenomena of the system can be interpreted as aspects of the concurrent system. Thus, the synchronization requirement determines which methods and when methods should be enabled or disabled.

In order to accomplish this, the authors viewed the synchronization abstraction as "composed of guards and postactions" (Constantinides et al. 2000). One significant observation was that "the activation order of the aspects is the most important part in order to verify the semantics of the system." For example, the synchronization aspect had to be verified before the scheduling aspect because a "reverse in the order of activation may violate the semantics." The authors also introduced a so-called Aspect Moderator Framework, which was based on the idea of "defining assertions (preconditions and postconditions) as a set of design principles." They observed that this approach is in the spirit of *design by contract*, in which a "software system is viewed as a set of communicating components whose interaction is based on precisely defined specification of the mutual obligations known as *contracts*. These contracts govern the interaction of the element with the rest of the world."

References

Agarwal, R., Jayesh, P., Tanniru, M., & Lynch, J. (2000). Risks of Rapid Application Development. *Commun. ACM*, 43(11), 177–188.

Allen, R. (2001). Workflow: an introduction. *Workflow Handbook 2001*. Workflow Management Coalition, Future Strategies, Inc.: Lighthouse Point, FL, 15–24.

Beck, K. (2000). *Extreme Programming Explained*. Reading, MA: Addison–Wesley.

Beck, K. et al. (2001). Manifesto for agile software development. Retrieved June 17, 2004 from www.agilemanifesto.org.

Boehm, B. (2002). Get ready for agile methods, with care, *IEEE Computer*, January, 64–69.

Clayton, C. (2000). *The Innovator's Dilemma*. New York: HarperBusiness.

Cockburn, A. & Highsmith, J. (2001). Agile software development: the people factor. *IEEE Software*, 131–133.

Cohn, M. & Ford, D. (2003). Introducing an agile process to an organization. *IEEE Computer*, 36(6), 74–77.

Constantinides, C.A., Bader, A., Elrad, T.H., Fayad, M.E., & Netinant, P. (2000). Designing an aspect-oriented framework in an object-oriented environment, *ACM Computing Surv.*, 32, Article No. 41, 12 pages.

Dagnino, A. (2002). An evolutionary life-cycle model with agile practices for software development at ABB. *Proc. 8th IEEE Int. Conf. Eng. Complex Computer Syst.* (ICECCS'02), 1 050-4729/02, 215–223.

Feller, J. & Fitzgerald, B. (2000). A framework analysis of the open source software development paradigm. *Proc. 21st Int. Conf. Inf. Syst.*, Association for Information Systems, 58–69.

Hamlet, D. & Maybee, J., (2001). *The Engineering of Software.* Reading, MA: Addison–Wesley.

Jeusfeld, M. & deMoor, A. (2001). Concept integration precedes enterprise integration. *Proc. 34th Hawaii Int. Conf. Syst. Sci.*, 9, 112–121.

Kiczales, G., Lamping, J., Mendhekar, A., Maeda, C., Lopes, C., Loingtier, J., & Irwin, J. (1997). Aspect-oriented programming. *Proceedings of 11th European Conference on Object-Oriented Programming '97.* Lecture Notes in Computer Science, Vol. 1, 241, Heidelberg: Springer–Verlag.

Kradolfer, M. (2000). A workflow metamodel supporting dynamic reuse-based evolution. Dissertation, Westfalischen Wilhelms University, Munster.

Martin, J. (1991*). Rapid Application Development.* New York: Macmillan.

Murphy, G.C., Walker, R.J., & Baniassad, E.L.A. (1999). Evaluating emerging software development technologies: lessons learned from assessing aspect-oriented programming. *IEEE Trans. Software Eng.,* 25(4), 438–455.

Weske, M., Goesmann, T., Holten, R., & Striemer, R. (1999). A reference model for workflow application development processes. *Proceedings of the International Joint Conference on Work Activities Coordination and Collaboration*, San Francisco, CA (USA). New York: ACM Press, 1–10; also published in: *Software Eng. Notes* 24(2).

Weske, M. (2000). *Workflow Management Systems: Formal Foundation, Conceptual Design, Implementation Aspects,* Technical University of Zurich.

Williams, L. & Kessler, R. (2003). *Pair Programming Illuminated.* Reading, MA: Addison–Wesley.

Winograd, T. & Flores, I. (1987). *Understanding Computers and Cognition.* Reading, MA: Addison–Wesley.

Chapter 5

An Assessment of Process Life-Cycle Models

5.1 Introduction

This chapter discusses the essential purposes and roles of software engineering processes. It begins with critiques of existing models and general proposals that have been made for assessing and evaluating models. The critical role of time as a factor in development is considered, including not only the various scheduling constraints on time to develop but also the business-driven parameter of time to market. The lack of an adequate integration between software and hardware technology, on the one hand, and business and social disciplines, on the other, is identified as a persistent shortcoming undermining the ability of the development process to attack real-world problems optimally.

Next, a series of questionable assumptions that have affected the historical development of software process models are considered, including suppositions about the primacy of the role of internal software factors; the relative independence of software development from the business process; separation of the software project as management enterprise from the software process; and a choice between process-centered versus architecture-centered development. These assumptions have illegitimately constrained and reduced the fundamental role that must be played by people, money, interdisciplinary knowledge, and business goals in terms of their impact on effective problem solution.

The elements of a redefined software engineering process are then identified based on the integration of critical process tasks or activities; required major interdisciplinary resources (people, money, data, exploratory and modeling tools, and methodologies); organizational goals; and the impact of time as components of an ongoing roundtrip approach to business-driven problem solving. The redefinition addresses limitations identified in the literature related to business evaluation metrics; the process environment and external drivers; and process continuation, as fundamental to process definition.

The idea of a software process model that fits every project seems farfetched because any project has so many aspects that it is difficult to capture every potential aspect in a single perspective (Liu & Horowitz 1989). However, this has not prevented the development of process models that have attempted to capture the essential benefits of previous software models in a unified manner. Humphrey (1988) observed that "since the software engineering process used for a specific project should reflect [that project's] particular needs, a framework is needed to provide consistency between projects." Liu and Horowitz (1989) argued against unification in models, but proposed essential features that every successful model should have. These included the ability to: describe the development process as a design process; address parallel processing in large-scale projects; map the diverse set of conditions that exist prior to development activities; debug the process by locating failed activities and resources; and allocate sufficient resources for each activity in the development project.

Some have argued against attempting to structure and manage the software development process because of the overwhelming differences that exist across different projects, firms, and cultures; however, Blackburn, Scudder, and Van Wassenhove (1996) argued to the contrary, observing that worldwide similarities in management of the process are more prevalent than differences. Considerable effort has been made to establish custom solutions based on existing process models. Although few of these efforts have tried to tailor or match process models to specific project needs, many have attempted to provide evaluation criteria or metrics; mechanisms for evolution and improvement; unified frameworks or taxonomies; and supporting tools and environments. Others studies have tried to address the general issue of process description or abstraction by constructing a conceptual process framework, rather than by evaluating existing process models (Armitage & Kellner 1994). These have served as a basis for the process representation or transformation that have assisted in the review, development, and improvement of process models. An understanding of these efforts will contribute to one of the main objectives, which is to build a more comprehensive taxonomy of process models.

In an overall sense, process models are used to enable effective communication; facilitate process reuse; support process evolution; and facilitate process management.

■ Humphrey and Kellner (1989) suggested that, to evaluate the effectiveness of a process model, one should consider its ability to represent the real-world application as well as the way in which work is actually done; provide a flexible, understandable, and powerful framework for representing and improving the software development process; and be refineable or resolvable to any required level of detail or specification

■ Curtis, Kellner, and Over (1992) identified five uses for process models: facilitating human understanding and communication; supporting process improvement; supporting process management; automating process guidance; and automating execution support. All of these uses can also be considered as evaluation criteria for process models as well.

■ Sutton (1988) asserted that, for a process model to be effective, it must exhibit "multidimensional" characteristics, including the ability for decomposition adequately to capture the details of the work to be done; the ability to provide complete coverage of all the activities of the software life cycle; the ability to reflect the distributed nature of the development process including the potential for sequential and parallel processing; and the ability to incorporate related interdisciplinary models from areas such as project and configuration management, software evaluation, and software acquisition into a single system development.

■ Madhavji and colleagues (1994) proposed a method for eliciting and evaluating process models that entailed understanding the organizational environment (organizational, process, and project issues); defining objectives, including model and project-oriented objectives; planning the elicitation strategy; developing process models; validating process models; analyzing process models; post-analysis; and packaging. According to these authors, the basic reasons for using software process models were to produce software of high quality that met budget and time requirements and to do so as far as possible by means of automated tools.

■ Khalifa and Verner (2000) focused on the Waterfall and prototype models in their empirical study, emphasizing the factors driving the usage of specific process models: depth and breadth of use and facilitating conditions (the size of the development team, organizational support, and the speed with which new methodologies were adopted).

■ According to Boehm and Belz (1990), the critical process aspects were requirements growth; the need to understand complex requirements; the need for robustness; available technology; and architectural understanding. They used these as a baseline for a software process model elicitation procedure.

■ Blackburn et al. (1996) identified the five most influential factors in the development process as development time; project characteristics; team size; allocation of time in project stages; and development language selection. The approach was based on a strong correlation between process optimization and software product metrics from a project management prospective.

Madhavji et al. observed that recognized benefits of life-cycle models included the ability to enhance process understanding; determine global activities; reduce cost; improve quality, methods, and tool effectiveness; and improve stakeholder satisfaction. Using estimation techniques, the models addressed problems of resource management such as time and manpower. They also provided predictive capabilities with respect to primary performance measures and captured some of the variability and uncertainty associated with the software development process (Martin & Raffo 1997). However, the models tended to fall short on overall problem comprehension, detailed description, and the ability to adapt or tailor to changing project requirements. They focused more on product engineering than the many elemental process building blocks essential to project management and control (Curtis et al. 1992).

Krasner et al. (1992) criticized the models for their tendency to "focus on series of artifacts that exist at the end of phases of the life cycles, rather than on the processes that are conducted to create the artifacts" in the first place. According to Madhavji et al., these traditional process models led to low software process maturity and difficulties in managing and controlling software processes. Their over-reliance on the Waterfall Model encumbered them with its negative side effects, such as enforcing one-way development by managers; inhibiting creativity based on design and requirements trade-off; and corrupting measurement and tracking systems in processes (Humphrey & Kellner 1989). The conventional models also tended to impose extensive documentation requirements without providing commensurate added value (Krasner et al. 1992).

Humphrey and Kellner (1989) attributed the problems with conventional process models to inaccurate representations on their part of the behavioral aspects of what occurs during software development because of an overly intense focus on task sequencing. Boehm (1996), on the other hand, attributed their weaknesses to factors such as a lack of user-interface prototyping; fixed requirements; inflexible point solutions; high-risk downstream capabilities; and off-target initial releases. According to Boehm, recognition of such problems "led to the development of alternative process models such as risk-driven, reuse-driven, legacy-driven, demonstration-driven, design-to-COT-driven, and incremental, as well as hybrids of any of these with the waterfall or evolutionary development models."

Ropponen and Lyytinen (2000) elaborate on the need for risk management in process model assessment, including risks related to scheduling and timing; system functionality; subcontracting; requirements management; resource usage and performance, and personal management. Madhavji et al. proposed combining process-detailed understanding and process support to address change or volatility in process-centered software environments. They identified several categories or perspectives from which a process model could be viewed in terms of its static and dynamic properties: process steps; artifacts; roles; resources; and constraints.

The analysis by Martin & Raffo (1997) recognized two major approaches in software development: process models and system dynamics. The latter is important in developing an intuitive understanding of how a project will behave under different management polices and alternatives and benefits significantly from simulation techniques. Abdel–Hamid and Madnick (1989) used system dynamics to model project risks such as delays, pressures, and unknown problems at different project levels; however, Raffo and Martin expanded this idea by introducing a continuous simulation framework (1997) that was consistent with the process improvement paradigm inspired by the CMM model (Martin & Raffo 1997; Paulk et al. 1993). Indeed, Boehm recognized the Abdel–Hamid and Madnick model as a realistic contribution to quantitative models of software project dynamics, although he was still concerned about the lack of a quantitative model of software life-cycle evolution (Boehm 1984). Clearly, project management and software economics perspectives have gained greater attention as critical elements in the assessment of process models.

Some of the research on model assessment has focused on classifying process models. Blum (1994) arranged development methods according to a matrix, depending on their focus of interest (the problem or product involved) and the form of representation used (conceptual or formal). Boehm & Port (1999) and Boehm & Belz (1990) addressed the conflicts that occur when a combination of product, process, property, and success models is adopted, leading to model clashes. They proposed a taxonomy of model clashes in an effort to resolve the resulting conflicts.

Over the past decade, the trend towards process improvement has been increasing and turning away from fixed, conventional process models. Thus, Bandinelli et al. (1995) observed that "there has been an increasing interest in the development of frameworks and guidelines to support the evaluation of software process maturity and to identify strategies and key areas of improvement." These authors built on experiences learned from the Capability Maturity Model, Bootstrap, Kaizen, QIP, SPMS, and other models in developing a feedback-loop model for software development organizations.

The model was intended to address problems with discrepancies; descriptions; comprehension; visibility; and traceability among the different process forms (desired, perceived, observed, and actual process). They used the feedback-loop model as a baseline in experiments aimed at improving process maturity. Two inferences can be made from their research. A process model is no longer a fixed model that fits in with a fixed problem definition, but instead dynamically evolves over time in response to changes in the problem until at some point it stabilizes. Second, the ability to capture a real-world situation (actual process) was and still is the most significant issue in assessing process models. The closer that a representation is to the actual situation, the more likely it is to be effective.

Basili and Rombach (1988) proposed the improvement-oriented TAME process model, which is based on a goal–question–metrics (GQM) approach. It includes separate components for characterizing the current status of a project environment; integrating planning for improvement into the execution of projects; executing the construction and analysis of projects; recording project experiences into an experience base; and distributing information across the model and its components. They claim such component integration distinguishes their model from traditional process models that have only partially addressed such issues. They assert that even recently developed process models have not been able to "completely integrate all their individual components in a systematic way that would permit sound learning and feedback for the purpose of project control and improvement of corporate experience."

Kadary and colleagues (1989) raised important questions about the need for or even possibility of a generic paradigm for software life cycles, aspects of such a generic model, and its potential role in industrial practice. Their challenge is difficult because the issue is not yet well structured and one can think of many alternatives that need further testing and assessment.

The research on assessments may be summarized as follows:

■ *Metric-oriented assessments* framed or synthesized processes and provided standards and metrics for further process enhancement and evaluation, as described in the work of Humphrey & Kellner (1989); Sutton (1988); and Curtis et al. (1992). The metrics took the form of factors or goals, as in Boehm and Belz (1990); Madhavji et al. (1994); Khalifa and Verner (2000); and Blackburn et al. (1996). Some assessments suggested elicitation procedures or plans as well (Jaccheri, Picco, & Lago 1998; Madhavji et al. 1994).

■ Unified model or *taxonomy-driven assessments* surveyed as many models as possible in an attempt to build a classification or taxonomy (Blum 1994) or make comprehensive conclusions regarding a unified process model derived through a broad selection and understanding of process models (Jacobson et al. 1999).

■ *Process improvement assessments* come from the perspective that existing models are insufficient and need enhancements and new architectures, as described in Bandinelli et al. (1995); Basili and Rombach (1988); El-Emam and Birk (2000); and Baumert (1994). The Capability Maturity Model has been the official reference platform for this approach, in addition to efforts to integrate it with ISO9000 standards. Some of the assessments have focused on dramatic change rather than incremental development.

■ Tool support and *software environment-based assessments* incorporated automated tools into process modeling. Some have even proposed frameworks for process model generation (Boehm & Belz 1990). These approaches have focused more on software development environments and included tool support to build more sophisticated process models using CASE tools and automation, as described in Osterweil (1997) and Ramanathan and Soumitra (1988). This and the process improvement category overlap substantially.

5.2 The Dimension of Time

Time has been the critical factor in software development from its beginnings; the original motivation for interest in computing was the computer's ability to carry out tasks faster than could be done otherwise. Computer hardware provided fast processing power and high-speed memories provided fast storage; software adapted this technology to the needs of individuals and organizations to address problems in a timely manner. It took only a while to recognize that building effective software required more than just the time needed to write the source code for a software product. Experience underscored the obvious: software was only valuable when it met people's needs and created value. Software came to be viewed as a system that emerged during the course of multiple, evolutionary, interdisciplinary life-cycle phases, rather than a one-shot effort composed from a largely technical perspective.

Accordingly, the objective of development shifted dramatically, from saving time in the short term to saving time in the long term, with software production recognized as a lengthy process that was engaged in developing solutions compliant with stakeholder requirements. This decisive attitudinal change was the first step in transitioning software development from coding to engineering, where business goals drove software construction and not vice versa.

Of course, the short-term effect of the time factor was not cost free. Software economics has underscored the importance of the time value of money in assessing the actual costs and benefits of a software project in terms of discounted cash flow, net present value, return on investment, and break-even analysis. Additionally, business and technology have undergone dramatic—even revolutionary—changes during the historic time-line of software development, creating new demands and facilitating new capabilities. From any perspective, time repeatedly plays a key role in software development and its evolution.

Thus, a firm's failure to respond to new business requirements within an adequate *time to market* can result in serious loses in sales and market share; failing to exploit new enabling technologies can allow advantageous advances to be exploited by competitors. Although it is derived from a business context, this time-to-market notion now plays a major role in software process paradigms. The implication is that short-term cycle time must become shorter and, at the same time, the features and expected quality of the final system must be retained. This is the new challenge faced by software development: building quality systems faster. The required acceleration of the software development process entails an extensive body of methodologies and techniques such as reusability; CASE tools; parallel development; and innovative approaches to project management.

5.3 The Need for a Business Model in Software Engineering

Software engineering faces several dilemmas. It has comprehensive goals, but limited tools. It demands broad perspectives, but depends on narrowly focused practitioners. It places a high premium on quality, but often has insufficient inputs to its problem-solving process. As a field, software engineering has yet to define theories and frameworks that adequately combine the disciplines of software and hardware technology with related business and social science disciplines to attack real-world problems optimally. Despite advances, software engineering tends to remain code driven and is burdened in testing for bugs, program errors, and verification, even though reusable objects, reusable applications, and CASE tools have long been available.

The engineering of software entails inviting software technology to help tackle human problems rather than just shoehorning human problems into a software solution. This requires reordering the relation between people and computers; computer programs are understood to play an important but limited role in problem-solving strategy. Such an approach to software engineering would still be software driven in the sense that it was driven by the need to develop software for automated as opposed to manual problem solving; however, it would view problems and evaluate solutions from a broadly interdisciplinary perspective in which software was understood and used as a tool.

Requirements engineering is supposed to address the problem part of software engineering, but it is part of the traditional view that looks at the problem-solving process as a phase in the software development life cycle, rather than at the software development life-cycle as part of the problem-solving process. The software development life cycle never ends with a solution, but only with a software product. Although one may assume that a software product should be the solution, in practice this never happens because software systems are only part of a total organizational context or human system; one cannot guarantee that these solutions are effective independently of their context.

5.4 Classic Invalid Assumptions

Four unspoken assumptions that have played an important role in the history of software development are considered next.

5.4.1 First Assumption: Internal or External Drivers

The first unspoken assumption is that *software problems are primarily driven by internal software factors*. Granted this supposition, the focus of problem solving will necessarily be narrowed to the software context, thereby reducing the role of people, money, knowledge, etc. in terms of their potential to influence the solution of problems. Excluding the people factor reduces the impact of disciplines such as management (people as managers); marketing (people as customers); and psychology (people as perceivers). Excluding the money factor reduces the impact of disciplines such as economics (software in terms of business value cost and benefit); financial management (software in terms of risk and return); and portfolio management (software in terms of options and alternatives). Excluding the knowledge factor reduces the impact of engineering; social studies; politics; language arts; communication sciences; mathematics; statistics; and application area knowledge (accounting, manufacturing, World Wide Web, government, etc).

It has even been argued that the entire discipline of software engineering emerged as a reaction against this assumption and represented an attempt to view software development from a broader perspective. Examples range from the emergence of requirements engineering to the spiral model to human–computer interaction (HCI). Nonetheless, these developments still viewed non-software-focused factors such as ancillary or external drivers and failed to place software development in a comprehensive, interdisciplinary context. Because software development problems are highly interdisciplinary in nature, they can only be understood using interdisciplinary analysis and capabilities. In fact, no purely technical software problems or products exist because every software product is a result of multiple factors related to people, money, knowledge, etc., rather than only to technology.

5.4.2 Second Assumption: Software or Business Processes

A second significant unspoken assumption has been that the *software development process is independent of the business processes in organizations*. This assumption implied that it was possible to develop a successful software product independently of the business environment or the business goals of a firm. This led most organizations and business firms to separate software development work, people, architecture, and planning from business processes. This separation not only isolated the software-related activities, but also led to different goals, backgrounds, configurations, etc. for software as opposed to business processes. As a consequence, software processes tended to be driven by their internal purposes, which were limited to product functionality and not to product effectiveness.

This narrow approach had various negative side effects on software development. For example, the software process was allowed to be virtually business free. Once the product was finalized, it was tested and validated only for functionality, as opposed to being verified for conformity to stakeholder goals. As a result, even if the product did not effectively solve the underlying business problems or create a quantifiable business value for the organization, it could still pass its test. Because software development was not synchronized with the business process, software problems could be "solved" without actually solving business problems.

5.4.3 Third Assumption: Processes or Projects

A third unspoken assumption was that the *software project was separate from the software process*. Thus, a software process was understood as reflecting an area of computer science concern, but a software project was understood as a business school interest. If one were a computer science specialist, one would view a quality software product as the outcome of a development process that involved the use of good algorithms, data base deign, and code. If one were an MIS specialist, one would view a successful software system as the result of effective software economics and software management.

This dichotomy ignored the fact that the final product was identical regardless of who produced it or how it was produced. The assumption reinforced the unwise isolation of project management from the software development process, thus increasing the likelihood of product failure. In contrast to this assumption, interdisciplinary thinking combines the process with the project; computer science with the MIS approach; and software economics with software design and implementation in a unified approach. Just as in the case of the earlier assumptions, this assumption overlooks the role of business in the software development process.

5.4.4 Fourth Assumption: Process Centered or Architecture Centered

There are currently *two broad approaches in software engineering; one is process centered and the other is architecture centered.* In process-centered software engineering, the quality of the product is seen as emerging from the quality of the process. This approach reflects the concerns and interests of industrial engineering, management, and standardized or systematic quality assurance approaches such as the Capability Maturity Model and ISO. The viewpoint is that obtaining quality in a product requires adopting and implementing a correct problem-solving approach. If a product contains an error, one should be able to attribute and trace it to an error that occurred somewhere during the application of the process by carefully examining each phase or step in the process.

In contrast, in architecture-centered software engineering, the quality of the software product is viewed as determined by the characteristics of the software design. Studies have shown that 60 to 70 percent of the faults detected in software projects are specification or design faults. Because these faults constitute such a large percentage of all faults within the final product, it is critical to implement design-quality metrics. Implementing design-quality assurance in software systems and adopting proper design metrics have become key to the development process because of their potential to provide timely feedback. This allows developers to reduce costs and development time by ensuring that the correct measurements are taken from the very beginning of the project before actual coding commences. Decisions about the architecture of the design have a major impact on the behavior of the resulting software—particularly the extent of development required; reliability; reusability; understandability; modifiability; and maintainability of the final product, characteristics that play a key role in assessing overall design quality.

However, an architecture-centered approach has several drawbacks. In the first place, one only arrives at the design phase after a systematic process. The act or product of design is not just a model or design architecture or pattern, but a solution to a problem that must be at least reasonably well defined. For example, establishing a functional design can be done by defining architectural structure charts, which in turn are based on previously determined data flow diagrams, after which a transformational or transitional method can be used to convert the data flow diagrams into structure charts. The data flow diagrams are outcomes of requirements analysis process based on a preliminary inspection of project feasibility. Similarly, designing object-oriented architectures in UML requires first building use-case scenarios and static object models prior to moving to the design phase.

A further point is that the design phase is a process involving architectural, interface, component, data structure, and database design (logical and physical). The design phase cannot be validated or verified without correlating or matching its outputs to the inputs of the software development process. Without a process design, one could end up building a model, pattern, or architecture that was irrelevant or at least ambivalent because of the lack of metrics for evaluating whether the design was adequate. In a comprehensive process model, such metrics are extracted from predesign and postdesign phases. Finally, a process is not merely a set of documents, but a problem-solving strategy encompassing every step needed to achieve a reliable software product that creates business value. A process has no value unless it designs quality solutions.

5.5 Implications of the New Business Model

The following consequences result when one refocuses from engineering software for the sake of the technological environment to engineering software for people's sake:

- Solutions will evolve only from carefully understood problems. The resulting solutions will be guided by their originating problems and considered successful only if they are able to solve those problems. The solution is never solely the software product, but everything needed to solve the problem.

- Problems will not be defined in terms of what the people want the software to do for them. Problem definition will address the relevant human needs regardless of the role of the software in meeting those needs. Subsequent to an interdisciplinary definition of the problem, an interdisciplinary solution will be proposed that will utilize the available, relevant human, financial, informational, technological, and software resources.
- The iterative software development process will become part of the synchronized business process and will in turn deliver business process total solutions. Thus, the business process will shape the software process in terms of its goals, metrics, and requirements.

5.6 Role of the Problem-Solving Process in This Approach

A solution represents the final output from a problem-solving process. To obtain reliable solutions, the problem-solving process must receive all the requisite inputs. The more comprehensive, carefully defined and well-established these inputs are, the more effective the solutions will be. Regardless of whether one uses a manual or computerized system to tackle a problem, the problem-solving process can properly operate only when it has sufficient relevant data, a well-defined problem, and appropriate tools.

5.6.1 Data

The importance of data, raw facts, or statistical summaries of raw facts in solving problems is decisive for the scientific method. Obviously, without adequate data, it is difficult to measure or estimate the "distance" from the current situation to a desired situation. Two basic problems that arise with data are:

- Data may be insufficient to provide a deep understanding of a problem domain or situation. It is hard to establish a solid point of reference in the context of insufficient data. Ambiguity may be substantial and uncertainty exacerbated.
- Data may be excessive, making it difficult to identify or distinguish which data is relevant or significant to the problem under consideration. An excess of data can lead to time wasted pursuing false directions, thus causing delays in solution and possibly allowing further development of system-degrading problems.

Defining an accurate context for business problems is critical to identifying and obtaining relevant data. Effective data capture requires data collection and data mining. Appropriate tools are needed to ensure the quality and speed of the collection and mining processes. In data collection, relevant data is explored to provide a comprehensive picture of the problems; this requires creative thinking and the use of diverse resources, disciplines, and skills. Interdisciplinary tools are essential. In data mining, the collected data is further examined and filtered to obtain the significant data. Once again, interdisciplinary tools are essential to extracting the relevant data.

5.6.2 Problem Definition

Once sufficient data is available, problems may at least potentially be properly defined. Problem definition is the foundation of an effective problem-solving process. It entails structuring, interpreting, and analyzing data. Subsequent to the initial data analysis, one can arrive at a reliable problem definition that captures the essential aspects of the situation. Problem definition depends heavily on data, so if data is inaccurate, incomplete, irrelevant, or insufficient, problems cannot be appropriately defined. On the other hand, determining which data to seek depends on the problem's initial definition, which sets the context or circumstance in which data is gathered.

5.6.3 Tools and Capabilities

Tools can support the problem and solution level of the problem-solving process, helping to automate and accelerate the entire process. Given adequate tools, accurate and reliable data can be determined and maintained. Tools can assist in data mining raw facts and elicit the important, relevant data. In the present context, tools encompass all the available capabilities that can be brought to bear during a problem-solving process; these tools are as critical as a knowledge base and personnel abilities. CASE tools are popular because of their applicability in the software development process, but the role of tools transcends software development. They encompass analysis, design, and implementation and extend to support the entire business process of an organization.

Interdisciplinary thinking is a necessity because a one-sided view of a problem will not reveal a comprehensive picture of a business or organizational problem. In an interdisciplinary approach to problem solving, a comprehensive diagnosis of the business problem is an essential part of the process. Interdisciplinary thinking not only permits a full analysis of a business problem, but also enables problem-solvers to take advantage of existing interdisciplinary abilities. An understanding of different disciplines is the basic enabling factor that allows incorporation of interdisciplinary thinking in problem solving. Bringing this knowledge to bear requires identifying and eliminating sources of ignorance about a problem. Interdisciplinary thinking also reflects an appreciation of the role of diversity. In fact, it can be viewed as a means for integrating diversity in a productive and effective manner. It allows recognition, measurement, and utilization of differences in terms of their positive role in problem solving. The following sections identify how ignorance and diversity influence problem solving.

5.7 Redefining the Software Engineering Process

The definition of the development process has long been disputed in software engineering literature. Computer scientists tend to view the process as one of providing a theoretical framework with the objective of systematically producing cost-effective software products. Project managers view the process as a way of partitioning projects into activities to provide guidelines for project managers. The problem with both views is their narrow focus on the activities that should be involved and on how the activities should be ordered or scheduled. Both views lack effective ways for optimizing the process to achieve real-world problem solving, which requires additional components beyond those that organize an identified set of activities in a particular order. These components include:

- A means for evaluating the process against the business goals of an organization
- A means for recognizing and responding to the diverse environmental, external, or interdisciplinary factors in the context of which the process functions or operates
- A means for identifying in what way the different process activities are interrelated or interdependent in terms of fulfilling organizational goals

Although many efforts have been made to establish or define metrics for assessing the quality of the software process and product, these metrics never seem to be part of the underlying process definition and rarely have clear connections to the external drivers in the surrounding environment. Consequently, software process definitions have generally lacked environmental interactivity and business purpose, although there have been some notable exceptions. For example, the Capability Maturity Model approach was introduced by the Software Engineering Institute partially in an attempt to define a process model responsive to changes and pressures from environmental factors. Overall, however, most approaches have paid little attention to ensuring that interdisciplinary resources are integrated into software process activities to advance business processes and goals.

5.7.1 Round-Trip Problem-Solving Approach

The software engineering process represents a *round-trip framework* for problem solving in a business context in several senses.

- The software engineering process is a problem-solving process entailing that software engineering should incorporate or utilize the problem-solving literature regardless of its interdisciplinary sources.
- The value of software engineering derives from its success in solving business and human problems. This entails establishing strong relationships between the software process and the business metrics used to evaluate business processes in general.
- The software engineering process is a round-trip approach. It has a bidirectional character, which frequently requires adopting forward and reverse engineering strategies to restructure and reengineer information systems. It uses feedback control loops to ensure that specifications are accurately maintained across multiple process phases; reflective quality assurance is a critical metric for the process in general.
- The nonterminating, continuing character of the software development process is necessary to respond to ongoing changes in customer requirements and environmental pressures.

5.7.2 Activities

The software engineering process comprises a set of interrelated activities that mutually require and support each another. Although the activities vary in terms of their names, labels, degrees of abstraction, or resolution, they always include the following steps:

- A well-defined process and project, as well as a well-defined problem identified through diagnosis and analysis
- A well-defined solution obtained through design and software architecture and based on the problem definition
- An accurate and precise execution of the defined solution obtained through implementation and installation

- Well-defined testing processes that use business and quality assurance metrics: testing, validation, verification, and quality assurance
- Continual improvement or adjustment of the implemented solution in response to customers, changes, competition, reengineering, and maintenance

5.7.3 Goals

The software engineering process must be guided, assessed, and evaluated by ongoing references to the business goals of an organization, which guide the entire process from beginning to end. These define the business case and provide the foundation for the requirements analysis process. They determine the economic and organizational feasibility of the software project. They serve as metrics to assess the performance and quality of the process and of the generated solution. Finally, they motivate continual improvement in the software engineering process.

5.7.4 Interdisciplinary Resources

The software engineering process integrates and uses interdisciplinary resources to execute its activities and meet its goals. Interdisciplinary resources encompass multiple disciplines and a diverse range of knowledge about people, money, data, tools, application knowledge, methodologies, time, and goals. This inclusive approach implies effectively executing each activity in the process and requires appropriate consideration of the pertinent interdisciplinary resources. Utilization of interdisciplinary resources is closely related to process performance and product quality. Failure to integrate interdisciplinary resources can significantly affect the success of process or project management, accuracy in problem definition, and the effectiveness of the final solution. The integration of interdisciplinary resources represents a critical recognition: namely, the importance of interdisciplinary thinking in software engineering in contrast to the prevailing attitude in conventional approaches. Interdisciplinary resources encompass multiple disciplines and a diverse range of knowledge about people; money; data; tools; application knowledge; methodologies; time; and goals, as described earlier.

5.7.5 Time

The software engineering process depends on time as a critical asset as well as a constraint or restriction on the process. Time can be a hurdle for organizational goals, effective problem solving, and quality assurance.

Managed effectively, time can support the competitive advantage of an organization, but time is also a limitation, restricting or stressing quality and imposing an obstacle to efficient problem solving. Time is the major concern of various stakeholders in the software engineering process, from users, customers, and business managers to software developers and project managers.

Time is closely correlated with money and cost, tools, and the characteristics of development methodologies like Rapid Application Development that aim primarily at reducing time and accelerating the software engineering process. These methodologies exhibit characteristics such as reusability, which emphasizes avoiding reinventing the wheel, object-oriented analysis, design, and implementation. Examples include assembly from reusable components and component-based development; business objects; distributed objects; object-oriented software engineering and object-oriented business process reengineering; utilizing unified modeling languages (UML); and commercial-off-the-shelf software. Other characteristics are automation (via CASE tools); prototyping; outsourcing; extreme programming; and parallel processing.

A redefined software engineering process must integrate the critical activities; major interdisciplinary resources (people, money, data, tools, and methodologies); organizational goals; and time in an ongoing round-trip approach to business-driven problem solving. This redefinition must address limitations identified in the literature related to business metrics, the process environment and external drivers, and process continuation, as fundamentals of process definition. A conceptual framework should emphasize the following characteristics for interdisciplinary software engineering. It must address exploring resources, external drivers, and diversity in the process environment to optimize the development process. It must overcome knowledge barriers in order to establish interdisciplinary skills in software-driven problem-solving processes. It must recognize that organizational goals determine the desired business values, which in turn guide, test, and qualify the software engineering process.

The process activities are interrelated and not strictly sequential. Irrelevant activities not related to or that do not add value to other activities should be excluded. The optimized software engineering process must be iterative in nature with the degree of iteration ranging from internal feedback control to continual process improvement. The software engineering process is driven by time, which is a critical factor for goals; competition; stakeholder requirements; change; project management; money; evolution of tools; and problem-solving strategies and methodologies.

References

Abdel–Hamid, T. & Madnick, S.E. (1989). Lessons learned from modeling the dynamics of software development. *Commun. ACM,* 32(12), 14–26.

Armitage, J.W. & Kellner, M.I. (1994). A conceptual schema for process definitions and models. *Proceedings of the 3rd International Conference on the Software Process,* Reston, VA. Washington, D.C.: IEEE Computer Society Press, 153–165.

Bandinelli, S., Fuggetta, A., Lavazza, L., Loi, M., & Picco, G.P. (1995). Modeling and improving an industrial software process. *IEEE Trans. Software Eng.,* 21(5), 440–454.

Basili, V.R. & Rombach, H.D. (1988). The TAME project: towards improvement-oriented software environments. *IEEE Trans. Software Eng.,* 14(6), 752–772.

Baumert, J.H. (1994). Process assessment with a project focus. *IEEE Software* 11(2), 89–91.

Blackburn, J.D., Scudder, G.D., & Van Wassenhove, L.N. (1996). Improving speed and productivity of software development: a global survey of software developers. *IEEE Trans. Software Eng.,* 22(12), 875–885.

Blum, B.I. (1994). Taxonomy of software development methods. *Commun. ACM,* 37(11), 82–94.

Boehm, B. (1984). Software engineering economics. *IEEE Trans. Software Eng.,* 10(1), 4–21.

Boehm, B. (1996). Anchoring the software process. *IEEE Software,* 13(4), 73–82.

Boehm, B. (2002). Get ready for agile methods, with care, *IEEE Computer,* 64–69.

Boehm, B. & Belz, F. (1990). Experiences with the Spiral Model as a process model generator. *Proceedings of the 5th International Software Process Workshop,* Kennebunkport, ME. Los Alamitos, CA: IEEE Computer Society Press, 43–45.

Boehm, B. & Port, D. (1999). Escaping the software tar pit: model clashes and how to avoid them. *Software Eng. Notes,* 24(1), 36–48.

Curtis, W., Kellner, M.I., & Over, J. (1992). Process modeling. *Commun. ACM,* 32(9), 75–90.

El-Emam, K. & Birk, A. (2000). Validating the ISO/IEC 15504 measure of software requirements analysis process capability. *IEEE Trans. Software Eng.,* 26(6), 541–566.

Humphrey, W.S. (1988). Software engineering process: definition and scope. *Proceedings of the 4th International Software Process Workshop,* Moreton-hampstead, Devon (U.K.). New York: ACM Press, 82–83.

Humphrey, W.S. (1995). *A Discipline for Software Engineering.* Reading, MA: Addison–Wesley.

Humphrey, W.S. & Kellner, M.I. (1989). Software process modeling: principles of entity process models. *Proceedings of the 1989 International Conference on Software Engineering,* Pittsburgh, PA. New York: ACM Press, 331–342.

Jaccheri, M.L., Picco, G.P., & Lago, P. (1998). Eliciting software process models with the E3 language. *ACM Trans. Software Eng. Methodol.,* 7(4), 368–410.

Jacobson, I., Booch, G., & Rumbaugh, J. (1999). *The Unified Software Development Process,* Reading, MA: Addison-Wesley.

Kadary, V., Even–Tsur, D., Halperin, N., & Koenig, S. (1989). Software life-cycle models—industrial implication. *Proceedings of the 4th Israel Conference on Computer Systems and Software Engineering,* Los Alamitos, CA: IEEE Computer Society Press, 98–103.

Khalifa, M. & Verner, J.M. (2000). Drivers for software development method usage, *IEEE Trans. Eng. Manage.,* 47(3), 360–369.

Krasner, H., Tirrel, J., Linehan, J., Arnold, P., & Ett, W.H. (1992). Lessons learned from a software process modeling system. *Commun. ACM,* 35(9), 91–100.

Liu, L. & Horowitz, E. (1989). A formal model for software project management. *IEEE Trans. Software Eng.,* 15(10), 1280–1293.

Madhavji, N.H., Holtje, D., WonKook, H., & Bruckhaus, T. (1994). Elicit: a method for eliciting process models. *Proceedings of the 3rd International Conference on the Software Process*, Reston, VA. Los Alamitos, CA: IEEE Computer Society Press, 111–122.

Martin, M. & Raffo, R.H. (1997). Considerations in selecting software process models. *Proc. Portland Int. Conf. Manage. Eng. Technol.* (PICMET), Portland, OR, July 21–24.

Osterweil, L.J. (1997). Software processes are software too, revisited. *Proceedings of the 1997 International Conference on Software Engineering*, Boston, MA. New York: ACM Press, 540–548.

Paulk, M.C., Curtis, B., Chrissis, M.B., & Weber, C.V. (1993*). Capability Maturity Model for Software, Version 1.1*, CMU-SEI-93-TR-24, Software Engineering Institute, Pittsburgh, PA.

Ramanathan, J. & Soumitra, S. (1988). Providing customized assistance for software life-cycle approaches. *IEEE Trans. Software Eng.,* 14(6), 749–757.

Ropponen, J. & Lyytinen, K. (2000). Components of software development risk: how to address them? A project manager survey. *IEEE Trans. Software Eng.,* 26(2), 98–112.

Sutton, W.L. (1988). Advanced models of the software process. *Proceedings of the 4th International Software Process Workshop*, Moretonhampstead, Devon, (U.K.). Baltimore, MD: ACM Press: 156–158.

Section II

Strategies for Solving Software Problems

Chapter 6

The Problem-Solving Process

6.1 Introduction

This chapter considers the relation between classic problem-solving concepts and software development, particularly in a business environment. A basic point concerns the advantages that accrue from exploiting diversity as a tool in problem solving, where diversity refers to the differences in cultural or personal background; professional experience; problem perspective; understanding; or technical and disciplinary capability. Diversity is a frequently overlooked resource that offers a unique opportunity for achieving a broader, more integrated approach to solving problem. Failure to capitalize on it undermines the ability of software development to address the complexity of real problems.

A related issue is that, because of their technical background, computer scientists may overemphasize the centrality of technical capability, but the correct identification of business goals is often the critical factor for effective development, with business goals providing the criteria and framework according to which the suitability of software systems can be properly assessed. Such an approach is user centered, or customer driven. It acknowledges the decisive importance of user perception and assumes solutions should come from a thorough understanding of user needs.

This chapter examines the impact of problem-solving concerns and principles on the development process because software development is closely linked to the concepts and strategies of problem solving. A review is presented of the basic ideas regarding problem solving and some of the kinds of problems that arise specifically in business environments, such as how to meet standards; selection from a set of alternative solutions; satisfying customer expectations; goal evolution; and improving organizational process. Finally, a brief review of the theory of problem solving, its concepts, methods, strategies, and their relation to approaches used in software development is given, together with some classic approaches used in business problem solving.

Problem solving can benefit greatly from incorporating an appreciation for diversity as a core value. In human terms, diversity manifests itself in the form of differences in cultural or personal background; professional experience; problem perspective; understanding; or technical capability. Although diversity has historically often precipitated conflict and exclusion, from a problem-solving point of view, it presents an irreplaceable opportunity to develop broader, more encompassing, and integrated approaches to solving problems. By learning to view diversity as an asset rather than as a barrier or obstacle, one can become motivated to understand problems in an interdisciplinary manner and to capitalize on the ability of diversity to identify and enable the creation of better solutions.

A diversity-driven framework can allow one to discover more aspects of a problem or solution than might have otherwise been recognized in a more unilateral or monochromatic framework. Clearly, such exposed or emergent issues should not be precluded from consideration and exploitation merely because of their interdisciplinary origin or character. A diversity-driven attitude may complicate the problem-solving process; however, this merely reflects the fact that previously unidentified aspects of a problem or sources for its solution are being recognized, accepted, and dealt with.

Consider, for example, the case of a business that uses software systems at every level of its manufacturing and sales processes. Suppose that the business has funded the development of an expensive software system intended to support its basic business functions; however, the cost of development has considerably exceeded its forecast benefits. The company's managers had assumed the new software would solve their business problems. The system's software developers had assumed the application would be successful because they had previously worked successfully with clients from similar industries. However, despite extensive communication between both sides, a standard framework that could be used as a common basis for solving the business problems encountered was never adopted. The software developers viewed the problem from a technical perspective, expecting a minimal need to tailor the product to the company's specific requirements. The company's managers conceived of the product as a software system that would operate like a black box generating the desired results when the needed inputs were provided.

The complexity of the real problem exceeded the capabilities of the software system. Here were hidden details, lurking behind the scenes, inadequately understood or recognized, and appreciated only by company workers, technicians, or administrative staff. Interdisciplinary factors contributed to problems in the business processes, encompassing financial, managerial, technical, psychological, legal, societal and educational issues. The background of the developers was not adequate to understanding the role of these problem factors in creating complexity. The managers never realized that the software solution could be so limited and inflexible, and they failed to grasp how much more time and money was required to have the system up and running as expected.

The company is the client, so arguably the software development team bears the brunt of the responsibility for resolving the problems. However, the software development process is tightly and inextricably coupled with business processes. The development team's expertise and training were not developed for the purpose of understanding the big picture view of a business problem. Simply put, the team's academic and professional preparation focused on how to solve well-structured problems that could be handled by developing appropriate software systems. As a consequence, the developers solved problems as perceived and not necessarily problems as they actually exist in an organizational context.

The business managers failed to appreciate that anything less than their complete and ongoing involvement could undermine the success of the software project. In fact, the entire organization should have been involved because every functional department of the organization would be affected by the software system under development; all those to be affected could have contributed to a more effective analysis of the business processes of the organization. An enterprisewide approach to problem solving was not done in this hypothetical company, resulting in an unsuccessful and cost-ineffective software solution.

Project management represents another interdisciplinary factor in software development. For example, reports from studies such as that of Glass (1998) indicate that almost 40 percent of software faults could be avoided by appropriate scheduling, thus reducing stress on the developers and also expediting the process. An additional one-third of problems can be attributed to human factors rather than to technical difficulties. The combined effects thus indicate that about 70 percent of all faults are directly related to project management. Figure 6.1 depicts the multidimensional character of business problems in terms of four underlying requirements: operational; human driven; business; and technical, as well as the impact of the degree of problem complexity. This ranges from the structured problems that arise at the operational level to the ill-structured problems

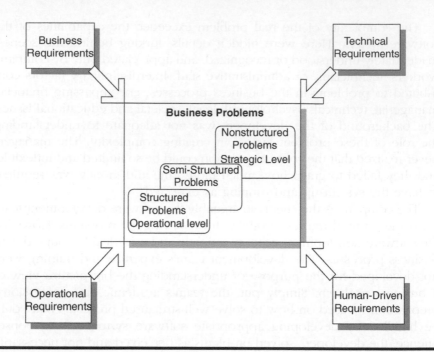

Figure 6.1 Multidimensional view of business problem (rarely realized by software developers).

arising at the strategic level of organizations, which affect the proper understanding of a business problem.

Computer scientists have in the past overemphasized the centrality of technical capability. Development time and effort were thus often expended in solving misperceived problems or providing software solutions to problems that did not need an automated approach. In such situations, misdirected software development not only wastes time, but may also exacerbate existing problems or introduce new ones. Of course, there have been many successful applications that reflected a thorough understanding of user requirements and organizational context or culture. However, these applications are not as well represented in the literature as they should be, so the replication of such accomplishments is hindered. Indeed, research or theoretical literature that situates such best practice within the context of a comprehensive and systematic framework for problem solving is currently rather limited.

The present chapter has the objective of introducing software engineering from such a comprehensive or global prospective. Rather than taking a highly focused, specialized approach, it will broadly address "computerization" as an enabling tool that assists in creating business value for any kind of organization. The software engineering literature is replete with frameworks and studies; however, most software development publications have tended to address the software crisis as a reaction to software project failures, instead of focusing on the underlying issues of business value that constitute the main rationale for using software.

Software systems introduced a new element in the historical evolution of problem solving. They provided new ways to accelerate, validate, communicate, secure, and enrich business problem solving. Using software systems, businesses could be monitored, understood, and controlled better. However, none of these outcomes is guaranteed without the proper use of software in terms of effective, efficient problem solving. Thus, the identification of business goals is the most appropriate perspective from which to view, evaluate, and apply software. Business goals provide the criteria and framework according to which software systems can be properly assessed. These goals should be the basic metric or measure of the distance from a problem to its solution. When business goals are accomplished more effectively, the distance becomes smaller.

Software should be viewed in this context as a capability that better enables businesses by bridging the gap between business problems and their solutions. Whenever software engineering is viewed as separate from business goals and strategies, the paradoxical outcome is that software may be improved without any corresponding impact on the value that the software is supposed to create for businesses. Software improvement is not the ultimate goal of software development. Understanding this relationship between business and software is the correct starting point for developing business software and the essential foundation for establishing more effective software engineering frameworks.

6.2 What Is a Problem?

The way to solve a problem is first to understand it. A problem exists whenever a gap is present between an initial or current state and a desired or goal state (Hewett 1995). Equivalently, a problem exists when a difference exists between an existing situation and a desired situation (Pounds 1967). These definitions imply that, by reducing the difference, a problem is solved or at least ameliorated. The process of problem reduction refers to the approach in which problems are partitioned or broken into smaller problems and perhaps iteratively further decomposed until one eventually arrives at reduced problems that can be easily or more readily handled. Such problem reduction is a core strategy in problem solving.

A more contextual way of looking at problem solving is as the difference between things as perceived versus things as derived (Gause

& Weinberg 1990). This is a user-centered or customer-driven approach because it acknowledges the decisive importance of user perception and assumes solutions should come from a thorough understanding of user needs. Acknowledging actual user needs can prevent developing expensive or unneeded solutions or solutions for the wrong problem.

A situation is problematic when things are not what one would like them to be but is not quite sure what to do about it (Eden, Jones, & Sims 1983). This definition views problems from a psychological or cognitive prospective, which involves uncertainty and equivocality as major manifestations of problems. Any situation in which an expected level of performance is not achieved and the cause of the unacceptable performance is unknown can also be considered problematic (Kepner & Tregoe 1981). This definition views the desired situation as a fixed reference standard or metric. It is derived from the feedback control-loop concept in engineering in which an existing situation and a desired standard are continuously compared. For control purposes in engineering, a problem is defined as a circumstance in which a change must be made to the current process to return it to an acceptable level. A problem occurs when a standard or metric has declined compared to a previous high point or agreed-upon standard. Problems are recognized when improvements are needed within the existing situation to return it to an original expectation.

A problem involves a situation in which a decision-making individual, group, or team has alternative courses of action available; the choice made can have a significant impact, but the decision-maker has some doubt as to which alternative should be selected (Ackoff 1981). This definition views a problem as a selection process among competing alternatives. It assumes that the alternatives are available and implies that the desired approach may be to use a set of weighted criteria to quantify the comparison process to reach an optimum solution.

Although many definitions for the word *problem* can be found in the literature, all of them depend on the notion of a difference, as illustrated in Figure 6.2. First, some *difference* is required to have a problem; otherwise, no problem exists and it is a waste of resources to solve nonexisting or misunderstood problems. The difference may be a desirable

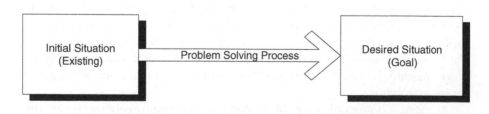

Figure 6.2   The problem-solving process from initial situation to final goal.

intermediate goal that leads to new, better goals, as can be seen in continuous and continual improvement approaches to problem solving. The difference may not exist in an initial situation because problems may not only reflect failures in existing situations, but may also arise because of evolution in a situation. For example, a difference can arise from a change in goals as well as from a decrease in satisfaction with an initial state. In business, a change in goals may reflect a change in experience; available tools and technology; policies and methods; market share; or the overall business environment.

A well-defined problem statement contains three principal elements: goal, givens, and unknowns; these are shaped by the process of problem solving into a solution. A problem may also contain additional important elements that must be recognized and defined, such as conditions, constraints, and operators. Identifying a problem's goal, givens, unknowns, conditions, and constraints, based on the current representation of the problem, is the first step in problem solving. One then proceeds to solve a problem by redefining it into subproblems and restating the goal in terms of subgoals (Duncker 1945; Newell and Simon 1972; Wickelgren 1974; Rubinstein 1975; Mayer 1983; Rist 1986). The most common terminology for problem solving is defined next, following Polya (1945), Duncker (1945), Newell and Simon (1972), Wickelgren (1974), Rubinstein (1975), and Mayer (1983).

A goal is what one wants to accomplish. It must be extracted from a problem statement by the problem solver and then represented appropriately. A well-defined problem statement begins with a representation of the specific facts that must be identified prior to solving the problem; these are known as the problem *givens*. Problem u*nknowns* are then identified and detailed. These are particular things that must be found out or resolved in order to accomplish the goal. As an example, consider the problem of sorting a list. The given is the unsorted list. The goal is to rearrange the list so that it is sorted. The unknown is the sorted list.

Conditions and constraints are qualifying factors that must be taken into consideration when solving a problem. Conditions tend to be logical restrictions, and constraints tend to be quantitative restrictions. Constraints include restrictions on the types of operators that can be used, their frequency, the conditions under which they can be used, or the sequence that they must follow (Wickelgren 1974; Mayer 1983). Subgoals are identified by restating the problem goal in terms of subproblem goals. The classic divide-and-conquer approach with step-wise refinement is one common method for identifying and integrating subgoals (Wirth 1971).

The stages of problem solving fall within the core of the software process stages (Page–Jones 1988), linking problem-solving methodologies and program development tasks. The problem-solving model defined by

Polya (1945)—to understand the problem, devise a plan, carry out the plan, and look back—is used as an example. Problem recognition, feasibility study, and requirements analysis are initial stages in the software process, and contribute mainly to understanding the problem, its needs, and scope. Design specification constitutes planning the solution. Implementation and integration are equivalent to carrying out the plan. Testing is performed by reviewing what was produced and done to solve the problem, and deployment presents the solution. Maintenance and retirement are postdeployment stages of the software process, essentially constituting the beginning of a new problem.

Obviously, a close relationship exists between software engineering and problem solving. For example, in the context of learning programming, beginners are frequently taught problem-solving techniques, even more so than being exposed to software engineering principles. One motivation is that, for those with little previous exposure to programming or problem solving, software engineering may represent a formidable, complex methodology; thus, learning general problem-solving methods provides a sensible compromise. The combination of problem solving with instruction in programming then affords many of the benefits provided by a basic understanding of software engineering, but without its attendant complexity.

Algorithmic problem solving, which is basic to programming and software engineering, uses techniques (such as subproblem decomposition) and facts (such as givens and unknowns) to produce an outline of steps leading to a problem solution. Programming is a kind of problem solving that requires representing solutions to problems in a coded manner suitable for processing by a computer. The relationship between problem solving and programming is simple: an algorithm is a precise step-by-step outline to solve a well-defined problem; a program is a sequence of syntactically and semantically correct instructions forming a solution for a problem. At a more advanced level, software engineers are trained in the details of software engineering methodologies that have been developed over the last 20 to 30 years.

One can identify five types of problems that occur in business environments: problems of meeting standards; of selection between alternatives; of customer satisfaction; of goal achievement; and of goal evolution. These problem types, illustrated in Figure 6.3, are discussed in detail next.

6.2.1 Problems of Meeting Standards

This type of problem is typically associated with fixed goals and is based on factual findings or empirical studies, as may occur in science or in business. The fixed goals may be related to adopted standards for an

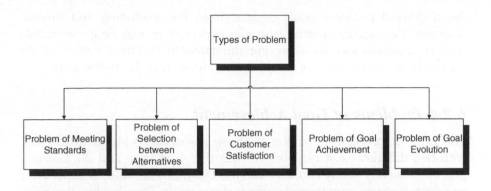

Figure 6.3 Types of problems based on different approaches in problem definition.

industry or be internal to an organization. The main characteristic of this type of problem is the long-term adoption of the goal. Examples range from controlling production lines in manufacturing processes, to adoption of ISO 9000 standards (ISO refers to the International Organization for Standardization—a consortium of the national standards institutes from 140 countries with a central office in Geneva that coordinates the system and publishes the finished standards), to feedback control in a management process based on fixed metrics for financial performance in terms of return on investment (ROI) or break-even point analysis (BEP).

6.2.2 Problems of Selection between Alternatives

This type of problem involves a composition of goals and alternatives in which the goals are usually specified in terms of weighted criteria. An evaluation matrix is constructed to quantify the comparison process and evaluate results quantitatively. The major difference involved in this type of problem is the availability of competitive alternatives. Often, the availability of a benchmark reference is beneficial to the evaluation process. Examples include selection of a best investment project, of a best purchasing offer, and of the best solution for a specific problem.

6.2.3 Problems of Customer Satisfaction

This type of problem overlaps the previous types but differs in that customer satisfaction can be identified as an independent goal regardless of the other goals adopted by an organization because organizational goals do not necessarily cohere with customer needs or requirements. Customers exhibit a broad range of needs, including psychological, social, financial, work-related, and personal requirements that go well beyond the traditional business goals derived from the marketing and finance domains. Thoroughly meeting customer expectations may be incompatible with or contradictory to achieving the tangible business values of an organization, so creation of a win–win solution may be problematic.

6.2.4 Problems of Goal Achievement

This type of problem is similar to those associated with standards, but with two differences: it can change over the short term and the learning process, which is tightly coupled with the evolution of business experience and best practices, significantly affects these goals. Despite this, the goals persist until existing goals prove to be outdated or external environments trigger a movement toward new goals. Examples of such semifixed goals are the internal goals of business firms derived from their prior experience.

6.2.5 Problems of Goal Evolution

The major distinguishing characteristic for this type of problem is the existence of a formal process of continuous improvement in an organization. The goals associated with these problems are constantly tested, validated, and improved in an iterative fashion. Therefore, the goals are continually changing based on performance results; competitive advantage; profitability; productivity; innovation; and similar aspects of a business environment. Examples occur in the practices of research and development teams and in the continuous improvement approaches found in quality management and business process reengineering.

6.3 What Is Problem Solving?

Interest in problem solving is not recent; formulations and developments that still affect current problem-solving methods reach back into antiquity. The work of Rene Descartes (1596–1650) on geometry was a milestone (Rubinstein 1975; Grabiner 1995). In his *Discourse on Method*, Descartes (1637) observed that the problem solver must go about things in the right way and must use the right method to arrive at a solution; otherwise, nothing will be discovered. Earlier, there was Alkowarazmi (A.D. 825), from whose name comes the word *algorithm* (Rosen 1995). Originally, Euclid's (300 B.C.) *Elements* were seminal for the systematic development of the scientific enterprise (Rosen 1995) and much later provided Descartes with the first problem on which he applied his new "method" (Grabiner 1995).

6.3.1 Models of Problem Solving

Deek (1997) reviewed a variety of different models of problem solving developed in the 20th century. The two earliest methods were introduced by Dewey (1910) and Wallas (1926) and represent opposite approaches. Dewey's approach essentially articulates a scientific method for problem solving; Wallas' represents a nonsystematic, creative view of problem solving. Models developed by subsequent researchers combined elements of both approaches. Principal among these was the method proposed and elaborated on in Polya's famous treatises on problem solving. The Polya model (1945, 1962) represents a problem-solving method that was extensively illustrated and supported by mathematical examples and documented in a series of books. Independently, Johnson's model (1955) refers to Wallas, and Kingsley and Garry's model (1957) elaborates on Dewey, with independent but similar models proposed in Osborn (1953) and Parnes (1967). Neither Johnson nor Kingsley and Garry introduced significant improvements over their predecessors. Despite the independence of these several methods, they were basically consistent in their approach—an important indication of the stability of the methodology over time.

A distinctive approach was introduced by Simon (1960), who viewed the process of problem solving as representing the interaction of a collection of cognitive abilities that included intelligence, design, choice, and implementation. More recently, methods were developed to provide mathematics, science, and engineering students with a method for problem solving. Generally, these models resolved the problem-solving process into a more finely specified process than those of earlier methods. Notable among these models is the work of Rubinstein (1975), who introduced an element of *reservation*. Reservation refers to withholding judgment at the problem-understanding stage in which one looks at possible solutions before finalizing the problem statement; a similar withholding of commitment occurs at the final problem solution stage. In other respects Rubinstein's method represents the standard view. Other popular methods are those of Stepien, Gallagher, and Workman (1993); Etter (1995); Meier, Hovde, and Meier (1996); and Hartman (1996), who presented models that basically follow the Polya model without significant change.

These problem-solving methodologies have stabilized over time, become clearer, and are demonstrably cognitively natural. The fact that the methods have settled down to a well agreed-upon and detailed form indicates that they provide a reliable theoretical framework for the present work. The naturalness of the methods, in the sense of psychological spontaneity, has been established (Duncker 1945; Newell & Simon 1972; Chi, Glaser, & Rees 1982) using thinking-aloud verbalization, protocol analysis, and related experimental techniques.

Newell and Simon did a careful phenomenological analysis, closely observing and monitoring how students thought about problems while attempting to solve them. The process that they identified was very similar to the methods reviewed, consisting of a series of stages. The problem solvers began by trying to understand what was expected of them and by gathering and organizing information. Facts about the problem were then used to examine and plan possible solutions. The plan was then refined, tentatively executed, and tested. If the putative solution was not confirmed, it was modified or new solutions were generated and the process was repeated.

In terms of tasks and procedures, problem solving can be defined as the process by which a situation is analyzed and solutions are formed to solve a problem, with steps taken to resolve, eliminate, or mitigate the problem. The current problem and situation are analyzed, potential solutions are generated, and a workable solution is determined and put into place. Problem solving is the process of analyzing situations of uncertainty to produce actual improvements or changes in the situation. In terms of methods and techniques, problem solving can be viewed as the strategy adopted to tackle problems to bridge the gap between one's current circumstances and a desired one.

Therefore, it is critical to determine existing capabilities (*what we have*) as well as requirements (*what we need*) to establish an effective foundation for problem solving. The "what we have" encompasses the enabling tools and the existing system. It has multiple roles. It reveals the true distance between the as-is (existing) system and the to-be system (the goal). It also helps to reach those goals through understanding requirements and exploiting capabilities. Without accurately identifying what is needed, there is neither a goal to achieve nor a problem to solve. If properly selected and carefully applied, strategies are the methods that make these theories work.

The problem-solving process, as illustrated in Figure 6.4, comprises many different elements that can be used in varying degrees, depending on the nature of problem to be solved. Typical elements include:

- Problem definition
- Situation analysis
- Idea generation
- Analysis of ideas
- Decision-making
- Determining the steps to be taken to introduce the solution into the workplace

Different problems require different uses of these elements, possibly in different orders or to different degrees. The structure of the process can

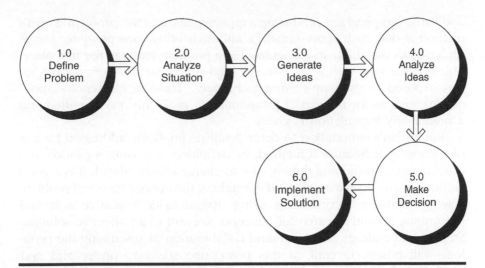

Figure 6.4 The problem-solving process.

vary greatly across different problems. One may need to make many attempts at problem definition to help establish the real question if the nature of the underlying problem is unclear.

6.3.2 Commonalities in Problem-Solving Models

One can identify a shared or common integrated model for problem solving based on the models just reviewed. Although the general form of the methodology is clear, it is beneficial to synthesize these methods into a common model of problem solving. The goal is to articulate the essential features of these problem-solving approaches and to provide an established, recognized framework, which can serve as the basis for a problem-solving method that can be adapted for program development. An integrated view of problem solving includes:

- Understanding and defining the problem
- Developing a plan for solving the problem
- Designing and implementing the plan to produce a solution
- Verifying and presenting the results

A synthetic view of the tasks involved by these objectives follows.

The key recommendations of the different methods concerning problem understanding and definition include the following. The essential ingredients were identified by Polya: state the question and identify the goal, givens, unknowns, and conditions. Kingsley and Garry and Osborn and Parnes emphasized producing a representation of the problem. Polya's method is one such representation, although others are possible. Simon underscores the ability to recognize that a problem exists in the first place. This is easily bypassed as an issue in academic contexts when people are first exposed to problem-solving techniques. Thus, in elementary applications such as for novices at programming, problems are identified and a preliminary formulation is given.

Rubinstein's exhortation to defer details is implicitly addressed by any of the methods because a method, by definition, encourages caution and clarification, constraining the impulse to charge blindly ahead. It is a good recommendation to keep in mind throughout the entire process of problem solving. Hartman recommends using diagrammatic cognitive aids and performing an initial search for concepts relevant to an effective solution. Stepien and colleagues recommend collaboration or discussing the problem with others. Overall, at this point, one seeks to understand and produce a description of the problem, gathering all relevant information (goal, givens, unknowns, conditions, and constraints). The objective is to identify and organize the pertinent facts about the problem and to ignore inessential aspects.

Regarding solution planning, the different methods include two key recommendations: identify alternative solutions and devise a plan. Almost all the methods explicitly emphasize the necessity of generating alternative solutions, which are then evaluated and one selected. Dewey early recognized the necessity of identifying several possible alternative solutions. Etter and Kingsley–Garry emphasize the explicit evaluation of alternatives prior to selection. Polya, in contrast, recommends examining similar or simpler problems and restating the problem. Though apparently different, this is in fact just a more fundamental recommendation than "finding an alternative solution" because it provides an actual technique for generating solutions by generating and examining simpler or alternative problems that one may be able to solve and whose solutions can then be adapted to the current problem. This provides a technique for accomplishing what Wallas, and later Johnson, recommended: gain insight into the problem and discover a solution, or for Rubinstein's recommendation to change the frame of reference and search for solution patterns.

Once a solution is selected, Polya provides the most inclusive recommendation: devise a plan by outlining a potential solution and breaking the problem into parts. The outline or plan for a solution is a high-level view of the solution that serves several purposes. It helps ensure the coherence of the implemented solution and its fidelity to the objective of the original problem by deferring premature or distracting immersion in implementation details. Once a high-level view is defined, the next logical step is to refine the plan by breaking the plan, problem, and solution into parts. Possible alternatives are assessed and a strategy for solving the problem is devised. The solution becomes more manageable when the problem is reformulated into a set or series of smaller subproblems. Therefore, the goal is refined into subgoals that are more easily achieved and the tasks to accomplish each subgoal are defined.

Regarding solution design and implementation, most of the methods explicitly emphasize the necessity to select a solution from the generated alternatives that is then refined and produced. The essential tasks were clearly stated by Polya in his *carry-out-plan* recommendation: refine and transform the plan into a solution and decompose tasks. The other methods also call for refinement, decomposition, and transformation (a form of implementation). For example, Kingsley and Garry, Osborn and Parnes, and Etter emphasize refining the solution; Rubinstein calls for transformations to simplify the process and Hartman recommends partitioning the problem into parts. In summary, the plan devised earlier must be implemented in order to produce the desired outcome. This is done by refining and transforming the plan into a solution to the problem. The transformation from a high-level solution outline to a precise solution may require further decomposition of subgoals, reorganization, and specification of an explicitly stated solution.

Regarding solution verification and presentation, the different methods include two standard recommendations: verifying the product and evaluating the process. All of the methods explicitly emphasize the necessity for verifying solutions, beginning with the early work of Dewey and Wallas and expanded upon by Polya, who refers to this as "looking back." This verification procedure includes testing the accuracy of results and the effectiveness and performance characteristics of the solution. Many methods, particularly Hartman's, additionally and separately emphasize the evaluation of the solution method and its suitability for other problems. This is the key to long-term productivity in problem solving because it brings the issue of ongoing learning explicitly into the picture. In other words, the process of solution should not only solve the problem at hand, but should also enhance one's ability to solve related problems in the future and improve one's adeptness at and experience with the problem-solving methodology. Stepien and colleagues and Meier et al. emphasize sharing and reporting results.

With the increasing emphasis on collaboration and the vastly expanded power to disseminate information in real time almost transparently provided by the Internet, the importance of the reporting phase is increasingly prominent. In summary, the main purpose of this objective is to produce an answer consistent with the goal of the problem. Therefore, the problem solver must look back and verify the correctness of the solution and evaluate the process of solution. This is done by testing the solution and examining the results. An equally important objective is to learn from the problem-solving experience, acquiring knowledge and skills that can be transferred to other problem-solving situations. Finally, the solution and the results are presented in a readable and organized manner.

6.3.3 Complex Management-Driven Strategies

Problem-solving strategies are the methods or approaches that people use to tackle problems. They are sometimes called problem-solving schemas. A problem-solving schema is an organized body of knowledge or information about the properties of a particular type of problem and the operations or steps required to solve it that is built by problem solvers. Hewett (1995) suggests that expert problem solvers develop a set of familiar problem schemas that are retained and called into play during problem-solving situations. In some familiar cases, schemas are activated without conscious efforts, providing reasonably efficient methods for solving commonly encountered problems. In more complex problem-solving situations, deliberate strategies and specific tactics are needed. Some of these strategies and heuristics are discussed next.

6.3.3.1 Problem Reduction (Decomposition)

Problem reduction is a strategic approach to managing complexity. A widely known method for solving large and complex problems is to split them into simpler problems and then iteratively apply this process until the subproblems are reduced to a level of complexity at which they are easily solved or at least exhibit an irreducible level of difficulty. This paradigm for solving problems is called problem reduction. In it, a problem in a given domain is decomposed into a structured set of subproblems in the same domain. As already indicated, each subproblem is evaluated (as illustrated in Figure 6.5) for suitability to be further decomposed until each subproblem is determined solvable. This problem reduction paradigm has been successfully applied to problems in a variety of application domains and in many phases of the process in which a top-down decision-making strategy is applicable (Porvin, Reynolds, & Maletic 1991).

6.3.3.2 Reusable Subproblems and Solutions

Despite its appeal, problem reduction can be expensive if the need arises to revise projects on a regular basis or invest additional resources in new projects. Often, the same process must be done repeatedly for a similar type of problem with only minor differences. As a result, problem reduction may

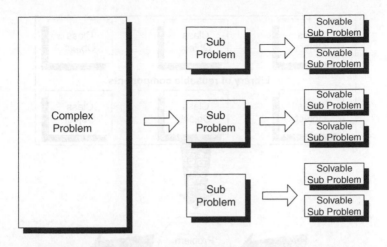

Figure 6.5 The decomposition of a problem.

cost even more over time as problems become more complex. One important approach to handling the side effects of problem reduction is to build reusable subproblems and solutions, instead of continually reinventing a related system reductive hierarchy. Such reusable subproblems and solutions can be stored in a components library and retrieved as required. As illustrated in Figure 6.6, complete solutions can then be obtained by using and reassembling appropriate subsolution components—an object-oriented approach that has achieved widespread popularity.

Building reusable components (class objects) can be done in a top-down fashion by means of specifications or in a bottom-up fashion by means of generalizations. Object-oriented technology reflects the prevalence of natural objects and functionally cohesive systems in the real world and the creation of artificial objects and constructs in domains such as engineering and mathematics. This technology is also consistent with an understanding of human cognitive psychology and is used in software systems and businesses as a technique for defining business processes in terms of "business objects."

6.3.3.3 Problem Expansion (Composition)

Problem reduction approaches may contain the hidden assumption that a problem has been fully understood and only needs to be analyzed by decomposition. This is often not true for problems of an interdisciplinary nature with root causes that must be carefully investigated. As discussed, business processes can be viewed from different perspectives, all of which

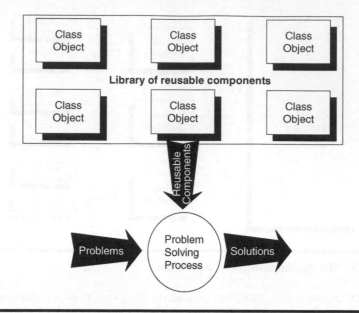

Figure 6.6   The problem-solving process using reusable components.

may be essential. In fact, missing any aspects of the larger business picture can result in ineffective problem solving.

A broader view of the problem may take the approach to solving a problem in a different, more relevant direction. An encompassing view of problem solving depends on a thorough analysis of stakeholder requirements and is also related to the interdisciplinary tools and knowledge used in recognizing the overall picture. The major difficulty in this approach is its dependence on a highly skilled organization with extensive and comprehensive human resource backgrounds and for innovative technical tools that incorporate a variety of techniques. Figure 6.7 illustrates the process of knitting together the interrelated aspects of a problem, from different perspectives, into a comprehensive solvable component.

6.3.3.4 Problem Misrepresentation

How problems are viewed is critical to how they are solved. Placing a problem in its correct context can make a difference in one's ability to solve it. Misrepresenting a problem results in unsuccessful solutions. Difficulties of problem misrepresentation can take several forms:

- *Language ambiguity*: using precise language in addressing a problem is essential. Vague language leads to ambiguity in understanding and ineffective and misleading communication.

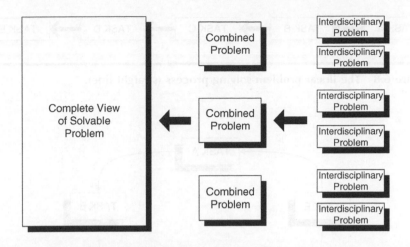

Figure 6.7 The problem expansion process.

- *Comprehension*: examining all the aspects of the problem is important. In many situations, a lack of problem knowledge or a misunderstanding of problem scope can distort recognition of a problem's complexity. Although the components of the problem may still be identified, other essential factors may be overlooked or ignored.
- *Preposition*: applying a previous solution derived for similar problems to a current problem is an important heuristic; however, doing so prematurely can lead to a prebiased perception that can negatively affect a complete understanding of the problem.
- *Context*: putting a problem in its correct context by looking at the problem from a technical as well as a human perspective can facilitate solving the problem.
- *Standardization*: standardizing problem presentation and adopting appropriate notations and modeling techniques can result in improved communication among problem solvers at different levels.

6.3.4 Strategies Driven by Task Structuring

These strategies are reflected in the topology of the path followed to solve a problem, independently of the tasks carried out or how they are composed or decomposed. The four basic modeling structures used in solving problems are the linear, iterative, parallel, and dynamic problem-solving strategies.

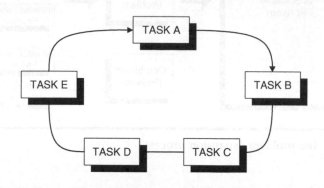

Figure 6.8 The linear problem-solving process (straight line).

Figure 6.9 The iterative problem-solving process.

6.3.4.1 Linear Problem-Solving Strategies

Linear strategies can be unidirectional or bidirectional. The corresponding linear solution path may be a straight-line path, a step-wise path, or a V-shaped path; it always has an open end indicating a time limitation for this type of strategy. Figure 6.8 shows a straight-line path for linear solution. Tasks are carried out sequentially with each task dependent on a proceeding one. In certain instances, variations of a linear structure allow a feedback control loop to exist between tasks, thus increasing the degree of interactivity between tasks and phases.

6.3.4.2 Iterative Problem-Solving Strategies

These strategies are often associated with continuous improvement and quality assurance approaches. The problem-solving topology is represented by a cycle (see Figure 6.9). The topology may include a single continuous cycle or multiple cycles in which external cycles emerge from internal ones. Although tasks in iterative approaches are still organized in a sequential order, this sequence is continual and does not stop at a fixed point in time. The iterative strategy may, however, be used as a part of a linear strategy.

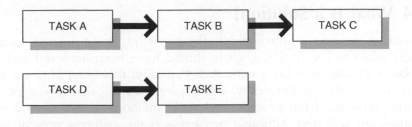

Figure 6.10   The parallel problem-solving process.

6.3.4.3 Parallel Problem-Solving Strategies

The parallel strategy is a technique for reducing cycle time for the problem-solving process. Unlike the sequential order for executing tasks, parallel tasks are assigned to parallel production lines in which all lines are processed simultaneously and independently. Of course, mixtures of parallel and sequential organizations are possible, with some portions of the process executed in parallel and eventually merging or synchronizing into a subsequent phase that depends for its initiation on completion of these earlier parallel phases. The most general form of such a topology is represented by an a-cyclic digraph (see Figure 6.10).

6.3.4.4 Dynamic Problem-Solving Strategy

In this approach, tasks are not organized in a regular or static shape but are dynamically structured based on interactions and interrelations between tasks.

6.3.5 Capabilities-Driven Strategies

Capability-driven strategies are determined by available or already incorporated resources. Although lack of capabilities may indicate a limitation or constraint on problem solving, the proper utilization of in-house or outsourced resources can expand organizational goals and optimize problem-solving performance. Technological capabilities are considered the most rapidly growing factor in problem-solving strategies because computerization can produce a notable difference in timing, control, competition, and solution quality. Knowledge-based expert systems, Internet repositories and search tools, and CASE (computer-aided software engineering) tools are important examples of these capabilities.

6.4 What Is a Solution?

A solution constitutes a final step in the problem-solving process. Ideally, when solutions are finalized, goals should have been achieved and the problem should have been mitigated. Typically, this is an outcome that exists only in theory. Practically, when a solution is realized, new phases in the problem-solving process, such as evaluation, validation, and verification, are activated. Although problem-solving strategies present vehicles to reduce errors and establish problem needs, the practical implementation of a solution is the ultimate way in which to verify its correctness.

6.4.1 Problems and Solutions in Context of the Old Business Environment

Many current organizational techniques for business problem-solving can be attributed, independently of the nature of the business, to the so-called old factory model described by Adam Smith. In 1776, Smith published his famous treatise "The Wealth of Nations," in which he described the management technique called "division of labor." This approach to problem solving—for example, in the context of a manufacturing environment—consisted of breaking problems into small units and allocating each unit to a human resource.

Smith described how a factory that made pins was restructured using this principle. Instead of having each worker make pins, the factory had been organized so that each worker specialized in one small part of the pin-making process. As a result, fewer workers could produce more pins than when each had to build the entire pin. The goal was higher productivity. Smith's approach encompassed fundamental notions such as the division of labor, departmentalization, and specialization. Various industries, from software development to airplane manufacturing, are still using Smith's approach in partitioning work and running the manufacturing processes.

Frederick Taylor (1856–1915) advanced this approach in the late 1800s by refining Smith's model with a scientific analysis that quantitatively examined work breakdown structures. Taylor's work revolutionized business by introducing the concept of the production line. The result was increased levels of productivity as well as greater and more systematic partitioning of work. Key elements of Taylor's contributions included standardizing work; unifying the methods used to perform tasks; matching workers with tasks; and constant overseeing of work. Henry Fayol (1841–1925) was Taylor's successor in management theory and introduced additional principles, such as organizing management by essential functions; utilizing line-staff organization charts; and emphasizing an underlying chain of command, formal authority policies, and the importance of a narrow span of control.

Max Weber in his "Theory of Social and Economic Organization" (1947) modeled the premise of administration in terms of an ideal bureaucracy based on rational, legal-authority systems. His principles were also rooted in the division of labor model. He believed that organizations gain legitimacy when they become rational and that this results in ensuring resources and support and building trust. So-called human relations theory later insisted that the productivity of workers is not affected solely by financial considerations. According to Mayo (1933), the informal organization of the workplace environment, social norms, acceptance, and the sentiments of a group are also critical factors of individual work behavior. Maslow (1943), McGregor (1960), Herzberg (1966), and others emphasized social relations in organizations and understanding that the social and emotional needs of workers and managers are important factors in managing organizations effectively.

After World War II, a pervasive and dominant trend was to solve business problems using quantifiable techniques; this trend emerged from the highly successful application of scientific modeling techniques in military applications during the war. This quantitative approach shifted the focus from decomposition theories to representative quantities, statistics, mathematical models, and operations research—all of which management information systems incorporated. The systems approach defined organizations as open systems that constantly interact with the external environment via inputs (resources and information); undergo transformation processes to produce outputs (products, services, information); and incorporate feedback.

Forrester's (1973) system dynamics, developed around 1960, involved exploring the "flows" within an organizational system. Forrester was especially concerned with feedback loops and the fuzzy behavior that occurs when a system acts in contrast to what common sense predicts. In the 1950s, Peter Drucker introduced a comprehensive strategy for business problem solving called "management by objectives" (MOB), which included key concepts such as setting measurable goals for each employee; directing employee goals towards organizational goals; and periodically reviewing progress.

Edward Deming in the 1940s introduced a comprehensive theory called "total quality management" (TQM) based on the following principle: the basic goal in a business organization should be to work continuously towards bridging the gap between the desired goals and the actual performance of the organization. According to TQM, customers—not producers—are the major drivers in product specification, and a customer can be defined as anyone upon whom the organization's product or service has an impact. The term *quality* is used in a broad sense to refer to the quality of the entire business system and not merely the quality of the end product or service produced by the organization.

The total quality movement arose partly as a reaction to the way in which some Japanese companies had demonstrated an ability consistently to create products quickly and with predictably high quality. Some analysts attributed this success to the adoption by these Japanese enterprises of the methods of the American management theorist Deming (1902–1993); others attributed it to a characteristic of Japanese culture. Total quality was adopted with considerable enthusiasm and some success. ISO 9000 evolved from TQM and became a standard for quality assurance. TQM views business problem solving from a comprehensive viewpoint in which all parts of an organization are responsible for maintaining the business system quality. According to TQM theorists, maintaining the quality of the system is the only way in which to ensure the ability to provide quality products and services consistently. Management commitment is essential to the success of the TQM process.

Over time, the complexity of business environments has dramatically increased. The partitioning of large business tasks has led to large numbers of functional departments with correspondingly smaller divisions. Manufacturing tasks been partitioned and fragmented, as have administrative, professional, and managerial tasks. The execution of individual tasks may have been made more efficient; however, the organization as a whole may have become less effective because of the delays, bottlenecks, and problems that occurred as work subproducts moved from worker to worker across organizational functions and divisions. The complexity caused by this fragmentation in the evolving business model created difficulties such as increased management costs and overhead as business firms attempted to plan and control increasingly large and fragmented organizations. A list of anomalies includes:

- Error rates increased due to the successive stages of production.
- A high degree of error rates had an increasingly significant impact on the quality of services and products.
- Delays and bottlenecks in the increasingly complicated process lengthened the cycle time of business processes as tasks moved through increasingly long chains of functions.
- Business organizations became overly large, overmanaged, bureaucratized, and departmentalized. Thus, organizations became inflexible and less responsive to the challenges of competitive markets.

The consequences of fragmentation and complication in business firm organization provided a strong motivation to rethink and redesign organizations to eliminate unnecessary work and to design businesses for flexibility and cost reduction. In 1990, Michael Hammer wrote an article called "Reengineering Work: Don't Automate, Obliterate," in the *Harvard Business Review*, that introduced the concept of reengineering. After studying the customary or standard way in which American businesses tended to be organized, Hammer concluded that, for the most part, they followed Adam Smith's principles (alluded to earlier). After two centuries of the division-of-labor era, Smith's principles exhibited limitations and lacked effectiveness. The resulting business models left firms with a hierarchical management; increasing specialization of workers; detachment from products, services, and customers; and an increasingly bureaucratic operation; these made it difficult for organizations to compete and handle business demands.

6.4.2 Problems and Solutions in Context of the Information Age

Existing economic and management theories are subject to adjustment because of the information technology revolution that has empowered individuals and groups. Innovative solutions to problems are enabled by the availability of advanced, powerful technology to accelerate a business process or to make products or services more accessible. The major effects of the use of information technology in businesses include new opportunities in sales and marketing; rapid product development and abbreviated product life cycles; changes in management methods and techniques; and reshaping of organizational structures to respond to global and local needs.

The role of information technology and associated IT staff is becoming more significant in organizations as information becomes one of the most important assets in business. The development of the Internet has also changed how organizations operate. Treese and Stewart (1994) underscore the convergence of the global Internet with commerce as fundamentally altering the business landscape. Dougherty (1997) observes that the Web is now part of any business and of the business infrastructure and has become a catalyst for change. Problem solving is the actual job of business management. Information technology plays a significant role in tackling business problems, but software alone cannot do the job. It must be incorporated into a comprehensive, enterprisewide, problem-solving framework in order to deal with the essential aspects of business problems and to tailor software systems to suit the actual needs of organizations.

References

Ackoff, R.L. (1981). *Creating the Corporate Future*. New York: John Wiley & Sons.

Chi, M.T.H., Glaser, R., & Rees, E. (1982). Expertise in problem solving. In R.J. Sternberg (Ed.), *Advances in the Psychology of Human Intelligence*, 7–75. Hillsdale, NJ: Lawrence Erlbaum.

Deek, F.P. (1997). An integrated environment for problem solving and program development, Unpublished Ph.D. dissertation, New Jersey Institute of Technology,

Descartes, R. (1637). Discourse on the method of rightly conducting the reason to seek the truth in the sciences, tr. L.J. Lafleur, 1956. New York: Bobbs–Merrill.

Dewey, J. (1910). *How We Think*. Lexington, MA: D.C. Heath.

Dougherty, D. (1997). The business of the Web is managing change, publisher, Web Review, Dec. 19, 1997.

Duncker, K. (1945). On problem solving, *Psychol. Monog.*, 58(5), 270.

Eden, C., Jones, S., & Sims, D. (1983). *Messing about in Problems*. Oxford: Pergamon Press.

Etter, D.M. (1995). *Engineering Problem Solving with ANSI C: Fundamental Concepts*. Englewood Cliffs, NJ: Prentice Hall.

Forrester, J.W. (1973). *World Dynamics*. Waltham, MA: Pegasus Communications.

Gause, D. & Weinberg, G. (1990). *Are Your Lights on? How to Figure Out What the Problem Really Is*, Dorset House Publishing Company.

Glass, R.L. (1998). *Software Runaways: Monumental Software Disasters*. Upper Saddle River, NJ: Prentice Hall, Inc.

Grabiner, J.V. (1995). Descartes and problem solving. *Math. Mag.*, 68, 83–97.

Hammer, M. (1990), July–August). Reengineering work: Don't automate, obliterate, *Harvard Business Review*, pp. 104–112.

Hartman, H. (1996). *Intelligent Tutoring*, preliminary ed. Clearwater, FL: H&H Publishing Company.

Herzberg, G.F. (1966) *Work and the Nature of Man*. Cleveland: World Publishing Company

Hewett, T.T. (1995). Cognitive factors in design: basic phenomena in human memory and problem solving. *CHI 95 Conference Companion*, 353–354

Johnson, D.M. (1955). *The Psychology of Thought and Judgment*. New York: Harper and Brothers.

Kepner, C.H. & Tregoe, B.B. (1981). *The New Rational Manager*. Princeton: Kepner–Tregoe.

Kingsley, H.L. & Garry, R. (1957). *The Nature and Conditions of Learning*. Englewood Cliffs, NJ: Prentice Hall.

Maslow, A.H. (1943). A theory of human motivation. *Psychol. Rev.*, 50, 370–396.

Mayer, R.E. (1983). *Thinking, Problem Solving, Cognition*, San Francisco: W.H. Freeman.

Mayo, E. (1933). *The Human Problems of an Industrial Civilization*. New York: The Macmillan Company (reprinted by Division of Research, Harvard Business School, 1946).

McGregor, D. (1960). *The Human Side of Enterprise*, New York: McGraw–Hill.

Meier, S., Hovde, R., & Meier, R. (1996). Problem solving: teachers' perceptions, content area models, and interdisciplinary connections. *School Sci. Math.*, 96, 230–237.

Newell, A. & Simon, H.A. (1972). *Human Problem Solving*. Englewood Cliffs, NJ: Prentice Hall.

Osborn, A.F. (1953). *Applied Imagination*. New York: Charles Scribner's Sons

Page–Jones, M. (1988). *The Practical Guide to Structured Systems Design,* 2nd ed. Englewood Cliffs, NJ: Prentice Hall.

Parnes, S.J. (1967). *Creative Behavior Guidebook*. New York: Charles Scribner's Sons.

Polya, G. (1945). *How to Solve It: a New Aspect of Mathematical Method*. Princeton, NJ: Princeton University Press.

Polya, G. (1962). *Mathematical Discovery,* New York: John Wiley & Sons.

Porvin, S., Reynolds, R.G., & Maletic, J.I. (March, 1991). Divide and conquer as a paradigm for program implementation: an empirical assessment. *Proceedings of 19th Annual ACM Computer Science Conference*, San Antonio, TX, 618–632.

Pounds, W.P. (1967). The process of problem finding. *Ind. Manage. Rev.*, 11(1), 1–9.

Rist, R.S. (1986). Plans in programming: definition, demonstration and development. In E. Soloway and S. Iyengar (Eds.). *Empirical Studies of Programmers: First Workshop*, (28–47), Norwood, NJ: Ablex.

Rosen, K.H. (1995). *Discrete Mathematics and its Applications*, 3rd ed. New York: McGraw–Hill.

Rubinstein, M. (1975). *Patterns of Problem Solving*, Englewood Cliffs, NJ: Prentice Hall.

Simon, H.A. (1960). *The New Science of Management*. New York: Harper and Row.

Smith, A. (1976). *An Inquiry into the Nature and Causes of the Wealth of Nations,* London: Methuen and Co., Ltd., ed. Edwin Cannan, 1904, Fifth edition.

Stepien, W.J., Gallagher, S.A., & Workman, D. (1993). Problem-based learning for traditional and interdisciplinary classrooms. *J. Educ. Gifted*, 4, 338–345.

Treese, G.W. & Stewart, L.C. (1994) *Designing Systems for Internet Commerce*. Reading, MA: Addison–Wesley Publishing Company.

Wallas, G. (1926). *The Art of Thought*. New York: Harcourt Brace Jovanovich.

Weber, M. (1947). *The Theory of Social and Economic Organization,* New York: Simon & Schuster.

Wickelgren, W.A. (1974). *How to Solve Problems*, San Francisco: W.H. Freeman & Co.

Wirth, N. (1971). Program development by stepwise refinement. *Commun. ACM*, 14(4), 221–227.

Chapter 7

Software Technology and Problem Solving

7.1 Introduction

Information technology has ubiquitously influenced business and affected management approaches to problem solving. A key manifestation of this technology is the software technology that has pervaded all aspects of life, from household appliances to entertainment devices, communication media, productivity toolware, learning systems, and portable devices that operate under the control of embedded, factory preprogrammed chips with settings and parameters controllable through easy-to-use user interfaces. The quintessential software characteristics of flexibility and adaptability have enabled manufacturers to create customized systems that respond to changing customer needs and allow tailoring technology to endlessly diverse business requirements. Problem-solving strategies increasingly depend on software technology as an enabling mechanism and for facilitating decision-making processes. In this context, software technology includes the complete software environment utilized in problem solving, covering application systems, the knowledge base, hardware facilities, and technical resources.

The introduction of information processing has changed the way in which people and organizations address problems. The previous chapter considered how problem-solving approaches are closely related to how software development is done. This chapter considers how the availability of software tools influences how problem solving is done. Software serves as the critical enabling technology that automates routine problem-solving

155

activities and interactions, facilitates visualization, supports collocated and distant collaboration, etc.

Because software is enabled by technology, advances in problem solving have become coupled with the rapid advances in technology. Software tools are now pervasively used to support classic problem-solving tasks from data exploration to communication. A similar pervasive adaptation of software and business processes is seen in the rapid reconceptualization of business operations reflected in the e-business revolution that is reshaping entire industries. The impact of the dramatically increasing portability of computing on business processes and the affect of enhanced digitally driven connectivity on development issues such as product cycle time will also be considered.

The flip side of the coin to the enabling power of computing technology concerns its limitations. Although software has provided business managers with capabilities that enhance continual growth, thus creating added business value and revolutionizing communication, portability, and connectivity, software does not represent a complete solution. The challenges to software-driven approaches to problem solving include:

- Diversity of user requirements
- Difficulty of capturing requirements
- Complexity of business and decision-making processes
- Lack of business experience and background among software specialists and developers
- Tight coupling between computer information systems and the people who use them

Some of the difficulties involved in adapting software to individual differences and changing organizational environments are identified, as well as difficulties that arise because, naturally, end users are not programmers. Consideration is also given to the fact that the introduction of new software systems in complex organizations is problematic for various interdisciplinary reasons. The effective business value that a software system adds to business performance tends to be neither explicitly addressed nor adequately quantified because the traditional focus in software development has been on technical metrics intended to assure the technical quality of the software product. Although project management and fiscally driven factors are part of the software engineering process, they are often not well integrated into the process. Thus, a gap remains between the discipline of management information systems and the software development disciplines; MIS looks at solutions from a managerial perspective, but for software development, technical concerns are more influential.

7.2 Software Technology as Enabling Business Tool—What Computers *Can* Do

The application of software technology to problem solving exhibits characteristics that are fundamental to business organizations. Software technology allows for the acceleration of the problem-solving process by automating tasks and reducing the need for repetition. This can lead to reducing human errors significantly and thus to more reliable solutions. From a human factors viewpoint, software technology

- Helps visualize problems so that they can be understood globally and intuitively and controlled effectively
- Facilitates communication among problem solvers and creates a collaborative environment for dealing with tasks, documents, conditions, and events allowing for the recording of knowledge and experiences
- Frees the problem-solving process from dependency on location, distance, or time
- Provides effective tools for collecting and analyzing data and for data mining

The specific impacts of software technology on business are elaborated in the following sections.

7.2.1 Exponential Growth in Capability

According to Moore's law, the density of digital chips doubles approximately every 18 months but cost remains constant, thus increasing computing power but not price. This in turn fuels software technology as software applications become increasingly powerful based on ever faster hardware platforms. No other problem-solving tool exists whose power expands so rapidly yet remains so cheap. When the objective is to reduce business product development cycle time under the constraint of limited financial resources, computer technology allows solutions in less time and with lower cost. Due to this correlation with technology, the issue of the development of problem solving is coupled with technological forecasting for the computer industry. Next, the implications for business problem solving of the evolving power of computing will be considered.

7.2.2 Business Problem-Solving Optimization

As people solve problems, they rely on computer hardware and software to store and retrieve data; explore solution alternatives; use communication technology to interact with others; utilize perceived if–then rules to make decisions; and process data, knowledge, and techniques to implement solutions. Software technology can shorten this process, potentially translating it into a single application requiring only a single stage of inputs with solutions delivered rapidly.

Database management systems and information retrieval systems can serve as dynamic relational memories that not only store and retrieve data, but also link related components together. Memory and retrieval systems may be supplemented by the ability to recognize manual inputs using techniques such as optical character recognition or voice recognition technology. Expert and AI-based systems can harness the knowledge developed by experts, and Web-based applications can facilitate almost instantaneous communication, dramatically enhancing the ability to collaborate with widely distributed team members and other human resources. Web applications can also serve as a repository to store, retrieve, and search for data and information. The navigation power of the Web transfers market power from producers and vendors to customers and helps suppliers to provide better quality products with shorter turnaround. Software technology has enabled breakthrough transformations in businesses and provided benefits that have included:

- Simplification of business structures
- Removal of unnecessary processes
- Overall quality improvement
- Reduction in time to market
- Organizational flexibility
- Cost reduction
- Bringing the benefits of a more innovative business culture

7.2.3 The E-Business Revolution

Metcalfe's law observes that networks increase in value with each additional node (user) in proportion to the square of the number of users. This relationship follows because, with n nodes directly or indirectly interconnected, $n(n - 1)/2$ total possible interconnections are available. The telephone network is a classic instance of the effect of this kind of utility behavior. When the network is small, its overall value is relatively limited. As the network encompasses more users, its benefit grows disproportionately, with the individual benefit growing linearly in the number of users, n, and the total network benefit growing quadratically in n.

E-business illustrates the impact of networking power on industry. E-business led to the generation of value-chain partnerships, new ways of interacting with customers and new services. This e-transformation introduced the concept of a virtual organization to business. One consequence is the acceleration of the decision–making process. E-transformation removed or changed the character of business boundaries, including those between the inside and outside of a company, and opened companies to partnerships from unexpected sources, including new relationships with partners, providers, and even competitors. Moreover, e-business capabilities enabled an integrated back-end–front-end architecture that allows online sales and physical activities to support each other in an almost real-time manner.

Web-enabled business processes in the network economy include front-end functions that cover business-to-customer transactions and back-end transactions that define relationships with vendors and partners. This includes interfunctional processes for internal data exchanges, viewing a business as having customers at both ends of its processes, and ensuring objectives are driven by customer satisfaction (Grover, Fiedler, & Teng 1994). Successful technological, Web-engineered processes triggered by the Internet have contributed to business the ability to slash inventories; customize products; bridge the communication gap between suppliers and individual customers; and even design personalized products that can be ordered online. All of these are part of the networked business process (Roberts 2000).

The general pattern of prior economic revolutions is recurring in the case of e-business: an enabling technology (Web engineering) has allowed the creation of a new (business) process that has sparked a global economic transformation (e-commerce). In commerce, such business processes can create an entirely new environment. Web-specific business processes transcend political, cultural, and social divisions to permit dynamic types of interaction between organizations and individuals when anyone anywhere can purchase or sell anything to anyone anywhere anytime via the Web.

Enabling Web solutions in businesses can reshape the entire business operation. The production process can be viewed from point of origin to point of delivery; emails generate inquiries and response turn-around accelerates (Roberts 2000). Therefore, efficient product management becomes a primary concern of the business process. Studies indicate that organizational strategy and sound management techniques result in quality products and profits (Elzinga et al. 1995) and thus are integral to the business process. However, continuous improvement is only sustainable given endurance in the technology transformation, and Web-engineering business processes are currently among the decisive factors.

Research also indicates that increased competitiveness is the greatest anticipated benefit of e-commerce as it improves products and makes enterprises more effective and, thus, more competitive (Lederer, Mirchandani, & Sims 1997). With respect to user relationships, integrating business processes with the Internet leads to far greater transparency between customers and suppliers (Roberts 2000). This confirms that user satisfaction is the most widely used single measure of information technology success (Grover et al. 1994). The literature on e-business suggests overall that an efficient business process in this environment can be achieved when processes are Web driven (or engineered): they are more competitive and more concerned with user relationships and satisfaction, and they require efficient product management.

Despite these revolutionary developments, the historic baseline for business remains the same as it has always been. In the final analysis, income statements and balance sheets remain the fundamental gauges or metrics of business performance. Mass manufacturing profoundly altered business processes, but the fundamental operations of business remained largely the same. Issues such as maintaining market share; ensuring adequate capitalization; sustaining profitability; controlling costs; and motivating workforces have always been primary challenges to managers. The same is true in the Web economy. Management strategies must therefore reconcile this global impact with the perennial need to keep their organizations growing and profitable.

7.2.4 Portability Power

One of the most notable characteristics of organizational problem solving is its frequent dependence on physical (as opposed to digital) resources: people, places, devices, connections, and work-flow documents; these extensively bind the problem-solving process to these resources. These bonds can restrict the ability of organizations to take advantage of opportunities that arise, for example, outside regular operating hours or beyond the physical location of the organization.

Information and software technology help transcend these boundaries by giving employees, decision-makers, and customers increased flexibility. Whether through LANs or wireless connections, one can be connected to the business environment regardless of location, time, or local technical infrastructure. Executive or expert systems that handle structured as well as routine connection problems provide backup for the communication and decision-making link. For example, online dynamic databases eliminate the need for live contact to check inventory or to process orders. Workflow application technology can support business processes and eliminate the need for physical paperwork through the use of smart digital archiving, thus reducing unnecessary organizational expense. These capabilities or opportunities can be further extended through portable devices such as laptops, PDAs, Internet-ready cell phones, optical scanners, etc.

Some conceptual and technological overlap exist between portability and the e-business transformation. However, portability focuses on expanding an organization's ability to work without physical limits, and e-business is related to extending external relationships with partners, vendors, and customers beyond traditional frameworks. E-business is Internet enabled; portability utilizes the Web and other technological capabilities in which information can be transported.

7.2.5 Connectivity Power

Software technology facilitates communication between devices in a multimedia fashion. A computer can be attached to a digital camcorder, TV, printer, scanner, external storage device, PDA, or another networked computer and to the Internet simultaneously. The architectural strategy of integrating these capabilities within a single platform can add more than mere entertainment or aesthetic value to business exchanges. It can lead to an environment in which the cycle time and costs of the business processes can be reduced via an all-in-one architecture. Multimedia data can be captured immediately, edited as required, stored on an electronic portable device, or sent to a vendor, customer, or business partner in almost real time.

Previously, such work required several departments, staff time, experience, and financial and technical resources. With the ability to represent and communicate multimedia information via a connected device with adequate software drivers installed, a well-equipped laptop can reproduce the functionality of an entire office or even an organization. Connectivity power provides unusual solutions to businesses such as manufacturing, engineering, medicine, and sports, as well as many other application domains in which demand for digital image processing, data mining, and feedback control is high.

7.3 Software Technology as a Limited Business Tool—What Computers *Cannot* Do

Software technology enables businesses to solve problems more efficiently than otherwise; however, as with any tool, it has its limitations. Solving business problems involves many considerations that transcend hardware or software capabilities; thus, software solutions can only become effective when they are placed in the context of a more general problem-solving strategy. Software solutions should be seen as essential tools in problem solving that are to be combined with other interdisciplinary tools and capabilities. This kind of interoperation can be achieved by integrating such tools with the software development process. Additionally, the software development process can also be used as a part of a larger problem-solving process that analyzes business problems and designs and generates working solutions with maximum business value. Some examples of this are discussed in the following sections.

7.3.1 People Have Different Needs That Change over Time

Software technology is limited in its ability to recognize the application or cognitive stylistic differences of individuals or to adapt to the variety of individual needs and requirements. These differences among individuals have multiple causes and include:

- Use of different cognitive styles when approaching problem solving
- Variations in background, experience, levels and kinds of education, and, even more broadly, diversity in culture, values, attitudes, ethical standards, and religions
- Different goals, ambitions, and risk-management strategies
- Assorted levels of involvement and responsibilities in the business organization's process

A software system is designed once to work with the entire business environment all the time. However, organizational needs are not stable and can change for many reasons—even over short periods of time—due to changes in personnel, task requirements, educational or training level, or experience. Designing a software system that can adjust, customize, or personalize to such a diversity of needs and variety of cognitive styles in different organizations and dispersed locations is an immense challenge. It entails building a customizable software system and also necessitates a continuous development process to adapt to ongoing changes in the nature of the environment.

7.3.2 Most Users Do not Understand Computer Languages

A software solution can only be considered relevant and effective after one has understood the actual user problems. The people who write the source code for computer applications use technical languages to express the solution and, in some cases, they do not thoroughly investigate whether their final product reflects what users asked for. The final product is expected to convert or transform the user's language and expectations in a way that realizes the system's requirements. Otherwise, the system will be a failure in terms of meeting its stated goals appropriately and will fail its validation and verification criteria.

In a utopian environment, end-users could become sufficiently knowledgeable in software development environments and languages so that they could write their software to ensure systems were designed with their own real needs in mind. Of course, by the very nature of the division of expertise, this could rarely happen and so the distance in functional intention between user languages and their translation into programming languages is often considerable. This creates a barrier between software solutions reaching their intended market and users and customers finding reliable solutions.

In many ways, the ideal scenario, in which one approached system design and development from a user point of view, was one of the driving rationales behind the original development of the software engineering discipline. Software engineering was intended as a problem-solving framework that could bridge the gap between user languages (requirements) and computer languages (the final product or source code). In software engineering, the user's linguistic formulation of a problem is first understood and then specified naturally, grammatically, diagrammatically, mathematically, or even automatically; then, it is translated into a preliminary software architecture that can be coded in a programming language. Thus, the underlying objective in software engineering is that the development solutions be truly reflective of user or customer needs.

7.3.3 Decisions and Problems—Complex and Ill Structured

The existence of a negative correlation between organizational complexity and the impact of technical change (Keen 1981) is disputed. More complex organizations have more ill-structured problems (Mitroff & Turoff 1973). Consequently, their technical requirements in terms of information systems become harder to address. On the other hand, information technology may allow a complex organization to redesign its business processes so that it can manage complexity more effectively (Davenport & Stoddard 1994).

On balance, a negative correlation is likely in complex organizations for many reasons. First, the complexity of an organization increases the degree of ambiguity and equivocality in its operations (Daft & Lengel 1986). Many organizations will not invest resources sufficient to carry out an adequately representative analysis of a problem. Therefore, requirement specifications tend to become less accurate and concise. Implementing a system based on a poor systems analysis increases the likelihood of failure as well as the likelihood of a lack of compatibility with the organization's diverse or competing needs. A demand for careful analysis and feasibility studies to allow a thorough determination of requirements might bring another dimension of complexity to the original problem.

Second, technology faces more people-based resistance in complex organizations (Markus 1983). This can occur because a newly introduced system has not been well engineered according to accurate requirements in the first place, as well as because of the combination of social, psychological, and political factors found in complex organizations. One further factor complicating the effective delivery of computerized systems in large projects is the time that it takes to get key people involved.

Finally, there are obvious differences in the rate of growth for complex organizations and information technology. Although information technology advances rapidly, complex organizations are subject to greater inertia and thus may change relatively slowly. Subsequently, incorporating or synthesizing technical change into an organization becomes a real challenge for individuals and departments and is affected by factors such as adaptability, training, the ability to upgrade, and maintainability. For such reasons, one expects a negative correlation between organizational complexity and the impact of technical change in terms of applying software technology and achieving intended organizational outcomes.

7.3.4 Businesses View Software Technology as a Black Box for Creating Economic Value

Although software systems play a significant role in business organizations in terms of business added value, the traditional focus of many organizations has been on their role in cost reduction because software automation can reduce error, minimize effort, and increase productivity. Innovative applications can enable organizations to achieve more than traditional software goals, including the ability to compete more effectively, maximize profitability, and solve complex business problems.

Business goals extend beyond direct financial benefits to include operational metrics involving customer satisfaction, internal processes, and an organization's innovation and improvement activities. Indeed, such operational measures drive future financial performance (Van Der Zee & De Jong 1999). Efficiency, quality, and market share and penetration are other important goals and measures of business vitality (Singleton, McLean, & Altman 1988) that can be dramatically improved by software systems. Moreover, research has shown that organizational performance can be maximized by clearly recognizing the interdependence between social and technological subsystems (Ryan & Harrison 2000). Software systems with Web capabilities can enhance business added value even more effectively through their ability to reach customers, affiliate with partners, and enrich information (Evans & Wurster 1999).

Although some small organizations use software systems only as one of many tools to achieve financial goals, many organizations have become partially or totally dependent on software systems. Comprehensive software solutions are becoming the standard in many large organizations in which carefully thought out, unified software architectures are used to address business problems in levels of complexity that range from the operational to upper management and strategic levels.

When an organization decides to assess whether it should develop a software system, a feasibility study is usually carried out to compare costs to benefits. Based on evaluating the appropriate organizational criteria and financial metrics, managers can decide whether to move affirmatively towards selecting an information system from among various alternative options. Organizations look at software as a tool that can make their businesses better, their customers happier, and their shareholders wealthier. Three criteria used in recent research on assessing business value for IT-based systems are productivity, business profitability, and consumer surplus (Hitt & Brynjolfsson 1996 and 1997).

However, when a software system is being developed, the effective business value that it adds to the business performance of an organization tends to be neither explicitly addressed nor adequately quantified. In general, the focus in software development is generally on technical metrics intended to assure the quality of the software product, mainly in terms of its reliability characteristics. This is because software value is typically measured in terms of its intangible rather than tangible benefits on business. If a software system is reliable and robust, is tested, and can be maintained efficiently, it is assumed that it has a business value regardless of the resultant business outcomes. The overall business effect on value is rarely considered, nor is the distance between the potential value of a system and its realized value (Davern & Kauffman 2000).

Requirements validation is also an important metric when building software systems; however, the traditional forms of requirements focus on direct users' needs and overlook business value in terms of comprehensive and quantifiable measurements. Although project management and fiscally driven factors are part of the software engineering process, they are often not integrated well into the process. Moreover, a gap remains between the discipline of management information systems and the software development disciplines: MIS looks at solutions from a managerial perspective, but technical concerns are more influential for software development. The direct connection between software development and business performance is inadequate and is not well quantified or recognized as a core

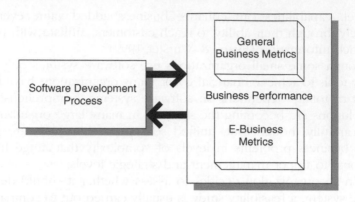

Figure 7.1 Relationships between the software development process and business performance.

concept. It is important to bridge this gap and identify the business value of software systems in terms of business metrics that are quantitative representations of business attributes (Krueger 1992).

Identifying business metrics for software systems will not only change how software systems are evaluated, but can also help improve the development process by more accurately mapping it to actual business goals and generating greater synchronization with business processes in organizations. When the development process becomes tightly coupled with business goals and metrics, business results will determine the feasibility of the process. Within this theoretical framework, technical metrics can only play the role of intervening variables (where applicable). Once these conditions are met, management by business results will be the driving force in the software development process (Singleton et al. 1988). This is increasingly important in an environment in which greater focus is put on the quality of products and services and total quality management and continuous improvement have become a necessity. A software system unable to deliver competitive-quality business value at the end of the value chain will no longer be an option.

Figure 7.1 depicts the interactive relationship between the software development process and business performance in general and in an e-business context. On the one hand, software systems are developed through a process and should be continually improved and tailored to adapt to changes in business requirements and environments. On the other hand, business goals are the critical measures of business performance, and thus business goals are the final evaluation criteria for business performance. Such business goals are called metrics when they become quantifiable as positive or negative indicators of business success. In such a framework, business performance can be categorized using two kinds of measures: general measures and e-measures. The arrows in Figure 7.1 are bidirectional because they reflect the mutual influences between the initial two variables of this framework. Business goals should be triggered to guide an optimal software development process. Thus, this framework represents a view of the initial impact of business metrics on the development process.

The effect of the development process on business performance is also a key concern. Although many problem-solving strategies are used in software process modeling, the overall software process can be viewed in terms of certain basic elements or resources, such as activities, time, people, technology, and money. To reduce costs or increase benefits, one can think of combining activities; minimizing the cycle time; reducing the number of staff involved; maximizing profit; restructuring the composition of capital and finance; managing risk; or utilizing more technology. When the software process is reconsidered in these terms, business performance and metrics become the decisive driving force for building software process models.

Consequently, the software process has two related roles. The first role is internal: to assure software project payoff with better return on the information system investment, as discussed earlier. The second is external: the software process should make an actual difference in business performance. The first role has been addressed extensively in the software development and project management literature. However, few research efforts have been dedicated to the study of the external impact of the software process on business performance. In fact, these roles should always be combined because external impacts cannot be studied without considering internal impacts. Figure 7.2 depicts this dual approach.

This view represents the integration of the process and project themes and describes the evolution of software process models over the last several decades. Business value has always been embedded implicitly or explicitly in almost every progress in software process modeling. Minimization of time was behind the Rapid Application Development (RAD) and prototyping models. Risk control and reduction were major issues behind spiral models. The efficient use of human resources lies behind the dynamic models. The impact of user involvement in software process models reflects the importance of customer influence. Achieving competitive advantage in software systems is a key business value related to users and customers. However, little empirical examination of the affect of the different problem solving strategies adopted in software process models takes place.

The interdependencies between the software process and business performance must be a key issue. The former is driven by the need for business value, and the latter in turn depends more than ever on software. Although the need to integrate or synchronize the software process with

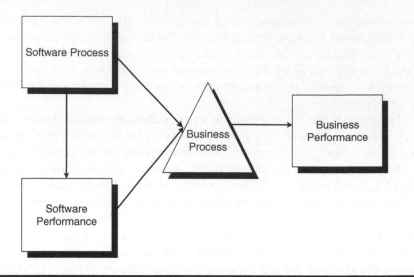

Figure 7.2 Dual role of the software process.

the business process is increasing, some organizations do not need even to separate these processes. This is particularly so for virtual organizations, which have little physical existence. Associated important research questions include:

■ Investigating the components of the business value of general software systems and of Web-based software systems
■ Determining how this business value can help define more realistic metrics for software systems and the relation between the software process and the business process
■ Determining the software process factors that are most responsible for adding business value to a firm and the difference between the problem-solving strategies embedded in software process models in terms of their impact on business value
■ Determining how business value can drive the structure of the software process model
■ Determining how the relation between the software process and the business process can be affected by increasing dependency on software systems
■ Determining how e-business solutions will contribute to this

7.3.5 Computers Cannot Work without People

Functional examination of any software system points to a high correlation with and dependence on people. The software development process is composed of people from end to end. This encompasses users, analysts, project managers, software engineers, customers, programmers, and other stakeholders. Computer systems are human inventions and do not function or interact without human input. Some manifestations of this dependency are:

- Software applications are produced by people and are based on people needs.
- Software applications that do not create value will not survive in the marketplace.
- Computers cannot elastically adjust to real situations (they work with preexisting code and prescribed user inputs).
- Computers do not think; in terms of expertise, they reflect if–then inputs or stored knowledge-based experiences.
- The main goal of software technology is to solve the problems of people.

This dependency on the human environment makes the automation that computers facilitate meaningless without human involvement and underscores the limits of computer systems. It also highlights the central role that people play in making software technology an effective tool for producing desired outcomes.

7.4 A View of Problem Solving and Software Engineering

Earlier sections presented a view of problem solving utilizing software technology and the impact of global problem-solving strategies on software-driven problem-solving strategies. They illustrated how global problem solving can apply a software-driven approach to enhance the efficiency of problem solving. The effectiveness of these approaches on business performance in terms of the business value created and software project optimization achieved was projected. Business value and project performance metrics were used to guide and reengineer the software-driven process modeling and the global problem-solving approaches.

This multidimensional, interactive, bidirectional view of global problem solving, software-driven problem solving, and business value is illustrated in the diagram in Figure 7.3. The software engineering literature has approached problem solving as a way of solving software problems. The view proposed here, as illustrated in this figure, uses an interdisciplinary approach to solving business problems in terms of software-driven technologies, tools, and capabilities. The objective is to create business value

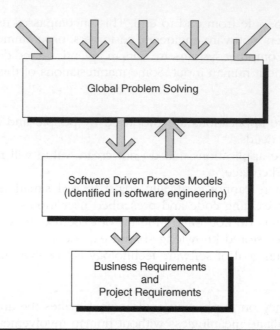

Figure 7.3   Interdisciplinary approach to problem solving.

rather than merely to overcome software development problems whose solution may not correspond to the creation of any business value.

Different factors have contributed to how business problems are solved. The introduction of information processing changed the way in which people address problems. Subsequently, software became an essential element of any problem solution for organizations. Software has provided business managers with capabilities that enhance continual growth, created added business value, and revolutionized communication, portability, and connectivity; however, software does not represent a complete solution. The challenges to software-driven approaches to problem solving include:

■ Diversity of user requirements
■ Difficulty of capturing requirements
■ Complexity of business and decision-making processes
■ Lack of business experience and background among software specialists and developers
■ Tight coupling between computer information systems and the people who use them

Software engineering is the science of computer-driven problem solving. The authors view software engineering processes as a preliminary background that needs to be appropriated and then enhanced to provide a comprehensive and problem-solving approach. This view combines business, technology, and other relevant domains into an interdisciplinary framework for solving business problems.

References

Daft, R.L. & Lengel, R.H. (1986). Organizational information requirements, media richness and structural design. *Manage. Sci.,* 32(5), 554–571.

Davenport, T.H. & Stoddard, D.B. (1994) Reengineering: business change of mythic proportions? *MIS Q.,* 18(2), 121–127.

Davern, M.J. & Kauffman, R.J. (2000). The value of decision technologies: discovering potential and realizing value. *J. Manage. Inf. Syst.,* 16(4), 121–144.

Elzinga D.J., Horak, T., Lee, C.-Y., & Bruner, C. (1995). Business process management: survey and methodology. *IEEE Trans. Eng. Manage.,* 42(2), 119–128.

Evans, P. & Wurster, T.S. (1999). Getting real about virtual commerce. *Harv. Bus. Rev.,* 77 (November–December), 84–98.

Grover, V., Fiedler, K., & Teng J. (1994). Exploring the success of information technology enabled business process reengineering. *IEEE Trans. Eng. Manage.,* 41(3), 276–284.

Hitt, L.M. & Brynjolfsson, E. (1996). Productivity, business profitability, and consumer surplus: three different measures of information technology value. *MIS Q.* 20(2), 121–142.

Hitt, L. & Brynjolfsson, E. (1997). Information technology and internal firm organization: an exploratory analysis, *J. Manage. Inf. Syst.,* 14(2), 81–101.

Keen, P. (1981). Information systems and organizational change. *Commun. ACM,* 24(1), 24–33.

Krueger, C.W. (1992). Software reuse. *ACM Computing Surv.,* 24(6), 131–183.

Lederer, A.L., Mirchandani, D.A., & Sims, K. (1997). The link between information strategy and electronic commerce. *J. Organ. Computing Electron. Commerce,* 7(1), 17–34.

Markus, M.L. (1983). Power, politics, and MIS implementation. *Commun. ACM,* 26(6), 430–444.

Mitroff, I. & Turoff, M. (1973). Technological forecasting and assessment: science and/or mythology? *J. Technol. Forecasting Soc. Change,* 5, 113–134.

Roberts, A. (2000). E-commerce/e-business/e-strategy. *IEEE J. Eng. Manage.,* 10(6), 250–251.

Ryan, S.D. & Harrison, D.A. (2000). Considering social subsystem costs and benefits in IT investment decisions: a view from the field on anticipated payoffs. *J. Manage. Inf. Syst.,* 17(1), 11–38.

Singleton, J.P., McLean, E.R., & Altman, E.N. (1988). Measuring information systems performance: experience with the Management by Results system at Security Pacific Bank. *MIS Q.,* 12(2), 325–337.

Van Der Zee, J.T.M. & De Jong, B. (1999). Alignment is not enough: integrating business and information technology. *J. Manage. Inf. Syst.,* 16(2), 137–158.

Chapter 8

Evolution of Software Development Strategies

8.1 Introduction

Software has altered how business is done, increased productivity, facilitated learning, and provided ubiquitous connectivity in every aspect of life. It has redefined geographic boundaries, accelerated the pace of business events, and helped people everywhere overcome social and cultural barriers. The underlying value of software lies in its ability to implement solutions to problems. The technical aspects of software development have become ever easier by building on the increasing automation available to developers that enables even nontechnical users to modify and customize applications to meet special requirements or user preferences. Creating a software application now requires less effort and time than in the early periods of software development. This progress can be attributed to a variety of factors.

Much of the frequently used code common to many applications has already been developed, so there is no need to reinvent it. The graphical user interface components available today in almost every development environment are an obvious example. The development of object-oriented programming languages and environments has provided very effective techniques for code reuse and distribution. For example, in current program development environments, many functions are available in predefined system libraries. The role of a programmer then consists largely of extending existing code to suit new applications. External or internal CASE tools can reduce coding time by automation, code generators, and

173

reverse engineering. Popular examples of external CASE tools include Power Designer, MS Visio Enterprise, and Designer 2000; examples of internal CASE tools include MS Access and Dream Weaver MX.

Web-based collaborative environments have provided an excellent platform for rapid, virtual communication among experts and developers, regardless of the physical location of the participants. Open-source development is a singular example of the potential of this concept. Rapid application development strategies have been widely adopted to reduce the lead time between the initial investigation and design phases and the later implementation phase. Examples range from concurrent development to evolutionary or throwaway prototyping to agile methodologies such as XP and SCRUM.

Although they have been available for quite a while, code generators are playing an important role in advancing the state of software development. Such tools are, in a sense, capable of transforming nonprogrammers into professional programmers; however, they depend on defining appropriate and unambiguous specifications, the creation of which may be similar in complexity to the difficulty of writing and verifying a program. A variety of design and analysis tools that generate code is currently available.

The actual advantage of code generators lies in their ability to allow developers to focus on the business problem rather than on coding. An error in identifying the business problem or process to be solved has the potentially most serious effects, so that is the most appropriate place to allocate maximum effort. The code produced by automatic generators may not be optimal—any more than the intermediate, assembly, or machine code created by compilers or assemblers would be. However, just as for those tools, the product of the automatic tools has a consistent quality, will be syntactically correct, and is on average as good as the kind of code generated by an average competent programmer.

8.2 Current Challenges to Software Development

The key challenge to software development today is not in creating new code, but in surviving an extremely competitive marketplace, which imposes stringent demands for software solutions that are on time, on budget, and on target. Other major challenges that software development encounters include:

- *User power and authority.* Business users and individual users are more powerful, experienced, and selective.
- *Market share.* Competitors are more aggressive, innovative, and knowledgeable.

- *Killer applications.* Applications are more customizable, interactive, dynamic, and stylish.
- *The anytime–anywhere factor.* Applications accommodate Web-based and wireless environments and an increasing number of portable devices.
- *The return on investment (ROI) factor.* Software is viewed as a true investment, not just a technical activity, and therefore is evaluated in terms of the value created rather than the functionality delivered.
- *The technology factor.* From CASE and Web-based tools to software–hardware integration to multimedia tools and applications, software technology evolves at an extremely rapid rate with which it is not easy to keep pace; nonetheless, it is essential to explore and understand such developments because new technologies can add significant competitive advantage if properly used.

These challenges have created a new view of software development that reveals a potential paradigm shift in software development ownership from technical individuals to management and business. This shift not only has motivated managers to adapt and take greater responsibility for managing the software development process, but also has motivated technical developers to increase their interdisciplinary skills to be better able to handle the business and human aspects of problems. Consequently, greater demands have been placed on software engineering education to extend its reach beyond traditional program development to develop an understanding of business-driven, total-solution approaches.

8.3 Competing Views of Software Development

Software and the business context are closely interconnected. They significantly affect each other's effectiveness, evolution, and structure, a view that reflects current realities and is often referred to as the tightly coupled relationship between software and business. A loosely coupled relationship between software and business is an alternative view that believes software is partially related to business, but not largely driven by it. This alternate view can be distinguished by two contrary perspectives:

- *Business can make software better.* In this view, software developers recognize opportunities for added business value. The software is initially developed independently of specific business needs, but is better appreciated in the context of delivering specific business value. This extends the traditional view of software engineering to include the impact of management information systems on software development. The inclusion of business metrics for evaluating the quality of software development reflects an awareness of this view.

▪ *Software can make business better.* In this view, a business recognizes an opportunity to apply software capabilities. The software is developed as a response to business needs, but only when business sees it as representing an opportunity for new business outcomes. According to this view, software is a valuable accessory to business. The applications are developed for specific needs. However, the software is not considered as a strategic value, even though the applications are recognized as supportive of business success. This view is disputable today: "Increasingly, software plays a strategic role in controlling and managing systems. Software is not just getting bigger; it is a crucial part of the products and services in almost all industries" (Humphrey 2002).

An isolationist or exceptional perspective is the technical one that often considers software as independent of business. This view implies that software can be successfully developed independently of business concerns. This autonomous attitude has been the traditional view in software engineering until recently. To the typical developer, *software* refers to the quality of the source code and algorithms that reflect the developers' technical skills. However, to the rest of the world, software is an end-user product that only makes sense when it adds a value to a business or to individual needs.

In fact, most users only interact with the front end of software systems and care little about how that software is technically developed or how it works internally. For most users, software is a black box. Indeed, if software ceases to be a black box, it usually means it is not performing its intended function, which ought to be transparent. Users of a product are uninterested in how a product is manufactured or how it actually works, unless some technical specifications are known to be tightly coupled with the desired features of the product, such as reliability and speed. The difference in nongeneric software applications is that users are actually involved in the cotechnical phases of the software development life cycle, such as analysis, design, and testing.

A similarly autonomous view considers business as independent of software. This belief contends that business can operate successfully without software. This attitude is noncontextual because it assumes a hypothetical world of guaranteed market share and zero risks in which no competitors use software for competitive advantage. If such conditions did exist and management ignored the potential cost reductions and revenue generation from using software, business could survive without software engagement. Of course, this is now impossible because software is no longer an option and competition is the major driving force in almost every business domain.

8.4 The Engineering of Software

The software engineering discipline emerged from the crisis of software development during the 1960s and the 1970s as a reaction to software project failures; economic losses; delays in schedules; increasingly competitive markets; and an increasing demand for functionality, quality, and reliability at the least possible cost. Today, software engineering still remains an emerging discipline, but it shows increasing maturity. As with other engineering domains, the engineering of software is invariably coupled with four key elements:

- Appropriateness: finding the best solution for a problem
- Value maximization: maximizing the value of the solution provided
- Effective strategy: adopting an effective strategy to develop the solution
- Modeling: designing a visual picture of a solution prior to its implementation

An Institute of Electrical and Electronics Engineers (IEEE) definition of software engineering says that it is "the application of a systematic, disciplined, quantifiable approach to the development, operation, and maintenance of software." The discipline encompasses frameworks, methodologies, techniques, and tools tailored to solve business problems. Although the software engineering discipline evolved academically out of departments of computer science, it has been influenced by other disciplines such as management, economics, and psychology. Over time, the impact of these disciplines on software engineering has redefined its character and broadened its scope to address more general objectives, especially in the business domain.

Today, many business schools and business practitioners view software engineering as part of a larger set of strategies for dealing with business problems in which the software development process is considered an essential element and critical success factor for the entire enterprise. Thus, as it has matured, software engineering has expanded beyond the confines of computer science to encompass a broader, interdisciplinary arena, in theory and in its applications.

To appreciate the breadth of software engineering, it is worthwhile to identify the disciplines with which it shares elements. These include, in addition to computer science, mathematics; computer engineering; industrial engineering; systems engineering; economics; management and management science; cognitive science; psychology; and human factors studies. The impacts of these disciplines have been important driving factors in the evolution of diverse software-driven problem-solving strategies for software process life-cycle models. Three successive layers or dimensions to software engineering might be thought of as:

- *The horizontal dimension.* This refers to effective software-driven problem-solving strategies and how they can be tailored to solve diverse business problems and meet various project needs. Examples include the Waterfall Model, the Spiral Model, prototyping, etc.
- *The vertical dimension.* This refers to the common components or phases of these strategies and how they can be efficiently addressed. Examples include the feasibility study phase, requirements analysis phase, design phase, implementation phase, maintenance phase, etc.
- *The methodological dimension.* This refers to the methods and techniques that can mediate the successful implementation of these problem-solving strategies and the common phases of the strategies. Examples include the structured-oriented methodology, the object-oriented methodology, CASE tools, etc.

8.5 The Process and the Model

Software engineering originated in early attempts by developers and theoreticians to provide guidelines for documenting program development. Initially, process flow charts were introduced for documenting manual business processes in the 1950s, when hardware suppliers began to offer guidance documentation to their clients. A process flow chart provided a high-level conceptual definition for an overall system process in terms of activities and roles. It visually recorded what happened in a business process: the sequence of activities, decisions, and actions of the as-is system and the to-be system alike, whether the system is providing products or offering services. The process flow chart is generally used in project documentation to help model the system before actual implementation.

By the mid-1960s, the provision of standardized, in-house methods for creating quality applications had already become a major concern for many organizations. Approaches were defined to identify how quality software production could be achieved in organizations. Because most applications at the time were produced under in-house development conditions, neither true standardization nor effective quality was realistically attainable for software applications. Indeed, the mix of new approaches and recommendations arguably only added further confusion and contributed to the crisis in the software industry.

By 1968, the recognition that a *software crisis* existed motivated the NATO Science Committee to sponsor two conferences to address the situation. These conferences, held in October 1968 and October 1969, led to significant outcomes. These included proposals for establishing sound engineering principles (methods) to economically obtain reliable software solutions that worked on real machines (Bauer 1972). This was to be accomplished by applying the principles of computer science and mathematics to developing cost-effective solutions to software problems and standardizing generic application components or notations so that they could be reused in other applications.

According to Osterweil (1997), a process is a natural transformation across activities needed to build an application from a known set of requirements or, as defined by the IEEE, a "sequence of steps performed for a given purpose" (IEEE-STD-610) (Paulk et al. 1993). A software process can be defined as a set of activities, methods, practices, and transformations used to develop and maintain software and the associated products, e.g., project plans, design documents, code, test cases, and user manuals (Paulk et al. 1993).

Alternatively, a software process is "the technical and management framework established for applying tools, methods, and people to the software task" (Humphrey & Kellner 1989). Software development embodies a process that transforms ideas, needs, and requirements into application programs. A process model can be defined as a specification of a real-world software process (Jaccheri, Picco, & Lago 1998). The term *software development life cycle* (SDLC) refers to the process and model used to develop software systems and describes the process that developers take in moving from problems to solutions.

A process can be characterized by a range of characteristics, from its complexity (Bandinelli et al. 1995), to its dynamic behavior, its activities, and how difficult it is to understand. A process may be discrete or continuous, sequential or nonsequential, hierarchal or distributed, or based on human action or routine computerized activities (Sutton 1988). Because processes often cross organizational functional or departmental boundaries, they lead to a description of organizational operations that identifies not only who is doing what, but also how and when these operations are accomplished. Thus, value-adding business processes represent the core to understanding business process re-engineering (Nissen 1994). The reliability and consistency of an organization's software process definition depends on an organization's maturity (Paulk et al. 1993). Furthermore, a software process must be continually improved by evaluating quantitative data about the performance of an organization's processes in order to guide its adoption of new information technologies and enhancement of the current process structure intelligently (Bandinelli et al. 1995).

Software product quality results from a combination of factors involving not only the product being developed but also the process that develops that product (Pressman 1996). As Jaccheri et al. (1998) observe, software processes are highly complex activities that affect critical factors such as final product quality and costs, so process control is essential. Effective process control is not intended merely for preventive maintenance or corrective action, but also for forecasting, scheduling, and reliability engineering, and to ensure quality assurance. In fact, controlling a process so that it attains the desired project objectives is the common, shared intention behind every process model approach.

Process control involves managing people, time, resources, and risks to make software production feasible and reliable. It is inextricably related to product metrics because defining software product metrics is the most obvious measurable way to achieve efficient control. These metrics also depend on project goals, a notion that can be formally addressed such as by the TAME method in a goal/question/metric approach (GQM) (Basili & Rombach 1988). Process models are obviously affected by the mechanisms for control and the software process concept overlaps project management in terms of control strategies and techniques.

It is essential to understand the interdisciplinary nature of software process control for the simple reason that tunnel-vision focusing on only one aspect of software process control will increase the chance of failure in software products. Such narrow approaches have in the past often resulted in a fundamental lack of understanding of the software development process and thus precipitated an increasing demand for a comprehensive approach in process models (Abdel–Hamid & Madnick 1989). Finance and economics, for example, are areas with impacts on the software process because they address project feasibility, cost estimation, risk assessment, productivity, planning, and control. Thus, integrating economics with process modeling helps provide an evaluation framework that can take into consideration the technical and fiscal aspects of a situation, especially in situations constrained by limited resources (Boehm 1984a,b).

Another aspect of the process concept is the cognitive aspect of modeling. Whether one adopts a managerial or technical approach to modeling software processes (Jaccheri et al. 1998), a model is an abstract representation of reality that is used to reduce the complexity of understanding or interacting with the modeled phenomenon by eliminating details that do not affect the phenomenon's relevant behavior (Curtis, Krasner, & Iscoe 1988). This notion is essential for effective process modeling analysis because models reflect the elements that their formulators believe are needed to understand or predict the phenomenon modeled. Thus, reverse engineering helps reveal the ideas or strategies behind existing process models.

8.6 Progression in Software Engineering Strategies

Software engineering originally emerged as a response to the software development crisis of the 1960s. It subsequently evolved as an engineering-like response to project failures, serious economic losses, scheduling delays, competitive markets, and increasingly demanding customers looking for functionality, quality, and reliability at minimum cost. The current state of software engineering strategies is the result of sustained progress as described in the following subsections.

8.6.1 The Era of Management Isolation

In the era of management isolation, considerable effort was devoted to optimizing the technical side of software systems with relatively little emphasis on the business side of software as part of the development strategy. This can be attributed to the backgrounds of software engineers of that period, who were primarily computer scientists and mathematicians. This was to be expected at that time because business managers had little or no involvement in the software development process; the entire software development process was directed, designed, implemented, and evaluated by technical specialists who dealt primarily with issues of automation.

A typical scenario for this era was for a business problem to be described quickly by a customer (or organization) while the software development team asked specific questions about the nature of the problem. The business representatives were then informed how long the software development process was estimated to last. Until the system was actually implemented, management involvement was limited to this extent unless a need for further information arose. This era was distinguished by the complete dependence of the business user on the computer professional. If the project overran an estimated schedule, the business users or company managers were relatively powerless except for expressions of dissatisfaction with service (Thomsett 2002).

In many cases, the resulting software solutions created more problems than they solved. For developers, software was naturally viewed as a goal rather than as a tool used to solve business problems in a way that should bring measurable value to a business. This period also witnessed the birth of the software life-cycle concept, with appropriate underlying technologies for each stage of the cycle. This was also the first time during which software development was viewed as a problem-solving process from a broader scientific perspective; it was seen a process governed by general rules that manifested itself in a tendency towards formalizing software development at increasing levels of rigor.

During this era, sequential and structured life-cycle models characterized the way in which software development was perceived, structured, and visualized. This structured approach reflected or imitated the organizational charts in conventional management structures in organizations according to which businesses were run by top-level management directives. Strong emphasis was placed on centralized control and closely restricted flexibility for middle and operational management.

- *Duration:* 1960s to late 1970s
- *Technology:* large computers
- *Management/business involvement:* lack of involvement and dependency on computer professionals
- *Software development process:* the value of software is in the software
- *Nature of applications:* large systems and structured problems (transaction-processing applications were common)
- *Team structure:* 100 percent technical team
- *Process life-cycle models developed:* Waterfall Model

8.6.2 The Era of Traditional Software Engineering

The development process was still under the relatively complete control of software professionals, but user and management participation was greater. Feedback loops were incorporated following the engineering model with quality measured as the distance between actual and desired results. This was seen in the modified versions of the Waterfall Model, which incorporated bidirectional relationships between different phases of the development. Examples of such modified models included waterfalls with overlapping phases and with subprojects.

The period still exhibited limited user inputs at the analysis and testing phases. Team structures sometimes allowed business specialists to represent the business requirements, but these specialists as yet had no clearly designated responsibilities, with a resulting lack of effectiveness.

Because the major challenge for software developers was to deliver a working system with appropriate functionality, little or no attention was given to measuring the business performance characteristics of the system. Correspondingly, there was a strong proclivity to test and evaluate information systems from a purely technical perspective regardless of their business value. Even when management desired to investigate the financial performance of an information system, often the software-related backgrounds among potential overseers or investigators were insufficient to carry out this role effectively.

- *Duration:* mid to late 1970s
- *Technology:* database, networking, and communications technology
- *Management/business involvement:* management or business involvement restricted to initial systems analysis, system testing, and documentation, but this involvement is on the terms of software professionals; bureaucracy marks this era
- *Software development process:* business metrics were implicitly incorporated with the emergence of more disciplined approaches to software development, project management, and quality assurance; yet, no incorporation of human-driven factors (social and political issues) was visible
- *Nature of applications:* management information systems (MIS) and decision support systems (DSS)
- *Team structure:* technical but sometimes allowing business analysts to get involved
- *Process life-cycle models developed:* modified waterfall models

8.6.3 The Era of Business Evaluation of Software Engineering

Software developers realized that computers did not solve business problems independently because those problems required more than technical skills. However, in this era, business managers also began to take control of software development. Although development teams were still technically oriented, their performance was assessed through the putative business outcomes that their products would bring, which included return on investment, net present value, break-even point, risk minimization, customer satisfaction, and added value for the long run.

This period also saw the birth of software economics. Information economics, which had begun to receive serious attention in the 1960s, played a significant role in the evolution of software economics. The roots of software economics go back to early 1970s (Boehm & Sullivan 2000). A fundamental difficulty with software economics is that most software engineers are unlikely to understand enterprise-level, value-creation objectives, and top and middle management often do not realize the success criteria for software development or how investments at the technical level are linked to value creation. One can argue that the inadequate financial education for software developers contributed significantly to the software crisis phenomena from the 1960s through the early 1980s. Despite this, the degree of internal involvement by business people was still limited. In fact, because those in control were not actually part of the process, this created new problems between technical and business domains due to incongruent goals and disparate interests and backgrounds.

- ■ *Duration:* during the 1980s
- ■ *Technology:* PC computing
- ■ *Management/business involvement:* the beginning of the strategic alignment between business and software development
- ■ *Software development process:* viewed as a critical investment in the organization that should be carefully evaluated from a business prospective
- ■ *Nature of applications:* desktop applications, packages, generic applications for organizations and individuals
- ■ *Team structure:* still technical but monitored by business managers; new responsibilities are strictly enforced in terms of feasibility studies, marketing vision, and customer service and support
- ■ *Process life-cycle models developed:* Spiral Model

8.6.4 Maturity Era: the Era of Business-Driven Software Engineering

This era is distinguished by a high degree of collaboration and partnership between the computing and business domains in which systems are analyzed and designed in joint application sessions. The rationale is to create value from diverse needs, backgrounds, and interests in well-managed, collaborative environments. The following characteristics distinguish this period:

The use of software process models and integrated environments (analyzing and supporting human factors)

Software process (process programming, Capability Maturity Model (CMM) by Software Engineering Institute)

Software Process Improvement

Integrated environments (tool integration)

Analyzing and supporting human factors (protocol analysis of human factors, communication support for consensus making and information exchange)

Object-oriented technologies (object modeling, design patterns, application frameworks, software components)

Distributed computing (concurrent object-oriented languages, distributed object-oriented languages, middleware, software agents, business objects, object-oriented business process reengineering)

Web-engineering (e-business applications, distributed collaborative software development, open-source software development, remote software testing and maintenance)

Agile development methodologies (radical project management, extreme programming, lean development)

- *Duration:* during the 1990s and on
- *Technology:* the Internet
- *Management/business involvement:* management partners with development teams in the software development process; high degree of user involvement in every phase
- *Software development process:* value creation-driven software process
- *Nature of applications:* Web-based, wireless, hardware–software combinations, enterprise-driven integration, heavy focus on user interface and real-time systems
- *Team structure:* interdisciplinary and tailored to the different needs of the various phases of the development process
- *Process life-cycle models developed:* Evolutionary Delivery, RPM Iterative Development, many versions of RAD, COTS, Agile, etc.

8.6.5 *Characteristics of Current Software Development*

There is currently significant pressure to incorporate exogenous factors and concepts in software development strategies. The presumption is that these concepts will balance the relationship between humans and machines. The social sciences have increasingly come to bear as the software industry recognized the relevance of software economics and human computer interaction (HCI), and financial, managerial, and psychological perspectives were recognized as important factors in software development. Extensive research, including field and laboratory studies, is being undertaken to explore the relation or correlation between software technology and its effectiveness in the real world. Another positive outcome has been the higher degree of interaction between computer and social scientists over the last two decades; this has enabled computer scientists to better appreciate the human, social, and organizational elements in the software development equation.

Software applications have evolved from isolated systems such as word processors, spreadsheets, and databases into networked tools that have radically and pervasively altered conventional business processes. Software was once primarily used to address well-structured data processing problems such as document and spreadsheet generation; however, software products are increasingly integrated into unstructured, day-to-day business operations. The expanded use and capabilities of these tools have enabled

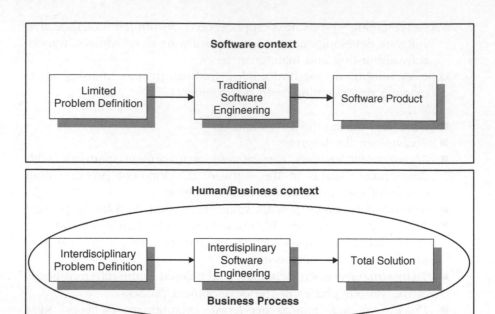

Figure 8.1   Traditional and interdisciplinary software engineering.

the design of reengineered business processes, allowing organizations to simplify business procedures and reduce cycle time. Developing software in this environment is an entirely different experience and requires synchronizing software and business processes with emerging information technologies.

An examination of software systems reveals characteristics that distinguish current information systems applications and software products from those of an earlier generation. Most current software applications are Web enabled or Web based; many interface with dynamic databases that are updated in little or real-time. Increasingly, the tendency is to build cross-platform software products that work with any operating system or environment, as well as truly evolutionary software products that have no final release version. Hardware has become more as well as less tightly coupled with innovative software applications; the user interface has become a major factor and rules for navigation, interactivity, and enhanced functionality are key elements for success.

Wireless and portable applications are gaining in importance, and issues of privacy and security are increasingly important criteria for development success. Personalization and customization also play an increasingly prominent role in the competitive advantage of software products; the presentation of facts, concepts, and ideas is now often accomplished through rich multimedia rather than unadorned text. The all-in-one or one-stop-shop concept has become a target for developing stand-alone and e-business applications alike and applications have become smarter, learn user patterns, memorize activities, provide feedback, measure performance, and track progress.

Enterprise application integration is designed to allow different departments to interoperate so that business processes can smoothly cut across multiple departments. Such applications also enable the enterprise to integrate its processes with partners, suppliers, and different levels of customers in the value chain. Finally, user interface design is increasingly becoming a critical factor in assessing the effectiveness of software products. Figure 8.1 illustrates the old approach to software engineering, in which emphasis was primarily given to processes associated with software, versus the latest interdisciplinary approach, in which human and business aspects play a major role in the problem-solving process.

References

Abdel–Hamid, T.K. & Madnick, S.E. (1989). Lessons learned from modeling the dynamics of software development. *Commun. ACM,* 32(12), 1426–1438.

Bandinelli, S., Fuggetta, A., Lavazza, L., Loi, M., & Picco, G.P. (1995). Modeling and improving an industrial software process. *IEEE Trans. Software Eng.,* 21(5), 440–454.

Basili, V.R. & Rombach, H.D. (1998). The TAME project: towards improvement-oriented software environments. *IEEE Trans. Software Eng.,* SE-14(6), 758–773.

Bauer, F.L. (1972). *Software Engineering. Information Processing,* 71, Amsterdam: North–Holland Publishing Co.

Boehm, B. (1984a). Software engineering economics. *IEEE Trans. Software Eng.,* 10.1, 4–21.

Boehm B.W. (1984b). Verifying and validating software requirements and design specifications, *IEEE Software,* 1(1), 75–88.

Boehm, B. & Sullivan, K.J. (2000). Software economics: a roadmap. In Finkelstein, Ed., *The Future of Software Engineering, 22nd International Conference on Software Engineering,* Limerick, Ireland. New York: ACM Press.

Curtis B., Krasner, H., & Iscoe, N. (1988). A field study of the software design process for large systems. *Commun. ACM,* 31(11), 1268–1287.

Humphrey, W. (2002). The future of software engineering: V. *The Watts New Collection: Columns by the SEI's Watts Humphrey.* Retrieved on Feb 11, 2004 from http://interactive.sei.cmu.edu/news@sei/columns/watts_new/ 2002/1q02/watts-new-1q02.htm.

Humphrey, W.S. & Kellner, M.I. (1989). Software process modeling: principles of entity process models. In *Proceedings of the 1989 International Conference on Software Engineering,* Pittsburgh, PA, New York: ACM Press, 331–342.

Jaccheri, M.L., Picco, G.P., & Lago, P. (1998). Eliciting software process models with the E3 language. *ACM Trans. Software Eng. Methodol.*, 7(4), 368–410.

Nissen, M.E. (1994). Valuing IT through virtual process measurement. In *Proceedings of the 15th International Conference of Information Systems*, Vancouver, British Columbia (Canada). New York: ACM Press, 309–323.

Osterweil, L.J. (1997). Software processes are software too, revisited. In *Proceedings of the 1997 International Conference on Software Engineering*, Boston. New York: ACM Press, 540–548.

Paulk, M.C., Curtis, B., Chrissis, M., & Weber, C.V. (1993). *Capability Maturity Model for Software*. Pittsburgh, PA: Software Engineering Institute, 1993. (Technical report CMU/SEI-93-TR-024).

Pressman, R.S. (1996). *Software Engineering: a Practitioner's Approach*, 4th ed. New York: McGraw–Hill.

Sutton, W.L. (1988). Advanced models of the software process. In *Proceedings of the 4th International Software Process Workshop*, Moretonhampstead, Devon, (UK), Baltimore, MD: ACM Press, 156–158.

Thomsett, R. (2002). Extreme project management. *E-project Management Advisory Service Executive Report, 2* (2). Retrieved on Feb 10, 2004 from http://www.cutter.com/consortium/freestuff/epmr0102.html.

Chapter 9

Diversification of Problem-Solving Strategies in Software Engineering

9.1 Introduction

This chapter examines factors that have promoted the diversification of software process models. The intention is to understand more clearly the problem-solving process in software engineering and to identify criteria that can be used to evaluate alternative software-driven problem-solving strategies for differing project requirements. A review of software process modeling is given first, followed by a discussion of process evaluation techniques. A taxonomy for categorizing process models, based on establishing decision criteria, is identified that can guide selecting the appropriate model from a set of alternatives on the basis of model characteristics and software project needs. These criteria can facilitate adaptability in the software process so that the process can be "altered or adapted to suit a set of special needs or purposes" (Basili & Rombach 1988).

The factors that have contributed to the diversification of software process models have often been related to the expansion in goals and capabilities in the software industry. The expanding goals that emerge

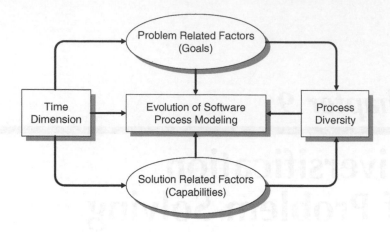

Figure 9.1 Process diversity as a function of problem and solution-related factors that evolve over time.

from new stakeholder requirements drive problem-related factors; the growth in software capability—which reflects the impact of emerging technologies, evolving methodologies, and increasing interdisciplinary impacts—drives solution-related factors. The impact of historical development and problem- and solution-related factors not only helps explain the changes that have occurred in process modeling but can also help project or forecast future developments in process modeling.

Figure 9.1 illustrates how the arrow of time continually pushes evolution in software process modeling and increased diversification of software-driven problem-solving strategies. The causative forces involve factors ranging from increased software development experience and more interdisciplinary background among software engineers to the degree of problem complexity; organizational goals; availability of technology; and changing cognitive styles in problem solving. Regarding the latter, for example, differing cognitive styles and paradigms of cognitive experience exist in every discipline and practice.

For example, in the domain of management information systems, an in-depth understanding of its models, cognitive activities, skills, and knowledge can lead to improved approaches for developing information systems and allow problems to be solved more creatively and efficiently (Benbasat & Taylor 1983). Bottom-up, reverse engineering of models (Tilley 1998) and cognate approaches may uncover original system design intentions. They can then be helpful when exploring the relationship among models in a specific discipline and can lead to establishing clearer frameworks for understanding.

9.2 Understanding Diversification in Software Engineering

At the problem level, the roots of diversification include:

- Scope and complexity of problems
- Types of requirements and forms of problems
- Need to learn and apply new capabilities
- Challenges of continuous change
- Impact of the consumer economy and interdisciplinary effects
- Development of e-business applications
- Multiplicity of stakeholders, project team skills, background requirements, and business goals

At the solution level, diversity has been driven by variations in:

- Project management approaches
- General standards
- Quality-assurance standards
- Hardware and software tools
- Networking tools
- Data mining and automation tools
- Nature, scope, and domain of applications
- Need for business-driven software engineering
- Secure software engineering
- "Killer" applications
- Mobile or wireless software engineering

9.2.1 Driving Forces of Diversity in Development Strategies

Diversity is a prevalent characteristic of the software process modeling literature. This reflects the evolution in software development in response to changes in business requirements, technological capabilities, methodologies, and developer experience. Process diversity also reflects the changing dimensions of project requirements, with process models maturing over time in their ability to address evolving project requirements. Diversification is also driven by the increasing importance of interdisciplinary views in modeling software processes. Figure 9.2 describes the combined effect of such temporal and interdisciplinary effects.

The temporal parameter is correlated with greater demands and changes that require ongoing adaptation and increased complexity. Time also introduces greater capabilities that afford better problem analysis and

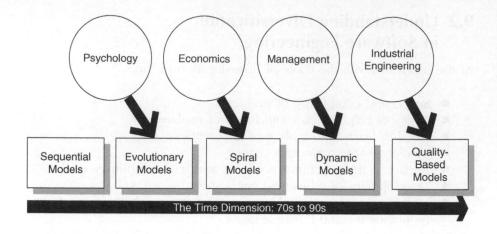

Figure 9.2 Impact of time and interdisciplinary impacts on the evolution of process modeling.

Table 9.1 Measures of Evolution in Software Process Modeling

Aspect	Illustrations from the Literature
Structure	Shift from sequential architectures in Waterfall Model to iterative architectures in spiral and prototyping models
Degree of control	Formal specifications—as in IBM Cleanroom—enable more validation and verification for user requirements as opposed to early traditional methods
Integration	Rational unified process and win–win spiral models offer comprehensive frameworks in which several process models were utilized
Automation	COTS, Cleanroom, the TAME and dynamic models utilize the emergence of CASE tools and simulation technologies to automate the development process
Visualization	The move from structured modeling paradigms to object-oriented modeling and use-case-driven paradigms enables greater visualization, especially with the availability of advanced modeling packages and simulation software

resources. There are numerous examples of measures that change through the development of increased capabilities, including methodology, technology, experience, and interdisciplinary impact, as illustrated in Table 9.1.

Technological capabilities seem to have the most influence on process modeling in terms of their impact on process automation, visualization, and degree of process control. Thus, although early process models were manual and sequential in structure, this changed with the introduction of fourth-generation techniques and languages. Process technology enabled the support of the rapid application development needed for iterative approaches with their greater emphasis on risk minimization and user satisfaction.

Time also increases the accumulated pool of experience in process modeling development. The movement from the traditional waterfall to the V-shaped model, or from the conventional spiral to the win–win spiral model over the decades are examples of the effect of accumulated experience on process modeling structure and definition. This capability measure is also a function of problem-related factors, with increases in problem complexity and business requirements affecting the collective pool of experience and altering how problems were solved.

The type of methodology adopted also has considerable impact on process modeling evolution. For instance, an object-oriented methodology supports the architecture-centric approach in rational unified process models in terms of structure, automation, and visualization, as distinguished from process-oriented methodologies. Although these two methodologies exhibit generic conceptual similarities in the earlier phases of the process model, they become more differentiated as implementation-related factors are considered or techniques and representational constructs are utilized (Agarwal, De, & Sinha 1999). The SOFL model of Liu and colleagues (1998) presents an integrated approach that adopts structured methodologies in the requirements phases and object-oriented methodologies in the design and implementation phases. The adopted methodology can be driven by quality assurance and associated with the evaluation of software systems. Gradual improvement approaches such as TQM view problems differently than highly dynamic approaches such as BPR (business resource planning). For gradual improvement, SEI-CMM; the Kaizen approach; QIP; and the BUTD approach have been introduced with significant effects on structuring and automating the development process (Bandinelli et al. 1995).

The software field originated with little attention paid to human factors. The importance of social context disciplines was only later appreciated, driven particularly by the increasingly widespread awareness of the high failure rate of software projects and its relation, at least in part, to social science-related factors. At that point, human factors began to be accommodated more seriously—for example, through the use of systems dynamics modeling and greater attention to cognitive effects and behavioral models. This reflected a more interdisciplinary understanding of software problem solving (Boehm, 1984).

Economic considerations were more systematically addressed by incorporating risk management in the prototyping, spiral, and other iterative process models; they were manifested in the development process with increased attention to feasibility assessment, cost estimation, risk assessment, productivity, and control. Industrial engineering and operations research are examples of other interdisciplinary influences affecting the evolution of process modeling. The application of quality-assurance standards to business processes is one example. Software modeling, in terms of development structure and process visualization, has also been affected by the increasing impact of customers on business. Thus, iterative structures substantially escalate user involvement and customer–developer communication becomes more effective with greater visualization. Thus, customer considerations have significantly affected process evolution. However, it is worth noting that working with small systems entails a different experience than working with large systems because modularization is not reliable without tailored approaches (DeRemer & Kron 1976). A schematic representation of drivers for the evolution of software process modeling is shown in Figure 9.3.

Several implications are worth noting here. For one, it is clear that the arrow of time is critically correlated with advances in software process modeling. Indeed, most of the influential drivers in process modeling evolution are time dependent, although time is inadequate to explain all the variation. Time can be thought of as a necessary requirement for problem- and solution-related drivers, acting as a trigger and a constraint. Although problem-related factors have been essential to precipitating changes, the availability of resources and capabilities (solution-related drivers) have had even greater impact on this evolution. This can be attributed to the impact of capabilities on problem-related factors. Thus, problem- and solution-related factors are not mutually exclusive, but depend on one other. The degree of automation, control, and integration and the extent to which changes in process structure take place can be used as measures of the evolution of software process modeling.

Another consideration has been the increasing degree of visualization provided for process models. Initial models, like the Waterfall, Evolutionary, and Spiral models, had a static view of the software development process, but later behavioral models explicitly portrayed the dynamic character of real-world software development processes. Indeed, with process improvement models and state-of-the-art advances in CASE tool technology, one is now able to monitor the development process in a multidimensional view, including full simulation of the dynamic behavior of the process. This advances the goal of efficiently controlling the software process. Figure 9.4 describes this evolution in visualization capability.

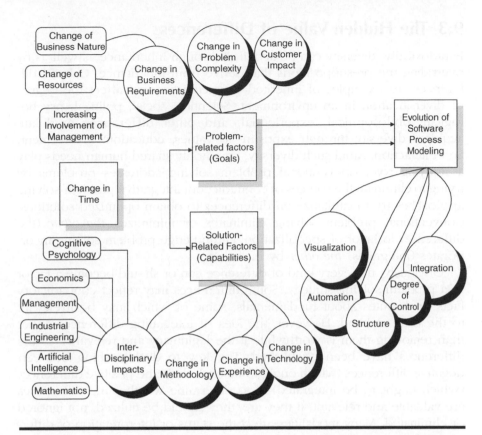

Figure 9.3   Schematic representation of drivers for software process modeling.

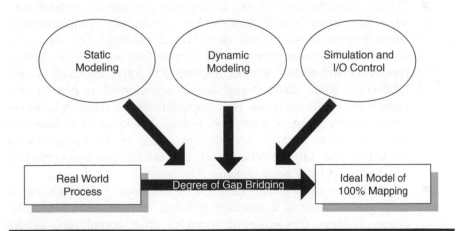

Figure 9.4   Evolutions of software process model capabilities for visualizing real-world development.

9.3 The Hidden Value of Differences

Paradoxically, diversity can be acquired through inheritance as well as by overriding the presuppositions that derive from inheritance. Cultural differences are examples of inherited characteristics that affect the degree of diversification in an environment. Scientific, social, political, psychological, philosophical, experiential, and other differences modulate acquired diversity through exposure to values, education, involvement, and interaction. Amid such diversity, commonly shared human needs play a unifying role. Conventional problem solving addresses problems by trying to eliminate the sources of contradiction; integrative problem-solving approaches try to capitalize on differences to obtain optimized solutions. Conventional problem solving eliminates or minimizes *the other* (the difference) in favor of specialization; cutting-edge problem solving incorporates (integrates) *the other* by inclusion.

Obviously, not every kind of difference can or should become a factor in a problem-solving strategy. Some differences may reflect contradictory facts or disputes about fundamentals, some of which may be irrelevant to the issue at hand. However, the idea of integrating differences rather than removing them is worthwhile if the legitimacy and relevance of the differences have been established. The key to distinguishing between negative differences (which ought to be excluded) and positive differences (which ought to be integrated) is to determine whether the differences are valuable and relevant. If they are, they should be utilized, not ignored or eliminated. Many modalities affect the status or interpretation of differences, for example:

- *The simultaneity factor.* Some differences can appear contradictory when they occur simultaneously, but are actually complementary when placed in sequential order on a timeline. For example, consider a false dichotomy such as whether analysis or design, process or architecture is more important in software development. Of course, when analysis and design are viewed as phases in a unified life cycle, each one is as important as the other. A business firm needs to diagnose a problem before providing an architecture for its solution, and an architecture needs to be tailored to a particular case. On the other hand, a good analysis is worthless if it is followed by a poor design.
- *The unique answer factor.* Differences can appear contradictory if only one element of a situation is taken as representative of the entire situation. This leaves no room for other contributing factors and no way to find relationships between diverse differences. For example, is a problem a technical or a business problem? Recognizing

that a situation may arise from business as well as technical errors is totally different from understanding the issue from only a single perspective. Different elements can contribute to a complete picture and they may interact with or complement each other. Thus, a technical problem may affect business factors and business factors may create technical problems. The failure of a commercial Website to generate revenue may have been caused by inadequate technical support, which led to frustrated customers. A lack of appropriate budgeting may in turn have been responsible for the shortfall in technical support.

9.4 Integration—Not Differentiation

What is really needed in solving a problem is to find out whether the relevant differences or diversities can or should be made to work together. The purpose in integrating differences is not only to ensure resolution of contradictory or conflicting factors. Indeed, diverse elements may not even be able to function independently of one another, and eliminating one element in favor of another may introduce other problems. To illustrate the integration of differences, consider another false dichotomy posed by the following question: "Which is more important: the process or the project?" This is a misguided alternative because it implies differentiation is the only choice and that integration is out of the question. In fact, no process exists without a project and no project can have a successful outcome without the guidance provided by a systematic problem-solving process. Thus, the project and the process must be integrated, combined, or synthesized—not differentiated in an exclusionary sense by sacrificing one element for the other.

In problem solving, it is tactically unwise to give priority to differentiation over integration because this tends to predispose developers to ignore or postpone examining the relationships among differences until they are compelled to do so by a roadblock in the solution effort. If differentiation is done first, a roadblock may occur after initial progress has been made in solving a problem when a difficulty related to some defect in the tentative solution is recognized. In this case, the process will be forced to backtrack, retracing its steps to determine what went wrong. By contrast, if one examines the potential benefit of integrating differences before selecting one of the apparent "alternatives," the risk can be reduced. Thus, a *differentiation-first* approach is more likely to entail a costly restructuring of an entire effort in order to debug and correct a faulty process, but an *integration-first approach* may require only a preliminary inquiry and relatively primitive tests to evaluate the potential benefits of integration.

9.4.1 Investing in Diversification

Diversity is an organizational asset. It embodies the *hidden value* of differences: a value that is frequently underestimated, underutilized, or obscured in traditional approaches. Appreciating diversity is the only way in which one can successfully implement interdisciplinary thinking in software engineering. The purpose of investing in diversity is ultimately to exploit and incorporate the interdisciplinary knowledge that it represents into a unified problem-solving framework. Diversity investment leads to a wider understanding of the role of diversity in software engineering and bringing it to bear on issues identified during the problem-solving process. It also implies identifying new, unrecognized, or underutilized areas of knowledge and exploring new aspects of problem definition.

One venue for doing this is by incorporating diverse requirements and capabilities into problem solving so that it is tailored to various kinds of business problems and project goals. For example, investment in diversity can be implemented by establishing training programs that prepare employees to think in an interdisciplinary way; to understand diversity; and to learn to incorporate diverse sources and types of knowledge to construct a broad-based approach to problem solving.

9.4.2 Factors That Affect Interdisciplinary Ignorance

For present purposes, the term *ignorance* refers to a lack of data or the presence of inaccurate data in a circumstance in which such a lack hinders the proper understanding and definition of business and human problems. Ignorance in this sense includes lack of knowledge about available information as well as about adequate or effective tools. This results in a problem-solving process that may have unreliable or insufficient inputs. Understanding the sources and varieties of ignorance can help reduce the failure rate in problem-solving processes. Just as in the case of domain knowledge, domain or process ignorance is also an interdisciplinary phenomenon; thus, overcoming this kind of ignorance requires an interdisciplinary response. Although a thorough grasp of a problem area and the solution domain results in success, ignorance masks or obscures the real situation and thus broadens the distance between actual problems and their appropriate solutions. The many sources of ignorance include unreliable sources of information; partial knowledge; lack of communication; and interorganizational ignorance.

9.4.2.1 Unreliable Sources of Information

This category includes inadequately accountable sources of information. Examples range from unconfirmed, inconsistent, suspicious, or doubtful resources to resources that are untrustworthy or lack qualification. Clearly, determining whether a resource is reliable requires examining the quality and credibility of the data and the data carrier; even computerized systems can be based on incorrect formulas, programming bugs, and inaccurate entries. Interdisciplinary capabilities are needed to eliminate or disqualify unreliable resources and to rate or rank sources, which can be human, digital, or hardcopy sources. For example, one can estimate the reliability of a human source by examining characteristics of subjects such as their skills, psychology, physiological criteria, etc. Technical testing may be required if data is delivered by electronic media. If a source involves specialized information, domain knowledge and expertise in the area may be needed to evaluate its reliability.

9.4.2.2 Partial Knowledge

This refers to aspects of an issue that have not been revealed (so-called in-breadth ignorance) or information about a specific aspect of an issue that is left incomplete (so-called in-depth ignorance). This type of ignorance may even derive from a complacent or self-satisfied attitude—"what we do not know does not exist."

In-breadth ignorance assumes that information can be gathered using only one or two paths of knowledge, with other aspects of the problem not even considered for relevancy. Failure to recognize all the dimensions of an issue can result in solving the wrong problem and thus leaving the real problem unsolved. For example, although the infamous Y2K problem was at one level a technical problem, it had in fact many managerial aspects. For example, solving the technical dimension of Y2K was arguably easier than finding sufficient staff capable of reviewing systems for relevant bugs. In this situation, because of the intense demand for qualified staff, managing the available human resources became a real challenge. The "technical" problem was indeed interdisciplinary, like most business problems.

In-depth ignorance may recognize the relevant aspects of an issue but not study them thoroughly enough to understand them effectively. For example, when considering the e-business readiness of a certain organization, a company may be deemed well prepared in terms of Web presence, design, and infrastructure, but may have overlooked the need to train and prepare its staff for the demands of e-business. Staff training is a key ingredient of e-business readiness—at least as critical as technical skills, written policies, or strategies. E-business needs to begin with solid technical preparation, but in the long run it requires sufficient staff support, involvement, and understanding. In-depth coverage means that each dimension or component of an issue is studied and analyzed fully.

9.4.2.3 Lack of Communication

Lack of communication is a major source of ignorance. Communication narrows the distance between the various elements of the problem in question. Lack of communication originates in factors such as failure to contact the stakeholders in a business problem; not using effective communication techniques; or not being able to carry out an efficient communication process. The effects of a lack of communication can be summarized as follows:

- *Ignorance of lack of sources.* Communication is the primary method for acquiring data from existing or prospective sources. Lack of communication reduces or omits sources of information.
- *Extracontextual ignorance.* Communication can ease tension between conflicting parties and improve common understanding. This is beneficial when gathering reliable data. Furthermore, the more that data resides outside an organizational context, the more difficult it is to obtain. Communication encourages an amicable and mutually accessible environment in which differences can be viewed as sources of data and knowledge. This also creates opportunities for transferring and exchanging data.
- *Ignorance of lack of communication channels.* Without appropriate communication channels, it is often difficult to deliver timely or on-time data. Late data delivery can make the problem-solving process less effective. This is especially important in achieving competitive advantage and responding to urgent situations.
- *Differentiation ignorance.* The current trend in business is to learn from competitors and to seek partnerships to achieve common goals. It is known that integrative approaches facilitate more effective problem solving roles in terms of gathering reliable data, compared to nonintegrative, differentiating approaches. Communication is the cornerstone for facilitating any integrative process.

9.4.2.4 Interorganizational Ignorance

The value of knowledge stems from its usability and adaptability, not from its mere existence. To be valuable, information or data must add value to an organization and to its problem-solving processes. Otherwise, it is tantamount to a form of double ignorance in which people do not know what they know but assume that they do (or, they do not know that they do not know). This can make knowledge expensive if one is in possession of unused data, or make an organization a victim of knowledge utilization delays that result from a lack of awareness or ignorance of ignorance. Knowledge-based ignorance can hide weakness behind apparent strength and business sickness behind an apparently healthy organization. This source of ignorance has many manifestations and degrees and even low levels can be damaging and costly.

Consider, for example, the sales transactions that a department store conducts with its customers on a daily basis. If this accumulated daily data is only stored until the end of the year and then used solely for purposes related to taxes and inventory, the opportunity to apply such critical information may have been permanently lost. For example, applied in a timely fashion, the daily data could have been utilized for a variety of purposes—including tracking inventory in order to avoid going below a repurchase point. If data is not processed on time for such tracking purposes, business sales can suffer because of out-of-stock occurrences on key saleable items, possibly resulting in a loss of strategic clients, alliances, or business partners. Ignorance at the inventory level can block a business from operating, partially or totally in a very short time. There-fore, even though this type of ignorance is associated with a low level of the structured business process, lack of use has a potential for major impact and so represents a serious risk.

Studying customer behavior in a manner that measures customer requirements on an accurate, predictive basis is another example of the applicability of such low-level data. Without analyzing daily sales data statistically, it may be impossible to cluster customers, products, or sales points so that the store can prosper and maintain its competitive advantage. Ignorance at the customer satisfaction level may not preclude a business from continuing operation, but it may put such a business at a competitive disadvantage. The level of *risk of ignorance* in this situation may be moderate, but the long-term effects may be critical. This situation belongs to the branch-level management class of business processes.

Conducting ongoing cost-benefit analysis to measure financial perfor-mance and to control share profit is also an important issue. Absence of knowledge critical to supporting decision-making processes may prevent an organization from effectively supporting strategic management deci-sions. Such knowledge is of strategic value and can only be derived from daily transactional data. A lack of knowledge of what is happening on a given day may be minimal in terms of risk; however, in the long term, this may mask critical risk factors lurking behind the scene that can lead to business failure.

Although many levels of ignorance are linked simply to lack of data, information, or knowledge, some ignorance can be attributed to vague, surface, or unused knowledge. Examples include:

- *Unprocessed data.* Data that is not transformed into useful information in the right form, at the right time, and provided to the right people represents unprocessed data. Unprocessed data makes what we know less effective, but still expensive. Many organizations are excellent at gathering data, but fail to relate it to their problems because they do not convert it to other, more meaningful forms of information or knowledge.

- *Unused data.* When data is not used to solve problems, it amounts to an absence of data. Unused data, regardless of its level of transformation or meaningfulness, merely represents an added cost created by careless business behavior. If this is related to data that has not been processed, it is a waste of time and money. If it is related to processed data known to be useful, then retaining this data without further examination or resolution is a problem and contributes to wasted time and resources. If data is unused due to lack of managerial commitment and despite the established value of the data, this transcends mere normal ignorance and rises to the level of culpable ignorance. Deliberate or culpable ignorance represents a type of business malfeasance.

- *Untailored data.* Utilizing data effectively requires an accurate problem definition, just as medication makes no sense without a proper prior diagnosis. Thus, understanding the problem and the solution domain is as important as knowledge of the data.

- *Vague data.* Data may be too low quality to be considered for processing. This is a case of ignorance of the data that one has. Such data may be uncertain, unconfirmed, unclear, or undefined, or need proper translation or adequate clarification. If the data is processed despite its errors or uncertainties, unreliable outcomes and inefficiencies in decision-making result.

- *Politically based ignorance.* Organizational politics can play a destructive role in obtaining reliable data. If nonscientific, nonrational, or biased motivations are behind the selection of data, this may preclude obtaining critical data. Such politically selected data cannot be considered representative. The excluded data may contain contradicting facts, clarifying statistics, or a more complete picture. Intentional and biased ignorance of this type affects the problem-solving process negatively. There must be a legitimate and objective reason, not based on political or economic interest, to justify exclusion of data. Biases are another kind of filter blocking accurate data acquisition; they represent a kind of color-blindness in viewing facts in which the interpretation of the data depends on whether it supports a position held in advance. This attitude inhibits seeing other viewpoints merely because they are the viewpoints of others.

■ *Technically based ignorance.* This refers to the lack of reliable tools that enable us to see, understand, and interpret phenomena correctly. Ignorance is strongly tied to such lack of tool support. One cannot be expected to make sense of data without reliable tools. When tools are unavailable, one should anticipate that the data may not be processed at all; may not be processed on time; may not be processed accurately; may be lost or destroyed due to lack of storage tools; may be used only at lower levels of management; or may not be recognized as enabling decision-making processes.

■ *Statistically based ignorance.* This refers to a failure to establish the right relationship between things in an interconnected environment. Ignorance is often not so much a failure to collect data, as a failure to explore the data or see how data is interconnected. For example, a change in organizational effectiveness that occurs in parallel with a newly adopted style of management may not be coincidental. Viewing data as isolated bits of information without making the effort to observe its correlations or interrelationships is a type of ignorance. The effectiveness of the problem-solving process strongly depends on the ability to observe, discover, or predict relationships between variables in an organizational context.

■ *Illusion-based ignorance.* Data is not always transparent; it may mask deception, illusion, imagination, or tricks that create false impressions. Major national corporations have gone belly-up as the result of this kind of ignorance. In order to distinguish facts from illusions, caution must be exercised when viewing available data. Figure 9.5 illustrates factors that influence interdisciplinary ignorance.

9.5 Diversity in Problem Solver Skills at the Project Management Level

Little empirical evidence is available about the skills required for a project manager to be successful or how the training or experience of managers affects the success of the projects that they supervise. However, there does seem to be a consensus on the kinds of skills required at a very high level, with technical competence a "given" for project managers; naturally, however, technical competence alone is not enough to be a successful project manager.

In addition, it is recognized that project managers also need various *soft* skills, including managerial and leadership abilities, relationship and interpersonal skills, and negotiation and sales skills (Moore 1996; Pressman 1996, 1998; Tatnall & Shackleton 1996; Bach 1997; Phillips 1999; Haggerty

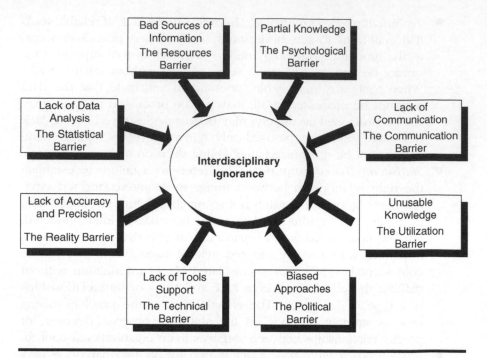

Figure 9.5   Factors that influence interdisciplinary ignorance.

2000; Potts 2000; Smith 2000; Reel 1999). Moore also observes that it is not enough to possess the skills: a project manager must understand how and where to apply different skills.

How skills are acquired is another important issue. Training project managers and software engineers can be a complex process. Learning the formal theory, techniques, and software needed to manage a project properly, as well as gaining experience from hands-on work and case studies, have value. Also, software managers are sometimes thrown into situations for which they are unprepared, leading to project failure. The consensus is that formal project management education alone does not produce effective managers (Pressman 1996, 1998; Liu et al. 1998; Moore 1996; Tatnall & Shackleton 1996; Bach 1997; Phillips 1999; Reel 1999; Potts 2000; Smith 2000). Tatnall and Shackleton identify a key problem with traditional education: formal education often involves a fixed scenario, unlike the case with real problems in which scenarios change dynamically.

9.6 Diversity as Value-Adding Tool in Problem Analysis

In business terms, human diversity has often been viewed as merely a phenomenon in the context of which individuals or peoples of different

Table 9.2 Levels and Types of Diversity Deployment

Type of Difference Deployment	Representation	Explanation
Difference activation	$X - Y = Z$	Diversity seen as potential problem
Difference neutralization	$X + Y = X + Y$	Diversity tolerated but not capitalized on
Difference optimization	$X + Y = Z$	Diversity properly deployed to create value

ethnicities, backgrounds, races, languages, or religions can at best learn to interact together in open or closed communities. However, it is gradually being recognized that human diversity can have different effects, depending on how it is approached. For example, if one looks at differences as problems (which will be referred to as *activating differences*), then one might try to mitigate the problems by eliminating or reducing the differences. Denoting the different characteristics by X and Y, the result of an activating-differences approach might be characterized as $X - Y = Z$, where the outcome Z is the result of excluding Y from X, or X from Y.

Alternatively, certain differences could be respected, tolerated, or accepted, in the manner of an agreement or arrangement (which will be referred to as *neutralizing differences*). The result of a neutralizing-differences approach might be characterized as $X + Y = X + Y$, corresponding to the situation in which X and Y coexist without producing the added value that could arise if positive interaction or cross-fertilization took place. Finally, differences can be recognized as a source of potential added value when differences make a positive contribution (which will be referred to as *optimizing differences*). The result of an optimizing differences approach might be characterized as $X + Y = Z$, where diverse patterns X and Y lead to a new pattern Z as the result of a positive interaction between X and Y. Table 9.2 illustrates the three approaches.

What kinds of diversity or difference can add value? The answer depends on the nature of the differences and on the effort applied to understanding them. The term *differences* as used here is not unequivocal; indeed, differences may be perceived as such only because of the language used to describe them. In modern businesses environments, difference or diversification is sought out because it can substantially enhance the quality of work and add significant value to problem-solving approaches. In order to add tangible value to a process, diversification can be optimized with respect to the following categories:

■ *Complementary differences* (diversity of components or ingredients) refers to elements that complete the picture when added together. This includes the different parts of a whole; different views of an object or issue; different dimensions of a structure; and different steps of a process or procedure. These types of differences can be used to add value and can be reproduced, reused, or instantiated to further enhance added value.

▪ *Interactive differences* (diversity of relationships) refers to elements that add value because of how they interact with one another.

▪ *Differences of degree, level, or version* (diversity of inheritance) refers to elements that are apparently different, but really only reflect differences of degree or level, or represent versions under a more comprehensive superclass.

In the case of software engineering, the different components of software engineering knowledge (theory, methods, techniques) and the different software engineering practices that tailor knowledge to specific requirements can add value to the problem-solving process (output or TO-BE). Furthermore, diversified resources can also add value to software engineering knowledge and to best practices (input or AS-IS). Thus, diversification can affect the AS-IS and the TO-BE levels of problem engineering. Existing differences can be brought together at the AS-IS level. For instance, diversified findings with regard to an existing system can be integrated in a complementary or interactive fashion. New inter-disciplinary resources can be incorporated to enhance the proper definition of existing business problems at the TO-BE level.

References

Agarwal, R., De, P., & Sinha, A.P. (1999). Comprehending object and process models: an empirical study. *IEEE Trans. Software Eng.*, 25(4), 541–556.

Bach, J. (1997). SE education: we're on our own. *IEEE Software*, 14(6), 26.

Bandinelli, S., Fuggetta, A., Lavazza, L., Loi, M., & Picco, G.P. (1995). Modeling and Improving an industrial software process. *IEEE Trans. Software Eng.*, 21(5), 440–454.

Basili, V.R. & Rombach, H.D. (1988). The TAME Project: towards improvement-oriented software environments. *IEEE Trans. Software Eng.*, 14(6), 752–772.

Benbasat, I. & Taylor, R.N. (1983). Behavioral aspects of information processing for the design of management information systems. *IEEE Trans. Syst., Man, Cybernetics*, 12(4), 439–450.

Boehm, B. (1984). Software engineering economics. *IEEE Trans. Software Eng.*, 10(1), 4–21.

DeRemer,F. & Kron, H.H. (1976). Programming-in-the-large versus programming-in-the-small. *IEEE Trans. Software Eng.*, 2(2), 80–86.

Haggerty, N. (2000). Understanding the link between IT project manager skills and project success: research in progress. In *Proceedings of the 2000 Special Interest Group: Computer Personnel Research Conference*, Evanston, IL. New York: ACM Press, 192–195.

Howard, A. (2000). Software engineering project management. *Commun. ACM*, 44(5), 23–24.

Liu, S., Offutt, A.J., Sun, Y., & Ohba M. (1998), SOFL: a formal engineering methodology for industrial applications. *IEEE Trans. Software Eng.*, 24(1), 24–45.

Moore, G. (1999). Surviving the project management battle. *Eng. Manage. J.*, 227–230.

Phillips, B.P. (1998). Successfully managing fast track engineering projects. In *Proceedings of the 1998 IEEE EMS International Engineering Management Conference*, May 3–5, San Juan, Puerto Rico: IEEE, 166–172.

Potts, K. (2000). The people and technology balance: getting it right for large projects. *Eng. Manage. J.*, 10(2), 61–64.

Pressman, R. (1996). Our worst current development practices. *IEEE Software*, 13(2), 102–104.

Pressman, R. (1998). Fear of trying: the plight of rookie project managers. *IEEE Software,* 15(1), 50–51, 54.

Reel, J.S. (1999). Critical success factors in software projects. *IEEE Software*, 16(3), 18–23.

Smith, G. (2000). The black art of project management. *IEEE Rev.*, 46(5), 39–43.

Tatnall, A. & Shackleton, P. (1996). IT project management: developing on-going skills in the management of software development projects. In *Proceedings of the 18th International Conference on Software Engineering: Education and Practice*, January 24–27, Dunedin, New Zealand: IEEE, 400–405.

Tilley, S.R. (1998). A reverse-engineering environment framework. Pittsburg, PA: Carnegie Mellon Software Engineering Institute 1998. (Tech. report CMU/SEI-98-TR-005)

Chapter 10

Strategies at the Problem Engineering Level

10.1 Introduction

Charles Kettering once said that "a problem well stated is a problem half solved." *Problem engineering* is concerned with the correct and complete definition of problems. Problem definition entails gathering the necessary problem-related data, processing this data effectively, and then generating a statement that accurately characterizes the problem. Particularly in a business environment, problem engineering goes far beyond the limited formulation of a problem definition in a number of ways.

The definition produced by problem engineering must be comprehensive in the sense that all aspects of the business problem must be identified and recognized. This includes the managerial, economic, human, and technical aspects of the problem. All the stakeholders of the business problem must be considered, including internal and external stakeholders, individuals, groups, communities, departments, partners, and other organizations. All essential versions, degrees, and levels of the problem must be reviewed, including degrees of problem complexity and levels of problem interaction with the different managerial entities in an organizational structure.

Problem engineering is expected to produce a problem definition that reduces uncertainty, equivocality, and ambiguity to the lowest feasible level. It must avoid overlap between problem definition and solution definition, as well as with the later design, implementation, and testing phases of the software development life cycle, which should not be confused with problem definition. The definition must be stated clearly, using any appropriate tools to express the problem. The problem definition must be verified and tested to ensure that the problem has been clearly understood.

Problem engineering must distinguish between problem symptoms and root causes. The risk of defining a business problem improperly should be assessed and a plan should be ready to minimize risk. Finally, problem definition involves utilizing tools to carry out a full-scale problem analysis. These tools include traditional and modern requirements-gathering techniques and CASE tools, as well as the use of interdisciplinary experts and knowledge; interdisciplinary resources; empirical studies; and tools that can be applied to help investigate problems carefully.

10.2 Identifying Interdisciplinary Resources and Comprehensive Problem Identification

The use of computers is increasing throughout industry as rapidly as it ever has and computer scientists with interdisciplinary interests are assisting other disciplines to use this information technology more effectively to solve problems and address new challenges (Grasso & Nelson 1997). As Hyde, Gay, & Utter (1979) have observed, every discipline has its own perspective as to what constitutes problem solving. Thus, it is important to understand how to discover appropriate interdisciplinary resources for attacking problems. Two basic methods that can be applied to identify relevant interdisciplinary resources effectively will be considered. The first method uses the *reverse engineering* of existing strategies and knowledge bases. The second involves finding relevant resources and performing *problem decomposition* for every phase identified in the problem identification process. These methods are explained in the following sections.

10.2.1 The Reverse Engineering Method

The *reverse engineering method* is defined by Buss and Henshaw (1991) as the process of analyzing a subject system to identify its components and their interrelationships and to create a representation of the system in another form or at a higher level of abstraction. The reverse engineering method can be carried out following the process depicted in Figure 10.1. Existing or legacy problem-solving experiences and outcomes (AS-IS) should be analyzed and then reverse engineered to extract their interdisciplinary resources. This will yield a detailed, in-depth synopsis of existing resources. The extracted interdisciplinary resources should then be reused,

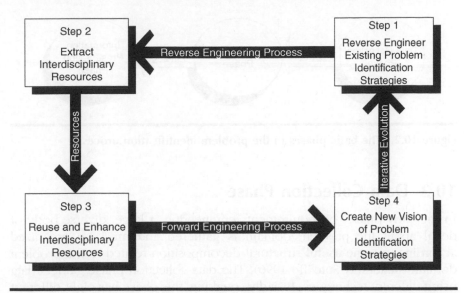

Figure 10.1   Identifying interdisciplinary resources to create new vision in problem identification

extended, and enhanced to support the new vision of the problem-solving process. A new (TO-BE) understanding of this process is created, iteratively extended, and updated to respond to changes in business requirements and technological capabilities. This process entails a dynamic response to varying requirements that adjusts according to the changed environment.

10.2.2 The Problem Decomposition Method

Problem decomposition serves two major functions. The first function or purpose is to exploit the advantage obtained by breaking bigger problems into appropriately defined smaller problems; this makes the problem complexity more manageable. The second purpose is to take advantage of the fact that the solutions from the smaller decomposed problems can be reused to help solve other problems (Jackson & Jackson 1996), and can exploit previously solved smaller problems. The problem decomposition method is illustrated in Figure 10.2 applied to the question or "problem" of problem identification. Problem identification is shown here as decomposed into three smaller, sequential subproblems or phases consisting of data collection, data processing, and an information presentation phase. These three phases characterize the typical problem identification process in problem engineering and are discussed in the next sections.

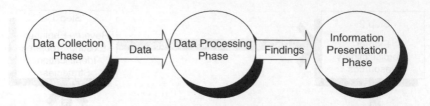

Figure 10.2   The basic phases in the problem identification process.

10.3   Data Collection Phase

In the early phases of requirements engineering, a large, diverse body of detail about the problem domain is gathered and must be organized according to some useful structural decomposition related to the problem domain (Maiden & Sutcliffe 1996). The data collection phase gathers data using different techniques. Broadly speaking, this phase has eight different elements:

- *Generate stakeholders list*: addresses the question of who is interested in this particular problem-solving process
- *Rationale for change*: identifies why these stakeholders are dissatisfied with the current situation
- *Measure risks of change*: identifies those aspects of the current situation that are still considered to be good or satisfactory
- *Thorough diagnosis*: identifies the root causes of the dissatisfaction with the current situation
- *Survey for benchmarking and setting evaluation criteria*: identifies the experience of others in the same problem domain and sector, as well as one's own experiences and those of competitors, customers, and employees
- *Initial functional requirements*: identifies what the stakeholders are looking for in a solution
- *Initial nonfunctional requirements*: identifies limitations on the solution
- *Tools identification and allocation*: identifies the tools and techniques available to gather requirements

10.3.1   Generate Stakeholders

The generate-stakeholders phase is concerned with identifying the stakeholders who are interested in the particular problem solving process. These include those who cause change as well as those affected by it.

All the stakeholders of the problem must be considered, including internal and external stakeholders, individuals, groups, or other organizations. The adequate, mutual, and sometimes opportune interaction of relevant stakeholders is of very high importance in the problem-solving and requirements engineering process (Sharp, Finkelstein, & Galal 1999). Proper identification is important; excluding a key stakeholder can undermine the process of problem solving because the relevant entities that can affect or be affected by the solution to the problem may be missed. Identifying stakeholders is also important in order to manage the quality attributes of the system under development—attributes related to "stakeholder-centric" conditions on the system (Preiss & Wegmann 2001).

10.3.1.1 Interdisciplinary Perspective

Stakeholder management allows the different members of an organization to improve their ability to work towards the common goals of the software development project; it is a form of collaborative management. Through this modality one tries to bring together the different stakeholders who are interested in and contribute to the planned change (particularly the end-users) around the specific project, for the purpose of identifying and acknowledging their differing perspectives. This collaboration helps develop an understanding of the details of the stakeholder needs and their requirements for the project and helps align the actions of individual stakeholders towards their shared goals. The process of identifying stakeholders also helps to build trust between the developers and end-users. This in turn helps generate the ability of the organization to sustain project commitment.

The task of identifying these stakeholder needs is not an easy one. In particular, it is not merely a matter of identifying the different stakeholders involved. It is also necessary to understand their specific requirements and how the manifold requirements of different stakeholders influence and interact with each other. In the end, tone must devise a plan to resolve any conflict in these competing requirements. A poor analysis of these relationships may lead to a failure in the entire problem-solving process (Robinson & Volkov 1997).

10.3.2 Rationale for Change

The *rationale for change* phase is concerned with identifying why stakeholders are dissatisfied with the current situation and why there is a perceived need to produce an alternative to the status quo. The weaknesses in the current situation need to be sought out and explicated in order to produce a careful analysis that accurately identifies the root causes of the perceived need or desire for change. This part of the analysis is essential to preventing or minimizing the likelihood of similar situations recurring in the future, as well as for correcting the recognized weaknesses in the present situation. In terms of software projects, these weaknesses or shortcomings are characterized by a potentially large set of attributes. The attributes must be chosen to address stakeholder needs, expectations, and aspirations. Therefore, it is necessary to understand the utility of a given project as perceived by its stakeholders (Giesen & Volker 2002).

10.3.2.1 Interdisciplinary Perspective

Dissatisfaction can arise from many sources. Dissatisfaction from a managerial viewpoint can be measured in terms of a failure to achieve organizational goals, failure to reduce cycle time, failure to increase productivity, lack of support for the decision-making process, etc. Dissatisfaction from an economic viewpoint can be measured in terms of a low return on investment (ROI), unacceptable results on net present values, high break-even point levels, a high degree of risk compared to the ROI, etc.

Dissatisfaction can be quantified through an empirical or statistical viewpoint. These views may be derived from experimental and field studies that reveal a failure of existing systems and identify the factors of dissatisfaction in organizational groups or systems. An empirical study can help quantify the evaluation of current systems and provide statistical evidence of the causes of system problems.

A human-engineering and psychological perspective can also identify sources of dissatisfaction. These can be measured in terms of human-factor goals such as the time necessary to learn how to use an environment; the speed of performance of the environment; rate of errors by users; retention over time; subjective satisfaction; and human–computer interaction or cognitive-based factors (Shneiderman 1987). Dissatisfaction from a technological viewpoint can be evaluated in terms of systems reliability, software quality, functionality, maintainability, performance, etc. Finally, dissatisfaction from a marketing viewpoint can be evaluated in terms of costs, channels of distribution, competition, promotion and prices, etc. (Applegate, McFarlan, & McKenney 1999).

10.3.3 The Measurement of Risks of Change

The measurement of the *risks of change* is concerned with identifying aspects of the current environment that are considered satisfactory, acceptable, or good. This is essential because every change has an associated risk. A risk analysis is always prudent before formal actions are taken toward any change. It is mandatory to assess the risk of alternatives to try to minimize problematic consequences. This is an essential element in maintaining the overall quality of the software development cycle, which is recognized as decisively affecting the quality of the final software product (Lam & Shankararaman 1998). Thus, although it may be advantageous or even essential to modify or change a system, it may not always be necessary to alter the existing system significantly. Indeed, it is often only necessary to fine-tune the current system to solve the perceived problems.

10.3.3.1 Interdisciplinary Perspective

Migrating to a new system always involves potential dangers, so it is not enough to evaluate a new system based only on its new features. It is also necessary to look at potential disadvantages of the change in terms of a risk of losing current functionalities or advantages. A new system requires added investment in terms of time, money, and effort, so its development should be undertaken only after positively establishing value creation by the new system. Just as in medicine, the first principle is to "do no harm" to the "patient."

In some cases, the existing system may need to be reengineered, still maintaining the advantages of the current system. Examining the positive aspects of the current system can introduce an interdisciplinary perspective in the same way as when assessing sources of dissatisfaction. Thus, the current and proposed systems should be thoroughly analyzed and evaluated. Because of the interdisciplinary underpinnings of any complex system, proposals for changing such systems will potentially add complexity to the system. An ad hoc or uncoordinated approach to managing change is inadequate for such situations; well-planned, thoroughly investigated, and focused attention on aspects of the change is necessary to increase the likelihood of a successful outcome from the change (Small & Downey 2001).

10.3.4 Thorough Diagnosis

The thorough-diagnosis phase is concerned with identifying the root causes of dissatisfaction with the current situation. A detailed and step-by-step diagnosis should be undertaken to understand the cause and effect of the current deficiencies. The diagnosis should involve detailed elaboration of the factors causing the dissatisfaction. Sometimes, the presence of a particular factor is required, yet the interaction of that factor with another factor may cause a problem. In such cases, one needs to nullify the effect of the interaction of the factors, rather than eliminate the factors altogether. Thus, a deep diagnosis is crucial to creating a workable, effective solution to the problem.

10.3.4.1 Interdisciplinary Perspective

Problem engineers are like physicians: they need to carry out a thorough diagnosis of a case to prescribe an appropriate treatment and must distinguish between the symptoms and the root cause of the disorder. A solution is useless unless it solves the right problem. Often, the cause of a problem may appear to be technical, but is actually human driven, or vice versa. To understand the causes of a problem, the problem engineer needs adequate domain knowledge. Business problems are usually inter-disciplinary; thus, a diverse background is essential, just as in the case of a physician who must appreciate the variety of factors that can contribute to an understanding of a specific case, help provide an effective solution, or even refer a patient to another physician.

10.3.5 Survey for Benchmarking and Setting Evaluation Criteria

Jones (1995) defines a *benchmark* as a collection of quantitative data used in comparing different organizations' practices and results. Benchmarking can also be done using qualitative data. The survey-of-benchmarking and setting-evaluation-criteria phase is concerned with identifying the experi-ence of others in the same problem domain or sector, as well as one's own prior experiences, and those of competitors, customers, and employ-ees. This involves identifying the positive aspects or advantages of these related experiences (which may then be included in the new solution) as well as the negative ones (which may be excluded from the solution). The Software Engineering Institute's (SEI) Capability Maturity Model (CMM) is an example of a qualitative benchmark that evaluates the performance of a software production organization on a five-point scale (Jones 1995).

10.3.6 Initial Functional Requirements

The initial functional requirements phase is concerned with identifying the needs of the stakeholders—the aspects and functionalities for which they are looking in the solution. Functional requirements are the end features that users want to see in a system. Often, prospective users of a system fail to illustrate specific functional requirements and instead define requirements on a compound system. Such requirements are deficient in explicitly stating what precisely the proposed system is supposed to do; therefore, they can portray an incomplete picture for developing the system (Kaindl, Kramer, & Kacsich 1998). Stakeholders can be a highly diversified group with disparate requirements. Defining all their diverse functional requirements at an early stage is important for effective problem solving because how a solution is evaluated as successful depends on whether the solution responds to the requirements of all its users.

10.3.6.1 Interdisciplinary Perspective

Functional requirements are the capabilities that software solutions provide for their users. Stakeholders are naturally diversified and represent inter-disciplinary viewpoints and their requirements will reflect this diversity, so it is natural to expect many categories of functional requirements. One such category is *management-based requirements*. Organizations develop strategic goals that evolve over time due to changes in the business' nature, competition, market needs, and other pressures emanating from within the organization or the external environment.

Functional requirements should reflect these goals and provide the ability to customize solutions to fit new demands. It is critical to understand the interorganizational structure so that the requirements can represent needs at different management levels, both horizontally and vertically. Horizontal requirements should meet departmental needs; vertical require-ments should match the needs of upper, middle, and operational man-agement. Management requirements include enhancing the ability to plan, control, coordinate, and evaluate business processes. They also include enabling the organization to manage, allocate, and utilize its resources effectively. Marketing requirements affect managerial needs because they are vital to accomplishing strategic goals.

An organization's *economic requirements* are important for understand-ing the business model according to which a company creates its financial value. Organizations have varied models or methods for making money; thus, functional requirements will reflect the strategies that a company uses to reduce costs; increase productivity; accelerate the cycle time of business processes; maximize profit; reach new customers; and achieve competitive advantage. Functional requirements at the economic level should include methods of monitoring, controlling, and evaluating the economic growth and performance of the business firm.

Technical requirements entail addressing the organization's software technology-related problems, such as lack of system reliability; poor functionality; absence of referential integrity; vulnerability in terms of security; low rate of productivity; bad error handling; unsuccessful user interface design; or slow communications. Technical problems have an impact on business performance and thus problem solvers must define the technical requirements clearly and precisely.

Businesses operate in an environment that is continually affected by human behavior. Accordingly, *human-based requirements* address the human-related aspects of the business problem, including its societal, psychological, political, legal, educational, behavioral, and environmental requirements. These requirements may be harder to identify because they are not normally specifiable in an explicit, quantifiable format. They require problem solvers to be knowledgeable in a range of areas to be able to identify and categorize them efficiently.

10.3.7 Initial Nonfunctional Requirements

The initial nonfunctional requirements phase is concerned with identifying the boundaries of the solution. Despite intensive efforts, it may be impossible to devise a comprehensive or totally satisfactory solution to a problem. The possibility of external factors affecting the operation of the solution is always present, as well as the possibility of loopholes, limitations, or bugs remaining unsolved. A solution may turn out to work only under certain constraints. Nonfunctional requirements do not identify direct operational actions of the system and do not possess any working features. Rather, they specify the system performance characteristics required for acceptance of the system by its stakeholders. A careful analysis and definition of these nonfunctional requirements is essential for correctly formulating a solution.

10.3.7.1 Interdisciplinary Perspective

Nonfunctional requirements are provisions that impose no demands on the direct functionalities of the software solution but impose external demands on the context, environment, or platform in which the system will carry out its operations. In other words, these requirements are properties that the product must have. They often overlap with functional requirements because the boundary between the two can be difficult to determine precisely and tend to be highly interdisciplinary because the system environment is usually diverse.

Nonfunctional requirements can be categorized in a variety of ways. One such category is *management-driven nonfunctional requirements*. This includes organizational requirements such as strategies; policies;

formal procedures; time consideration requirements; total quality management requirements; performance requirements; and marketing and standards requirements. *Technically driven nonfunctional requirements* form another category. These include requirements for implementation; efficiency; hardware; software (operating system, browser, DBMS, etc.); space; and reliability. *Environmentally driven nonfunctional requirements* include legal and ethical requirements; legislative and regulatory requirements; and privacy and safety requirements. *Supply chain management nonfunctional requirements* include logistical requirements; delivery requirements; order fulfillment requirements; partnership requirements; and portability requirements.

10.3.8 Tools Identification and Allocation

The tool identification and allocation phase is concerned with identifying the tools and techniques available to gather the requirements. Techniques used to gather requirements vary from the traditional to the modern. Some of these use advanced technologies such as joint application design (JAD), and others use simple methods such as interviews.

10.3.8.1 Interdisciplinary Perspective

Using interdisciplinary capacities can provide extensive support to the requirements gathering and determination process. Although this support can make a significant difference, the availability of the tools and techniques is the determining factor. Many of these techniques require multidisciplinary knowledge, so background plays a significant role in facilitating such capabilities. This part of the requirements collection phase can overlap with the next, the data-processing phase.

Traditional information-gathering techniques include questionnaires; interviews; document archaeology; protocol analysis; and observation of patterns and structures. Modern techniques include brainstorming; cognitive maps; use-case scenarios; story boarding; snow cards; business event workshops; electronic requirements; video; prototyping; role playing; and CASE tools. The various types of CASE tools may include:

- Information engineering
- Process modeling and management
- Project planning
- Risk analysis
- Project management
- Requirements tracing

- Metrics and management
- Documentation
- System software
- Quality assurance
- Database management
- Software configuration management
- Analysis and design
- Interface design and development
- Prototyping
- Programming
- Integration and testing
- Static analysis
- Dynamic analysis
- Text management
- Client or server testing
- Reengineering

10.4 Data-Processing Phase

Data gathered in the data collection phase must be further investigated, evaluated, mined, prioritized, and structured. Clearly, interdisciplinary skills and backgrounds come into play in a significant way here as well. Because requirements vary widely across interorganizational levels and specialties, processing requirements data implies producing different versions of outputs that can be tailored to different kinds of needs. This requires data mining and structuring requirements to reflect the desire of each level of management, each department, and each specific category and subcategory of organizational goals and demands. Sometimes, even this level of specificity is not sufficient and requirements must be personalized to suit the requests of individuals, groups, or units in the organization with very specific needs and expectations from the software solution. The data-processing phase consists of the following subphases (see Figure 10.3).

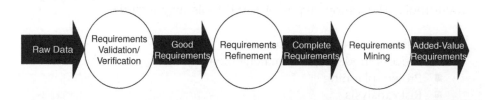

Figure 10.3   Subphases of the requirements gathering process.

10.4.1 Validation and Verification Subphase

In software engineering, validation and verification have different connotations. Validation refers to the need to make sure that the right product is built: the product that stakeholders desire. One achieves this by matching the model against the specified problem. Verification implies that the model should be compared internally with itself. Its data must be subjected to quality assurance tests to ensure that identified requirements are accurately represented. In other words, the requirements must reflect what stakeholders want. This effort is made to ensure that functional and nonfunctional requirements have been completely established. The data should map solution requirements to the problem specification. This involves the refinement of data by means of quantitative and qualitative evaluation techniques such as statistics, data mining, and protocol analysis. Programming is a problem-solving process, so determining the validity of the solution is part of this process; thus, integration of validation with software development is crucial for success (Adrion, Branstad, & Cherniavsky 1982).

10.4.1.1 Interdisciplinary Perspective

Research methods, statistics, and data mining are useful tools for quantitative evaluation of requirements. Cognitive psychology, psycholinguistics, and human–computer interaction can be helpful in protocol analysis as qualitative methods for assessing system requirements.

10.4.2 Refinement Subphase

Requirements are further fine-tuned to exclude any that may be recognized as unneeded or to include additional requirements as needed. Those deemed to be irrelevant, redundant, mixed, or nonsignificant should be excluded. After detailed review, requirements overlooked or unrecognized in previous rounds can be included in this subphase.

10.4.2.1 Interdisciplinary Perspective

Overlooking the multidisciplinary aspects of business problems can lead to missing organizationally significant requirements. Thus, carrying out an interdisciplinary review of business problems can reveal further requirements needing consideration. The different stakeholders in a business process generate or pose different requirements pertinent to the stakeholders' specific domains. These disparate needs may have interaction effects with each other that may, in turn, precipitate additional requirements arising from this mutual interaction. Thus, a further, second-order analysis may identify supplementary requirements to be gathered and recorded.

The requirements may overlap significantly and these redundancies or incompatibilities need to be pruned. Exclusion of irrelevant requirements is as important as capturing significant requirements for the cohesiveness of the model developed. This kind of refinement process can be viewed as a backtracking-based review, process steps are retraced to carefully reexamine the steps covered so far for the purpose of bridging any gaps and discarding unnecessary details.

10.4.3 Data Mining Subphase

Requirements vary broadly as one crosses the boundaries in an organization, so different versions of outputs need to be produced to cater to the different stakeholders. Requirements must be grouped, categorized, structured, and redefined in order to generate organizationally meaningful output that reflects the needs of each level of management, each division, and the varying classes of stakeholders. The requirements at this level are fully integrated in the software development process to guide the next steps effectively and efficiently.

10.4.3.1 Interdisciplinary Perspective

Software applications evolve continually as the result of bug patches, functionality upgrades, and security updates. During this updating process, the original system requirements mutate as well. Readjusting the requirements is a challenge. The rationale underlying an application's motivating design and development is distributed or scattered between the application source code and stakeholders (El-Ramly, Stroulia, & Sorenson 2002). Interdisciplinary skills can provide criteria that help structure, group, prioritize, and make sense of these requirements. Requirements of a similar nature are grouped together in order to form an overall structure that represents the functional as well as nonfunctional requirements of the users. This helps formulate a cohesive set of requirements.

10.5 Information Presentation Phase

After problem-solving data has been carefully examined, verified, evaluated, and structured, it is ready to be presented in a standardized or formal way. Formal methods of presentation vary from one organization to another based on local standards. Requirements can be represented in a natural language or using mathematical and graphical models. Natural language provides an avenue for informal representation and helps in communicating information uniformly among people with different backgrounds. However, relying on natural languages imposes the danger of ambiguity and imprecision (Meyer 1985). Mathematical models provide a formal way to represent requirements, but can be abstruse and thus difficult for nonexperts in this domain to understand. Graphical models such as the Unified Modeling Language (UML) bridge this gap. UML is a standardized language for specifying, visualizing, constructing, and documenting the intricacies of software systems and for modeling business processes and other nonsoftware systems.

10.6 Strategies in Software Engineering

The issues considered in this chapter raise important questions about software engineering, such as the role strategies that should play, or whether the discipline should be viewed as providing a handbook of prescriptions for software-driven problem solving. Is software engineering supposed to be a dynamic, knowledge-based engine that provides strategies and approaches to problem solving? Is it an input to the problem-solving process? Is it an output of extensive experience in and knowledge of problem solving? Is it some combination of these? Some of the literature on software engineering presents it as solely an input to the problem-solving process or a guide for producing successful software solutions. Bruckhaus (1992) observed that, as knowledge of how to create software evolved, the term "software engineering" was introduced and reflected the belief that *sound engineering* approaches should be applied to the development of software. It is now widely agreed that, to produce high-quality software products, one needs to engineer the software processes well, by means of software engineering methods, tools, and techniques.

Overall, software engineering tends to be understood as an input to the problem-solving process that provides a roadmap for software development problem solving. There are several consequences to this view. Software engineering is seen as a fixed, standardized discipline that evolves slowly, a view reflected in the often repetitious or redundant character of recent software engineering methods. One could argue that software engineering should provide a TO-BE approach rather than an AS-IS approach to problem solving. One way to improve the effectiveness of software engineering would be to ensure that it dynamically adapts to change. Tracking and monitoring change would then become essential components of software engineering. An adaptive response to dynamic requirements that adjusts according to changing environments can lead to a better solution.

The theory of software engineering adjudicates the reliability of software processes and products; however, software engineering is rarely evaluated, as demonstrated by the general lack of empirical studies of software development. Because software engineering provides standards, descriptions, and characterizations of what and how software solutions should be carried out, it is viewed as an AS-IS discipline. However, the processes that it proposes rely on many hidden assumptions and uncertain evidence. Software engineering theories are often not supported by scientific proof that justifies them or the extent to which they should be used. Such a justification must go beyond feasibility studies to include empirical evidence gathered from experimental investigations.

The assumption that the field of software engineering is largely the outcome of the application of limited, disciplinary sources—an assumption reflected in the separation in software engineering of the systems analysis and design domains—is flawed and inaccurate. To the contrary, the literature of software engineering strongly reflects the cumulative impact of challenges and changes in business requirements and technology. The interdisciplinary impact of these forces on software engineering is evident. Despite this, the recognition of the multidisciplinary character of software engineering, in a manner that would more effectively promote the inclusion of and interaction with other disciplines as part of a well-defined strategy, still remains problematic.

These issues reveal the difficulties associated with viewing software engineering from a purely input perspective. When viewed as input, software engineering cannot effectively solve problems using static structures, approaches, and strategies. It needs to expand continually to reflect developing needs and requirements, changes, challenges, and opportunities in the scientific and business worlds. Problem solving in the real world is too complex for a fixed theory tailored to specific situations and environments that arose at particular times. Software engineering must be viewed as more akin to a knowledge-base or inference engine that provides problem-solving support. The underlying objective is to maintain a result-driven structure—one that includes knowledge and tailorability, and alternates between input and output roles. In other words, software engineering should be a dynamic structure capable of adaptively solving business problems efficiently, accurately, and reliably. Such a result-driven model is illustrated in Figure 10.4.

Figure 10.4 shows how software engineering can be viewed as a TO-BE approach, as opposed to a traditional AS-IS approach. In the TO-BE approach, software engineering strategies develop iteratively, gathering

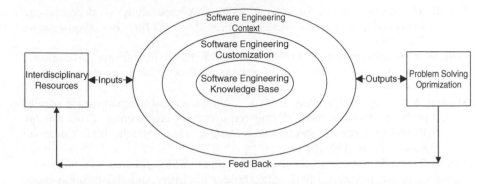

Figure 10.4   The dynamic structure of software engineering.

more knowledge of methods, techniques, and tools, in order to respond to changes, adapt to new situations, utilize interdisciplinary resources, and produce better problem-solving strategies.

References

Adrion W.V., Branstad, M.A., & Cherniavsky, J.C. (1982). Validation, verification, and testing of computer software. *ACM Computing Surv. (CSUR)*, 14(2), 159–192.

Applegate, L.M., McFarlan, F.W., & McKenney, J.L. (1999). *Corporate Information Systems Management.* (5th ed.). New York: McGraw–Hill.

Bruckhaus, T. (1992). Software engineering environment: towards a computer-aided process engineering environment. *Proc. 1992 Conf. Centre Adv. Stud. Collaborative Res.*, 1, 499–512.

Buss, E. & Henshaw, H. (1991). A software reverse engineering experience. Proc. 1991 Conf. Centre Adv. Stud. Collaborative Res., 55–73.

El-Ramly, M., Stroulia, E., & Sorenson P. (2002). Reverse engineering: recovering software requirements from system–user interaction traces. *Proc. 14th Int. Conf. Software Eng. Knowledge Eng.*, Ischia, Italy, 447–454.

Giesen, J. & Volker, A. (2002). Requirements interdependencies and stakeholders preferences. *Proc. IEEE Joint Int. Conf. Requirements Eng.*, 206–209.

Grasso, M.A & Nelson, M.R. (1997). Interdisciplinary computer science: introduction. Issue on interdisciplinary computer science, *Crossroads,* 4(1), 2, New York: ACM Press.

Hyde D., Gay, B., & Utter, D. (1979). The integration of a problem solving process in the first course. *Proc. 10th SIGCSE Tech. Symp. Computer Sci. Educ.* (table of contents), 54–59.

Jackson, D. & Jackson, M. (1996). Problem decomposition for reuse. *Software Eng. J.*, 11(1), 19–30.

Jones, C. (1995). Software benchmarking. *Computer* 28(10), 102–103.

Kaindl, H., Kramer, S., & Kacsich, R. (1998). A case study of decomposing functional requirements using scenarios. *Proc. 3rd Int. Conf. Requirements Eng.,* 156–163.

Lam, W. & Shankararaman, V. (1998). Managing change in software development using a process improvement approach. *Proc. 24th Euro Micro Conf.,* 2, 779–786.

Maiden, N.A.M. & Sutcliffe, A.G. (1996). A computational mechanism for parallel problem decomposition during requirements engineering. *Proc. 8th Int. Workshop Software Specification Design,* 22–23 March, IEEE Computer Society Press, 159–163.

Meyer, B. (1985). On formalism in specifications. *IEEE Software,* 2(1), 6–26.

Preiss, O. & Wegmann, A. (2001). Stakeholder discovery and classification based on systems science principles. *Proc. 2nd Asia–Pacific Conf. Qual. Software,* 194–198.

Robinson, W.N. & Volkov, S. (1997) A metamodel for restructuring stakeholder requirements. *Proceedings of the 19th International Conference on Software Engineering,* Boston, May, Washington, D.C.: IEEE Computer Society Press,140–149.

Sharp, H., Finkelstein, A., & Galal, G. (1999). Stakeholder identification in the requirements engineering process. *Proc. 10th Int. Workshop Database Expert Syst. Appl.,* 387–391.

Shneiderman, B. (1987). *Designing the User Interface: Strategies for Effective Human–Computer Interaction.* Reading, MA: Addison–Wesley.

Small, A.W. & Downey, E.A. (2001). Managing change: some important aspects. *IEMC '01 Proc. Change Manage. New Ind. Revolution,* 50–57.

Section III

Interdisciplinary Factors in Software Development

Chapter 11

People and Software Engineering

11.1 Introduction

Multidisciplinary thinking helps us understand problems better and therefore solve problems more effectively. Previous chapters have illustrated this at the *process* level and examined process structure, process models, process activities, and problem analysis as initial components of the problem-solving process. This chapter considers multidisciplinary thinking at the resource level, specifically in terms of its *people* dimension (see Figure 11.1).

Traditionally, software engineering has considered people as a resource only if they were explicitly involved in carrying out software development tasks—analysis to design to implementation. In interdisciplinary software engineering, the concept of people as a resource extends beyond those who are immediately involved to encompass all the individuals who play a significant role in the problem-solving process, regardless of whether they are officially affiliated with the development team. This more inclusive concept comprises those informal but nonetheless critical human resources without whose cooperation the problem cannot be adequately solved: informal resources engaged through a process of collaboration rather than formal affiliation. Examples of collaborative human resources include such stakeholders as customers, managers, and group clients.

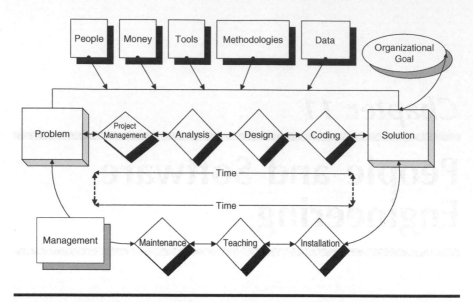

Figure 11.1 People in the software development process.

11.2 Interdisciplinary Background

Advantages of an interdisciplinary approach in helping to redefine the role of human resources in the problem-solving process include:

- *Representation and structure.* This refers to representing and restructuring the resources of software engineering to allow better use of human talents, techniques, and knowledge as explicit operational components of a unified problem-solving framework. The concept of *people* in conventional software engineering has generally been problematic because of its diffuseness, which makes it hard for beginners to appreciate, and illusive, which makes it hard for practitioners to apply effectively.
- *Relevance and knowledge.* Expanding understanding of the problem relevance of people allows one to apply a broader variety of techniques and knowledge to problem solving. Recognizing that people are a software development resource entails an understanding of project management. Recognizing that people are customers entails an understanding of marketing and consumer cognitive psychology. Recognizing that people are managers entails understanding the skills needed for managers to run a project successfully. Recognizing that people participate in interacting groups entails understanding group communication, social psychology, and even political science.

▪ *Extended knowledge.* This refers to applying an extended knowledge base to the entire problem-solving process, thus allowing the problem to be viewed from many alternative angles so that the solution receives a sufficiently broad analysis.

11.3 The Importance of People in the Problem-Solving Process

People are at the core of problem solving because business problems are solved by people for people. The problem solvers are not just the software developers; business problem solving is collaborative and requires ongoing management support, commitment, and understanding. It also requires significant cooperation from the relevant organizational units and employees of a business. In some cases, an organization may constitute a team to work formally with a development group. This is especially so for software solutions that must comply with organizational quality management rules and standards. The structure of the group and its efficiency of communications, style of management, and cohesiveness are critical factors in the effectiveness of the team.

11.3.1 The Roles of Users in Problem Definition

The term *user* is too narrow to reflect adequately the variety of stakeholders who can affect or be affected by the evolution of a problem's definition and its eventual solution. Figure 11.2 provides an overview of the kinds of people involved in this process.

At the staff level, for example, many kinds of direct and indirect users need to be considered. A system operator, responsible for inputting and updating data, monitoring progress, and generating reports, represents the simplest example of a direct staff user. Salesmen interoperate with systems at a mobile or remote level in order to access inventory, check prices, and close deals. Inventory personnel track data, input updates, and initiate new requests. The accounting department interacts with the system at the financial level. Marketing, legal, personnel, and other administrative departments also input relevant data, output reports, and monitor progress from their specialized perspectives. System engineers, database managers, and software or hardware specialists use the system and view its problem domain from very different viewpoints.

The current or potential customers of an enterprise are also key stakeholders and may be direct or indirect users of a system. A user receiving only outputs from a system, such as payroll reports or account

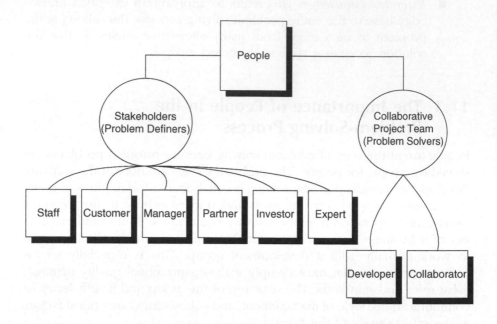

Figure 11.2   People involved in the problem definition and problem-solving processes.

statements, is indirectly using the system through other direct users (corporate employees). When customers interact directly with the system, their desired level of involvement in the problem definition becomes more critical. With the increasing availability of competitive, Web-based support services, the growing number of computer- and Web-literate customers, and the low cost of using Web services, more customers are shifting from indirect patterns of usage to direct usage of computer systems.

In fact, in an effort to reduce operational costs, many businesses are substituting automatic, dynamic Web services for employees. This has significantly increased the direct customer use of software systems. The customers involved may be individuals, groups, or business customers; each type imposes its own kind of varying system requirements. For example, a software solution that accommodates the functionality of a university registrar system imposes quite different requirements than would a business-to-business relationship between a pair of organizations.

Management is another major category of stakeholder. As used here, the term ranges from operational supervisors, to middle managers, to strategic decision makers. Each level of management deals with a different kind or degree of problem definition and complexity, which in turn strongly affects the nature of their expectations about solutions. As indicated previously, problem complexity is typically low at the operational level because operational problems are likely to be well structured; however, at the tactical and strategic management levels, problems tend to be semistructured or ill structured. Management requirements vary widely from department to department because their variation in needs and different contexts lead to diverse problem definition views.

Thus, financial managers want systems that help assess the financial performance of the organization. Research and development managers want the ability to examine the quality of products and services and track operational costs throughout an organization. Production managers want software solutions that support resource planning in terms of required labor and materials and that assist them in reducing errors and maximizing productivity. Marketing managers look forward to software solutions that provide descriptive and inferential statistics across geographic locations, and among various salesmen and different products and brands.

The business partners or collaborators in the supply chain are other essential stakeholders. Many organizations currently link their corporate intranets to extranet systems accessible to their business partners. Although security and privacy considerations apply, these extranets can be extended to larger geographic or metropolitan areas through metronets. Defining a problem at an intranet level is obviously less complex than defining a problem at a metronet or global level, and the risks involved may have a very different character.

Investors and owners are also significant stakeholders who make demands on a system in terms of financial goals, net present values, break-even points, and return on investment. Experts and consultants are another stakeholder class who can strongly affect problem definition. Whether experts are sought from within an organization or from outside, their experiences make their viewpoints of key value to the entire process, possibly representing the difference between project success or failure and minimally offering insights that can save time and money.

11.4 Human-Driven Software Engineering

The most critical resource in the problem-solving process is *people*. Whether they are staff members, customers, managers, partners, investors, or experts and whether their involvement is direct or indirect, their role in functional and interface requirements at the problem definition and solution construction levels is essential. Thus, if one is to achieve success across the software development process, the following people-driven issues must be addressed effectively:

- *Stakeholders.* The various requirements of all the stakeholders must be satisfied.
- *Customers.* To attract customers away from alternatives, the product must not just be competitive and of high quality, it must also be in time to market, have appropriately attractive features, and be priced well.
- *Development team.* It is a given that the development team must be qualified and skilled, but the team must also have sufficient multidisciplinary skills to truly meet the underlying project requirements.
- *Project manager.* The project manager must have interdisciplinary skills beyond the customary prerequisite ability to manage, coordinate, control, plan, and communicate effectively.
- *Partners.* Partners are an essential part of supply chain management. The partners may be identified as stakeholders or as a component of supply chain management.
- *Groups.* There are groups of developers, groups of customers, groups of managers, and so on. These groups must all exhibit successful communication, collaboration, and management mechanisms.

To utilize human resources efficiently, one must identify and locate the people who are important to truly understanding a problem and assisting in its solution; who are able to document the information needed in order to build a knowledge inventory for the entire problem-solving process; and who can bring this information to bear to guide the proposed solution of the problem. One must also obtain feedback in order to validate and verify that needs and expectations are reflected in the proposed solution. In addition, it is necessary to train those who will work on the development team or collaborate at the organizational level to accomplish the system goals and deliver the expected business value. Figure 11.3 illustrates the role of the people factor in the problem-solving process.

11.5 The People Factor—Multidisciplinary Aspects

The multidisciplinary aspects of the people factor manifest themselves at the problem and the solution level. At the problem level, the issue is which people-related disciplines can help one better understand the underlying problem. At the solution level, the main concerns are the people-related disciplines that enable one to address problem solving better. Table 11.1 offers an overview of these issues.

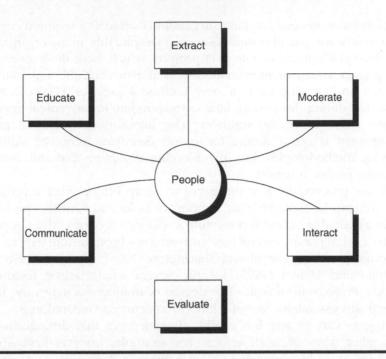

Figure 11.3 The people factor in the problem-solving process.

Table 11.1 Drivers and Disciplines

Interdisciplinary Driver	Relevant Discipline	Utilization
Customers	Marketing	Discover more subcategories of customers and other stakeholders Explore systems requirements from a marketing perspective
Development team	Project management	Structuring the development team
Users	Cognitive psychology	User interface design

11.5.1 *People as Project Managers*

Project management is increasingly important in enterprises because enterprises are more than ever affected by IT issues and capabilities. During the decade of the 1990s, organizational success became decisively dependent on information systems, making successful IT projects a required common denominator for overall business success. Despite this, many organizations experienced a high failure rate in IT projects, which made the improvement of IT project management even more critical. However, although extensive research and development of new methodologies for IT projects was conducted during this period, little corresponding improvement appeared to take place in IT development. The implication is that IT project management is not a simple matter of identifying requisite skills and applying methodologies, but an emerging discipline that still demands extensive further research.

Before proceeding, it is necessary to recap briefly what a project is. A *project* can be thought of as a group of tasks and activities performed within a definable period and meeting a specific set of objectives. A project involves a temporary assemblage of resources brought together to solve a specific problem. Tatnall and Shackleton (1995), Rosenau (1998), and Meredith and Mantel (1995) identify several characteristic features of projects. Projects are unique. The degree of uniqueness may vary, but all projects are essentially one-of-a-kind, nonrecurring undertakings.

Projects vary in size but exhibit characteristics that distinguish them from other types of work efforts. For example, projects have specific objectives, must be completed within a given budget, and are carried out by teams. The assignment of people to a project team may be on a full-time or part-time basis, depending on the specific needs of the project. Projects must be completed within a specific time period and have well-defined beginnings and ends. Correct project definition is critical to project management. The project definition helps establish a clear scope for the project and serves as a basis for project planning.

The steps needed to define a project begin with describing the opportunities that brought about the project in the first place; supplying a description of the background that established the need for the project; and then defining the goals for the project. After identifying the stakeholders and available resources, one must also identify any related projects that will affect or be affected by the project under consideration. One then identifies the criteria for deciding whether a project is viable, including understanding project constraints, assumptions, and risks, as well as the implication of such constraints and assumptions for the project risks.

Project management can be defined as a set of principles, methods, tools, and techniques for planning, organizing, staffing, directing, and controlling project-related activities in order to achieve project objectives within time and under cost and performance constraints. The project management process faces the often daunting task of assembling a project team that has the expertise needed to implement a project; establishing the technical objectives of the project; dynamically managing changes in order to meet requirements; and planning and controlling the project so that it completes on schedule and within budget. Project management is applicable in any situation in which resources must be efficiently applied to achieve demanding goals under significant time and cost constraints, and serious ramifications will occur if the expected results are not met on time, on budget, at required standards, and to stakeholder satisfaction. One can classify project management activities according to the phase of the project:

- *Project conception.* The purpose of the conceptual phase is to determine the feasibility of the project. Objectives are examined in the context of the business environment, alternatives are defined and evaluated, and preliminary estimates of cost, schedule, and risk are done. This phase culminates in a decision as to whether to proceed with the project.
- *Planning.* The performance, cost, and schedule estimates are refined to a point at which detailed plans for project execution can be made. Budgets and schedules are developed, the project team is formed, and a project management system is established to guide the management of the project.
- *Execution.* The program manager's responsibility is to manage the resources necessary to accomplish the objectives. The emphasis of responsibilities shifts from planning to control.
- *Termination.* The project activities are phased out. This can be triggered by premature termination or by successful achievement of the goals. In either case, certain activities are necessary to wrap up the project.

The success of project management depends on factors ranging from managerial leadership and the availability of business and technical documents that properly establish and communicate plans, to organizational or institutional support for developing the managerial skills that enhance people and project management. The most frequently cited management-related difficulties in project management include poorly defined goals and specifications; lack of an adequate project plan; and unrealistic deadlines and budgets.

The effectiveness of the project manager is critical to project success. The qualities that a project manager must possess include an understanding of negotiation techniques, communication and analytical skills, and requisite project knowledge. Control variables that are decisive in predicting the effectiveness of a project manager include the manager's competence as a communicator, skill as a negotiator, and leadership excellence, and whether he or she is a good team worker and has interdisciplinary skills. Project mangers are responsible for directing project resources and developing plans, and must be able to ensure that a project will be completed in a given period of time. They play the essential role of coordinating between and interfacing with customers and management. Project mangers must be able to

- Optimize the likelihood of overall project success
- Apply the experiences and concepts learned from recent projects to new projects
- Manage the project's priorities
- Resolve conflicts
- Identify weaknesses in the development process and in the solution
- Identify process strengths upon completion of the project
- Expeditiously engage team members to become informed about and involved in the project

Studies of project management in Mateyaschuk (1998), Sauer, Johnston, and Liu (1998), and Posner (1987) identify common skills and traits deemed essential for effective project managers, including:

- Leadership
- Strong planning and organizational skills
- Team-building ability
- Coping skills
- The ability to identify risks and create contingency plans
- The ability to produce reports that can be understood by business managers
- The ability to evaluate information from specialists
- Flexibility and willingness to try new approaches

Feeny and Willcocks (1998) claim that the two main indicators of a project manager's likely effectiveness are prior successful project experience and the manager's credibility with stakeholders. The underlying rationale for this is that such conditions, taken together, help ensure that the project manager has the necessary skills to execute a project and see it through to completion and that the business stakeholders will continue to support the project; see also Mateyaschuk (1998) and Weston & Stedman (1998a,b). Research also suggests that the intangibility, complexity, and volatility of project requirements have a critical impact on the success of software project managers.

11.6 The Team Factor

A *team* can be defined as a group of individuals who have been organized for the purpose of working together to achieve a set of objectives that cannot be effectively achieved by the individuals working alone. The effectiveness of a team may be measured in terms ranging from its outcomes to customer acceptance, team capability, and individual satisfaction. Organizational and individual inputs significantly affect the team's inputs. The team work process is characterized by the efforts exerted towards the goal; the knowledge and skills utilized; the strategy adopted; and the dynamics of the group. Team construction and management are a critical challenge in software-driven problem solving. They require:

- Goal identification
- Strategy definition
- Task management
- Time management
- Allocation of resources
- Interdisciplinary team composition
- Span of control
- Training
- Team communication
- Team cohesiveness
- Quality assurance and evaluation

The main characteristics of successful teams include:

- *Shared goal.* There must be a shared awareness of the common team goal among all the team members. This shared goal is the objective that directs, guides, and integrates the individual efforts to achieve the intended results.
- *Effective collaboration.* A team must work as a team. This entails collaborating, individuals making contributions, exchanging their ideas and knowledge, and building interpersonal relationships and trust. The project environment should facilitate and encourage effective collaboration and interoperation.
- *Individual capabilities.* Each team member must be trained and guided so as to be able to cooperate with the other team members towards the common goal.

Some other characteristics of well-functioning teams include:

- Sharing the mission and goal
- Disseminating complete information about schedules, activities and priorities

- Developing an understanding of the roles of each team member
- Communicating clear definitions of authority and decision-making lines
- Understanding the inevitability of conflicts and the need to resolve them
- Efficiently utilizing individual capabilities
- Effectively deploying meetings
- Accurately evaluating the performance of each team member
- Continually updating individual skills to meet evolving needs

Additional indicators of effective operation include a high level of project management involvement and participation; a focus on purpose; shared responsibilities; a high degree of communication; strategically oriented thinking; and rapid response to challenges and opportunities. These team performance characteristics require every team member to contribute ideas; operate in an environment that contains a diversity of skills; appreciate the contributions of others; share knowledge; actively inquire to enhance understanding; participate energetically; and exercise flexibility.

11.7 The Customer Factor

It is a truism that, in a customer-focused economy, software engineering must also be customer driven. This section considers some characteristics and techniques typical of a customer-driven software development environment. These include:

- *Customer-driven development is requirements intensive and features driven.* Because customer needs are the highest priority, they must be carefully gathered, identified, specified, visualized, and internally prioritized among themselves. As a consequence, requirements engineering becomes the key strategic phase across the software engineering process.
- *Customer-driven development is iterative in nature.* Iterative development is essential because it allows extensive feedback and development response to the feedback.
- *Customer-driven development aims to develop killer applications.* The only way to survive in a highly competitive market is to develop winning applications—not ordinary applications that merely pass the test of basic viability.
- *Customer-driven development strongly values time to market.* Time means opportunity, so applications must be engineered expeditiously enough to capture time-dependent marketing opportunities.

- *Customer-driven development attempts to achieve multistakeholder satisfaction via win–win situations.* Every software development activity involves many participants, each of whom has his or her goals and views of what constitutes value; therefore, the effective reconciliation of conflicts over system requirements becomes a key factor in assuring customer satisfaction.
- *Customer-driven development focuses on quality in products and services.* Quality assurance implies managing software processes in such a way that the developer and the customer are satisfied with the quality and consistency of the goods or services produced or provided.
- *Customer-driven development views customers as partners—not merely as buyers.* In order to assure that customer expectations are met, customers should team up with developers at each phase of the software development process. This can significantly minimize risk and reduce cycle time throughout the development process.
- *Customer-driven development is customizable, personalized, and adaptable to individual needs and changes in needs.* No two businesses or individuals are identical (demands and needs vary and evolve even across a single organization), so recognizing individual differences and organizational diversity is crucial to providing effective solutions.
- *Customer-driven development is driven by cognitive psychology.* Cognitive psychology can be thought of as the language for the source code of the software customer's mind. Therefore, a customer-driven software development approach should examine the extent to which software design accurately reflects the needs of customers as perceived by the customers.
- *Customer-driven development is informative and accessible.* Designing a software solution in the "customer age" requires full customer service and support in terms of well-documented help, interactive Web assistance, and state-of-the-art means of communication. Applications that do not provide support information are subject to customer complaints, dissatisfaction, and rejection.
- *Security and privacy are concerns in any customer-driven solution.* To earn customer trust, software engineers must design reliable systems that are less likely to be vulnerable to privacy invasions or security hackers. Security and privacy are key concerns of software customers.

References

Feeny, D. & Willcocks, L. (1998). Core IS capabilities for exploiting information technology. *Sloan Manage. Rev.*, 39(3), 9–21.

Mateyaschuk, J. (1998). Project managers learn the value of business skills. *Inf. Week*, 712, 166–167.

Meredith J.R. & Mantel, S.J. (1995). *Project Management*. New York: John Wiley & Sons.

Posner, B.Z. (1987). What it takes to be a good project manager. *Proj. Manage. J.*, 18(1), 51–55.

Rosenau, M.D. (1998). *Successful Project Management: A Step-by-Step Approach with Practical Examples*, 3rd ed. New York: John Wiley & Sons.

Sauer, C., Johnston, K., & Liu, L. (1998). Where project managers are kings: lessons for IT from construction industry. *Proj. Manage. J.*, 32(4), 39–49.

Tatnall, A. & Shackleton, P. (1995). Project management software—the fourth tool? In *Software Education Conference*, Los Alamitos: IEEE Computer Society Press.

Weston, S. & Stedman, C. (1998a). Forget ROI—just install it. *Computerworld* 32(15), 1–14.

Weston, S. & Stedman, C. (1998b). It's a brand new ball game as business workers fill IS jobs. *Computerworld*, 32(14), 8–9.

Chapter 12

Economics and Software Engineering

12.1 Introduction

The software business is no different from any traditional business: one must invest money and assets in order to generate returns. Software development represents a strategic investment whose purpose is to create a marketable generic software solution or to solve an in-house business problem. Morrissey and Wu (1979) observed that the production of software can be viewed as an economic as well as an engineering process. To begin with, software-driven problem solving uses money as an input resource in order to produce a solution. Money subsequently serves as a key performance indicator calibrating the success of the solution or product. However, money does not adequately represent what is invested or what is expected in return. Software investments entail capital costs, time, a variety of developer and managerial talents, development effort, and so forth. The returns expected can be expressed in terms of attaining the maximum possible value-creation objectives, including market share, company and product image, technological leadership, etc.

This chapter discusses the economic aspects of software engineering and the fundamental role that financial resources play in the software problem-solving process. It also presents a fairly detailed review of software cost development techniques such as the Constructive Cost Model (COCOMO) and the use of function point analysis.

Erdogmus et al. (2002) described software development as an ongoing investment activity in which developers and managers continually make investment decisions requiring the expenditure of resources such as time, talent, and money. They viewed the overriding purpose of this activity as geared towards maximizing business added value, subject to its equitable dispersement among the participating stakeholders. Money plays a role in every aspect of the problem-solving process. Business problems often originate from money-related causes and may be resolved or ameliorated by efficient management of financial resources such as cost-cutting or increasing productivity. Because money is affected by time and delays, secondary effects are related to the time value of money (TVM). Money is needed to manage, hire, and train the human resources needed to do development and is used to purchase systems, software, equipment, and supplies. It is the basic reference metric used to evaluate whether a solution accomplishes the intended organizational goals.

12.2 Economics and the Development of Software

Although most definitions of software engineering describe the discipline in terms of cost effectiveness, budget considerations, and customer orientation, the software engineering literature generally does not adequately address these concepts or the magnitude of their impact. For example, a review of 16 texts on software architecture and object-oriented design turned up only two books that even included the word *cost* in the index (Boehm & Sullivan 1999). Major economic concepts, such as production points, economies of scale, net present value, marginal analysis, or statistical decision theory, were not mentioned in the software engineering literature for decades after the emergence of the discipline. Cost estimation approaches took a long time to appear; benefit estimation approaches are only now beginning to be considered.

The area of economics called *information economics*, which first received serious attention in the 1960s, played a major role in the development of software economics. Software economics goes back to the early 1970s with Sharpe's (1972) publication of *The Economics of Computers*, which briefly addressed cost estimation and referred to the seminal study in this regard done by the System Development Corporation (SDC) of the U.S. Air Force. The SDC study formulated a linear regression model for cost estimation based on an extensive empirical analysis of software development projects. Although the model was not especially accurate, it nonetheless did serve as a foundation for subsequent cost estimation models (Boehm & Sullivan 1999).

One barrier to applying software economics more widely has been the fact that software engineers may be unlikely to understand enterprise-level value-creation objectives and may lack formal business training. On the other hand, top and middle management may not understand the criteria for the success of a software development project or the relation between business value creation and investments made at the technical development level. Indeed, the lack of financial education among software developers was arguably a significant contributing factor to the software crisis phenomenon of the 1960s through the early 1980s. The major challenge facing software developers during that period was to deliver a working system with appropriate functionality, so often little attention was given to measuring the business performance of such systems. Instead, the strong (even prevalent) propensity was to test and evaluate (for example) information systems from a solely technical perspective regardless of their business value. Even when management wanted to investigate the financial performance or impact of an information system, it often lacked sufficient software-related background to carry out that task effectively.

This missing link between finance awareness and software development has had unfortunate consequences for a variety of reasons. For example, actual financial planning or assessment often does not occur *prior to* starting software development because a detailed feasibility study may not be carried out. This situation can lead to extremely poor project management caused by the resulting high levels of uncertainty and equivocality. Furthermore, business evaluation for an information system may not be conducted *even after* the software system is developed except for its evaluation via traditional technical metrics. This has the paradoxical result that the software product may be successfully verified, validated, and deployed even though it actually adds no significant value to an organization.

Additionally, when decisions are made during the design stage, alternative options or sufficient flexibility may not be provided to meet potential challenges resulting from ongoing market dynamics. Because business metrics may not even be considered in guiding modular designs and phased project structures, management may fail to stop or terminate projects even when new information would indicate the projects have manifested a low probability of achieving success in a timely fashion. Another point is that conflicts among the decision-makers are more likely to occur because of the lack of adequate, value-driven guidance for resolving arguments—for example, which technical conditions are more appropriate or which decision best creates the desired value for an organization.

Furthermore, the use of technical measurements to define the criteria for the success of software development and production is neither sufficient nor effective. Although metrics and measurements must provide criteria relevant to building and evaluating software systems, such criteria make no sense if they merely lead to the delivery of bug-free systems that add little or no business value. Finally, there has been a recurrent failure to utilize not only powerful new technologies, but also organizational tools, regulations, tax, market, and other mechanisms and structures within the context of which the software is developed and used (Boehm & Sullivan 1999). This failure extends to the ineffective use of important capabilities provided by the wider economic environment, such as the ability to exploit third-party components or buying and selling software risk through marketplace instruments.

12.3 The Rationale for Software Economics

Software cannot be engineered without using business metrics to guide its technical requirements and measure its success. Indeed, the originating idea behind software engineering was to bridge the gap between software technology and business in terms of cost effectiveness and return on investment. Therefore, any discussion of traditional software engineering concepts such as scheduling, planning, quality assurance, validation, verification, testing, or development strategies is meaningless without linking it to relevant business values. In order to establish such linkages, one must systematically incorporate software economics throughout the entire software development process, although the work done so far to realize this goal has been limited.

The reasons for demanding a significant focus on software economics are clear. These include the fact that the dynamics of technology innovation have become focused on highly competitive commercial markets. Value measurement and value creation have also become more complex because of the increasing importance of time to market and other market-related factors. Business firms are also more critically dependent on software-enabled change than ever before. Not only does software development need to satisfy business metrics to deliver value, but business processes must also be software-enabled to create value. There is an increasing need to establish a comprehensive approach that articulates the impact of software-driven investments across an organization into a single framework—as opposed to approaches that only address partial software expenses that lead to ineffective global investment patterns (Boehm & Sullivan 1999).

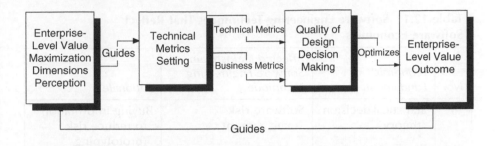

Figure 12.1 Framework for relation among technical criteria, design decision-making, and enterprise-level value maximization in software development.

Another factor is the state of permanent or continual change in the business world and technology that leads to unpredictable risks during software development and the software product life cycle. Thus, demand for reliable strategies able to deal with uncertainty, lack of knowledge, and competition are in demand. Such strategies are important to creating and maximizing value. The complexity of value is another reason for developing dynamic strategies. Change is the driving factor behind many risks and has also made the measurement of value more complex than ever.

Figure 12.1 depicts a framework for the relationship among three major variables in software economics: technical criteria; quality of design decision-making; and enterprise-level value maximization. The framework is based on the idea that guidance on enterprise-level value maximization can enhance technical metrics and criteria as well as help establish improved business metrics. This integrated approach criteria can improve the quality of design decision-making in software development. This in turn can enable management to act and react in a dynamic and flexible manner and respond more effectively to changes in the market. Value creation can be seen, for example, in canceling a failure option before it is released; searching for a real opportunity option; or creating a new prospective opportunity option.

12.4 The Influence of Software Economics on Software Engineering

A serious need exists to develop additional business metrics that can measure, guide, structure, and evaluate software development; however, conventional software economics has already left its imprint on software engineering. Table 12.1 illustrates a number of widely used software

Table 12.1 Software Engineering Techniques That Reflect Software Economics

No.	Economic Fundamental	Affected Mainstream Software Engineering Technique	Rationale
1	Statistical decision theory	Software risk management	Buying information to reduce risk (prototyping, testing, formal verification) (Boehm & Sullivan, 1999)
2	Risk and product value considerations	Spiral, iterative and evolutionary development models	Sequence increments of capability
3	Basic economics	Software reuse	Productivity and cost reduction
4	Net present value, return on investment, and break-even point analysis	Economic feasibility study in project management	Evaluating software investment in advance in terms of cost-benefit analysis
5	Satisfying multistakeholders criteria	Participatory design Join application design Stakeholder win–win requirements engineering	Shared-based value as opposed to win–lose and lose–lose situations
6	Dramatic reduction in cycle time	Extreme programming	Adopting cost minimization strategies
7	Opportunity cost	Rapid application development (RAD)	Rapidly bringing product to market considering the opportunity cost of delay in shipping a product in a competitive market place
8	Minimal cost strategy	COCOMO and most other cost and schedule estimation models	Capturing direct resources required to develop a project

Table 12.1 Software Engineering Techniques That Reflect Software Economics (continued)

No.	Economic Fundamental	Affected Mainstream Software Engineering Technique	Rationale
9	Time-to-market factor	COCOMO II extension (CORADMO)	Support reasoning in regard to rapid schedules for smaller projects
10	Productivity	Component-based development Commercial off the shelf (COTS) Very high-level languages (VHLL) Systems of systems CASE tools-supported development	Boosting software productivity to reduce cost, time, and human resources

engineering techniques that implicitly reflect the influence of fundamental concepts from software economics.

12.5 Software Economics

Maximization of value at the enterprise level is ultimately the decisive criterion for determining how scarce resources are to be invested because, at the end of the day, creating value is the only justification for incurring expenses. Although a reduction in cost or an increase in benefits may enhance the value of an organization, the mere implementation of a cost reduction does not automatically lead to value creation. Furthermore, value transcends direct financial effects and includes nonmonetary benefits such as organizational prestige, workforce morale, or even amelioration of societal problems. Such indirect benefits are usually called *intangibles* and may ultimately lead to an indirect financial return on the original investment. This section provides a brief overview of some of the fundamentals of software economics as a guide to its application in software development.

12.5.1 Value Maximization

Value maximization is traditionally related to profit maximization. In microeconomics, profit maximization is typically used as the target metric for a business; value maximization emphasizes the effective utilization of capital resources with minimum regard for time-related considerations. For example, a project manager could easily increase profits in a local time frame by eliminating activities in research and development that might be considered of lower priority. Of course, this may work in the short run, but it is not likely to be in the best long-term interests of the organization. This is especially the case in a software development context, so it is important to account for such effects in any realistic measure of value maximization. In particular, two major effects that should be addressed are *uncertainty* and *timing*. Profit maximization is also incompletely addressed unless consideration is given to shareholder wealth maximization as a key factor in measuring maximization of value for a firm, project, or investment.

The concept of value in the business or organizational sense has become increasingly complex because of the impact of highly competitive business markets. The sources of value include:

■ *Conventional value creation via current configurations.* This refers to the present value of uncertain future gains through cash flow streams from consistent traditional sales. Value at this level is created by producing profit based on current configurations.

■ *Realistic options value creation via new configurations.* This refers to potential gains from the exercise of realistic options. Real options are not limited to current configurations; potential opportunities are more significant. However, such opportunities require new configurations to take advantage of them. In software development, this implies the ability to change software, architecture, and technical properties in order to be able to enter new markets.

■ *Value creation via process reengineering.* This refers to reengineering design processes to enable effective competition. This can significantly accelerate the speed of product innovation and even have a significant impact on the economy and technology.

■ *Value creation via enhancing decision flexibility.* This refers to selecting and integrating process models to create value in the form of decision flexibility. This allows restructuring, redirecting, canceling, or modifying phased project structures or modular designs in order to meet time-to-market requirements. Decision flexibility can be achieved through mechanisms such as options pricing, by applying utility theory, and by using dynamic discounted cash flow.

■ *Value creation via portfolio management.* This refers to creating a portfolio of realistic options through a specific modular design. To create value from such an approach, its benefits must be greater than the investment in the architecture or process used to produce it. An alternative is to evaluate possible portfolios corresponding to different modularizations.

■ *Value creation via nonmonetary results.* In modern economics, value is not measured purely in terms of money. Money is used in many cases as a critical enabler to create value in other domains such as safety, employee morale, or in situations that can have a positive impact on society. Some of the highest ranked profit-making companies do not value money as their highest goal.

12.5.2 Evaluating Investment Options

Every software project can be considered as representing an option that can be initiated, cancelled, modified, or adopted. In deciding whether to undertake a project, it is critical to evaluate its prospective financial performance. Projects are evaluated as investments because they involve costs and benefits; thus, the objective is to analyze the ability of the project to maximize value for the business firm. A criterion used to evaluate project or investment alternatives or options should include a method to: distinguish between what is accepted and what is rejected; be able to resolve choices among alternatives; be applicable in all cases; assign a higher value for options that generate better, quicker profits; and be able to rank options based on their potential performance.

Because the evaluation of investment alternatives is considered a decision support issue applied prior to project initiation, one is most likely to find this topic under the *capital budgeting* area in finance literature. The methods used to evaluate and compare projects and investment options can be classified into two categories: projects that have equal risks and projects that have different risks.

12.5.2.1 Projects with Equal Risks

This category can be further subdivided into two classes. The first concerns the evaluation of projects with a high degree of certainty and no consideration given to the time value of money. The two basic evaluation criteria for this category are the pay-back period and the accounting rate of return. The second class concerns the evaluation of projects with a low degree of certainty for which one does consider the time value of money. The two widely used methods for evaluating investment projects and options under this category are net present value (NPV) and return on investment (ROI).

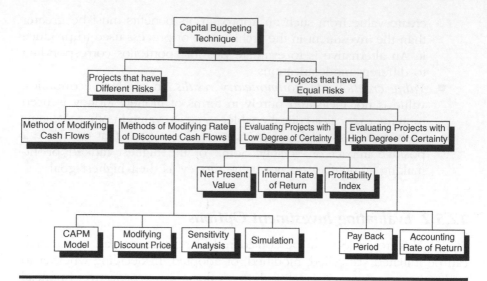

Figure 12.2 Taxonomy of capital budgeting techniques in finance.

12.5.2.2 Projects with Different Risks

This category can also be subdivided into two classes (see Figure 12.2). The first concerns methods for modifying the rate of discounted cash flow. This encompasses four methods for evaluating investment projects: Capital Asset Pricing Model (CAPM); modifying discount price; sensitivity analysis; and simulation. The second class concerns methods for modifying cash flows.

12.6 Risk and Return

Investment is made in order to obtain a return. Of course, there is no free lunch and thus return is always acquired at some risk and is threatened by the possibility that something may go wrong. Regardless of the nature or cause of the failure, the chance of failure is called *risk*. In financial terms, risk is defined as the probability that the actual return will be lower than the expected return. The greater the risk involved, the greater the return expected in the event that things go well.

Important relevant concepts are the *operating leverage* and the *financial leverage*. Operating leverage is fixed operating costs divided by total operating costs. The total operating cost includes fixed and variable costs. Financial leverage is the degree to which a business is exploiting its borrowed money. Companies with high leverage may incur higher risks; however, a higher degree of financial leverage is not always injurious because it can increase the stakeholder ROI. Risk is frequently coupled with other characteristics that qualify its meaning: expectation, deviation, probability, and uncertainty, which are defined as follows:

- *Expectations.* Risk concerns what might happen in the future. Even though risk is related to the future, its estimation or (risk) assessment is based entirely on past or current experiences. This assessment involves analysis, forecasting, and planning—none of which can succeed without appropriate data. Thus, data about prior or existing experience forms the basis for any risk assessment.
- *Deviation.* Because risk is focused on problem, error, or failure, it can only be examined when metrics and checkpoints are in place. Risk requires that an organization or business firm has already set its goals clearly and precisely. Such tactical or strategic goals are the basis for metrics and measurements. Risks are viewed in terms of the extent to which future results may *deviate* from the goals or metrics of an organization.
- *Probability.* Risk is about what events can possibly happen and what the probability of the occurrence of the events is. High risks are those that combine the most severe adverse consequences with the highest probability of occurrence. Probability expresses risk in a quantitative fashion, allowing statistics to be used intensively to weigh, prioritize, and manage risks.
- *Uncertainty.* As a rule of thumb, one cannot control things that one ignores. Lack of knowledge and conflicting or confusing information lead to uncertainty and enhance the expectation of risk. Uncertainty is usually defined as the expected fluctuation or volatility in the cash flow of an investment option according to some probability distribution. However, some financial resources differentiate between risk and uncertainty according to the extent to which each reflects realistic historical data or even personal speculation. In this sense, *risk* relies on historical data, as opposed to uncertainty, which is more tied to personal expectations.

For a practical or applicable understanding of the concept of risk, consider an informal definition of risk as the possibility of the occurrence of events that are hard to predict and can have adverse effects or consequences on business and software processes. *Actual return* refers to the return on the investment that actually takes place at the end of a period of time. *Expected return* refers to the return that an investor anticipates to occur at the end of a period of time viewed from the investor's perspective at day zero. Two factors make risk more significant: probability and magnitude. These relate to the following important questions:

- *How risky is a project?* This refers to the degree of volatility as measured statistically.
- *What is the magnitude of the adverse effects that result from risk?* This refers to the nature of the effects that may result from risks.

12.7 Traditional Software Economics

The traditional or conventional approach used in software economics has several characteristic features largely focused on cost-benefit analysis. Little consideration is given to risk identification or minimization and clearer emphasis is put on cost estimation than on benefits analysis and estimates. Generally, benefits are not well addressed in classical software economics literature and few connections are available between business and technical metrics in evaluating software systems. In fact, it is rare to find any focus on business metrics. Additionally, benefits are generally only measured at the financial or tangible level; competition is not viewed as a driving force in software design decisions, so time-to-market strategies are not incorporated; and the conventional approach offers no clear strategy for addressing the impact of changes in business and technology.

12.7.1 Problems with Conventional Software Economics

One of the most fundamental considerations in software economics concerns risk and return. A serious problem with traditional approaches is that they frequently assume equal risks between competing options or projects. Consequently, they rely on non-risk-sensitive measurements such as net present value (NPV). Another problem is that even the newer approaches that do include risk in their evaluations fail to distinguish between systematic and nonsystematic risks. *Systematic risks* cause volatility in the expected rate of return to all existing or suggested investment projects across an entire industry. Systematic risks are often called *undiversified risks* because they cannot be eliminated or reduced by diversification. On the other hand, nonsystematic risks cause volatility in the expected rate of return to all existing or suggested investment projects only in a specific firm or across a particular business domain. Such nonsystematic risks are often called diversified risks because the risk can be eliminated by diversification.

12.8 Software Cost

Cost may be defined as the total amount of money, time, and resources associated with an activity that, in the context of software engineering, encompasses problem solving and software development processes. Cost is a strategic concept in software development for the following reasons:

- *Project management.* Estimating cost is critical to correctly carrying out project management activities such as scheduling, planning, and control.
- *Feasibility study.* Making investment decisions about software projects requires a full cost breakdown and analysis. The identified recurring and one-time costs are included in a financial feasibility study in terms of a cost-benefit analysis.
- *Cost reduction.* Because software engineering proposes to provide cost-effective software solutions to business problems, many processes and project-related activities are designed or reengineered to achieve cost minimization.
- *Evaluating business performance.* Cost is an essential ingredient in calculating many of the financial ratios introduced earlier and is used to evaluate financial performance for a business firm.
- *Leverage.* Cost plays a significant role in operating as well as financial leverage with respect to risk and return. Relying on fixed costs as opposed to variable costs can boost operating leverage, and financing with high-percentage, debt-based costs may boost financial leverage.

12.8.1 Cost Estimation

More projects are doomed to failure by poor cost and scheduling estimates than by technical, political, or organizational problems. It should therefore be no surprise that few companies appreciate that software cost estimating can be a science and not merely a rough art. In fact, it is known that software cost estimation is able to predict development life cycle costs and schedules accurately and consistently for a wide array of software projects. Estimating software costs typically involves trying to model the effect of the following factors: the complexity of the software project; the size of the project; the effort needed to complete the project; the time needed to complete it; and the risk of failure and uncertainties involved.

Of course, any predictive model that intends to project development costs and time must combine such putative driving factors into an algorithm. A relatively direct algorithm is one based on formulae with parameters that can be statistically estimated from previous project or organizational experience, or possibly from a functional decomposition analysis of the project to be done. However it is done, that parametric formula then defines the predictive model. The important factor of risk has still not been adequately incorporated in most cost estimation models for software systems.

Despite some differences, the cost estimation models tend to be more or less based on the following kinds of relationships:

- *Complexity determines size*: that is, the complexity of the project determines the software size in terms of kilolines of code (KLOC).
- *Size determines effort*: that is, the KLOC determines the effort required for the project in staff-months with a given level of productivity.
- *Effort determines time*: that is, the predicted effort determines the time required for a project for a given mode or model.
- *Effort determines the number of people required*: that is, the effort for a project determines the number of people required, assuming the prior existence of a trained, full-time, software development team.

The initial estimates of the software development cost of a project are sometimes called *investment appraisals* and act as key elements of a feasibility analysis. Although an extensive body of knowledge on cost estimation techniques exists, most of these techniques explicitly or implicitly view cost as a function of project complexity. In Boehm's (1981) early COCOMOs, complexity referred to the project size or program size, which was assumed to be estimated in KLOC. In later estimation models and COCOMO II, complexity was recognized as a combined function of the inputs, outputs, interfaces, files, and queries required by a software system. This complexity estimate was then adjusted based on a variety of added-complexity factors with the final estimate obtained using parameters from a standard table.

The calculations in a basic cost estimation model are straightforward. They estimate the required project effort in terms of the man-months required for the project. The term *man-months* (also referred to as *staff-months*) means the number of months required to complete the entire project, assuming that a single person were to carry out the mission. This variable is the reference variable for all the software cost estimating models, especially those that derive from Boehm's (1981) well-known Constructive Cost Model.

COCOMO estimates the total effort in staff-months using two variables: how many thousands of lines of source code (KSLOC) the programmers must develop and what effort is required per KSLOC (the linear productivity factor). Combining these variables gives the staff-months of effort required for the project. This is generally a reasonable estimate if the project is relatively small. For larger project sizes, a size penalty factor is incorporated, which may be quadratic in the team size.

The outputs from a COCOMO analysis give the estimated total effort (in staff-months); the project schedule (in months); and the staff requirements for the project (in terms of the number of personnel). In later COCOMO models, the effort, schedule, and staff estimates are broken out or distributed for each of the project phases. Hamlet and Maybee (2001) very simply and insightfully illustrate the handiness of such basic COCOMO guidelines. For example, they summarily observe that

> Projects in the range of 100,000 LOC take about two years to complete, and the required effort is about 20 percent for requirements/specification, 50 percent for design/coding, 30 percent for test. The staffing and distribution of schedule depend more on the type of project but is about 500 total man-months, but this is distributed 30:40:30 percent among the phases.

The total effort for a project depends significantly on the type or so-called *mode* of the project (semidetached, embedded, or organic, as described later). For example, the most complex type—an embedded project—may require three times as much effort as does the least complex type of project—the organic type. On the other hand, although the level of effort varies significantly with the project type or mode, the distribution of that effort over the various project phases is relatively invariant in the project type. However, this is not the case for the project schedule. For example, in an embedded project, the requirement or specification phase may take twice as much time (as the organic mode), but may spend only 70 percent as much time on the design or coding phase (Hamlet & Maybee 2001).

This kind of rationally based planning estimate is extremely useful for giving managers and engineers a persuasive grasp of the likely resource requirements of a project. Indeed, it provides a software engineer who is interfacing with management a singular opportunity to have a major impact on his work environment with very little effort—almost a pencil and paper calculation. The projections can also be used for understanding the implications of various scenarios. For example, Hamlet & Maybee (2001) mention the following instructive illustration.

Suppose management wants a project to be completed in nine months rather than the two years initially forecast by the COCOMO model. To accomplish that, the initial 20 percent of the effort required for requirements and specification, applied to the approximately 500 man-months originally estimated by the model, will imply that about 100 man-months will have to be accomplished for the project just in those first three months (20 percent of 500). Because this effort is indeed spread over three months, the staff requirement will be for 30 people. Even more people will be needed later during the even more effort-intensive design and code phase, for which similar calculations will indicate that a total of 80 staff will be required. As an additional complication, assuming a management-to-staff ratio of (say) eight to one, these 80 people will entail a further addition of ten new managerial resources to the project. Furthermore, even such an expedited model estimate is only a lower bound on the required resources because it completely ignores the unavoidable pitfalls that will be encountered in trying to parallelize activities that may not really lend themselves to parallelization.

The parameters used in the classic COCOMO model are, of course, not pulled out of thin air. Rather, they are based on a detailed statistical analysis that was originally developed by Boehm using extensive historical project data for 63 software development projects undertaken at TRW. *The value of this type of estimation model is clear. It uses simple, statistically validated correlations between project resources (such as time, effort, and people) and project type and size to project the key manpower, schedule, and total time requirements for a project in a relatively simple way that can be easily implemented by COCOMO estimation software.* The model has the advantage of being highly transparent and can help provide an intuitive understanding of the impact of different factors on the effort that will be needed to be expended.

COCOMO is the most widely used model to estimate the cost and schedule of a software development project. Its estimate is based on the size of the software to be developed. The COCOMO model is categorized into three levels: *basic; intermediate*; and *detailed*. These three categories have different degrees of precision (or at least of model specificity) and involve different levels of cost factors. The basic COCOMO model separates software development into three kinds or *modes* and provides different equations for each to estimate the project cost and schedule. The modes (as mentioned earlier) are organic, embedded, and semidetached.

- *Organic* projects are relatively simple software development projects that can be efficiently undertaken and developed by small project teams. This type of project is usually undertaken in house by a team that has a detailed knowledge of the working domain of the product to be developed and of the relation of the product to organizational goals. The requirements and other processes involved in this type of project are flexible and are usually negotiated and adjusted on a fairly regular basis during the product development cycle. The software size is typically at most 50,000 delivered source lines and the project application is typically not innovative.

- *Embedded* projects, on the other hand, are complex projects in which software development is done under a set of complex hardware, software, and functional constraints. The project team must adhere to rigid requirements and possibly stringent regulations, and may possibly face significant uncertainties in problem definition. Embedded projects are typically "embedded" in larger, preexisting systems or environments. A classic example is a military application for an embedded navigational system. A complex banking system is another example. If the product is new or original, then the development team involved in the project may not have extensive experience with the environment and thus the system may require intense design. The project may have considerable scope and require scientific innovation.
- *Semidetached* projects lie between organic and embedded projects in complexity and their size is usually no more than 300,000 delivered source lines. The software requirements are also a mixture, lying between the rigid requirements of an embedded project and the flexible requirements of an organic project. The development teams also have members with a mix of experience levels.

The *basic COCOMO* model required an estimate of effort for development that was measured in man-months (PM). It used the following empirically derived formula to estimate effort:

$$\text{Effort} = a \times (\text{KDSI})^b$$

where the term *KDSI* denotes thousands of delivered source instructions. Thus, only source lines that are delivered as a product are considered; other lines (e.g., test drivers, support software) are excluded from this scope. To estimate the software product development schedule in months, the basic COCOMO model uses the formula:

$$\text{Schedule} = c \times (\text{Effort})^d$$

Table 12.2 gives the equations for estimating development effort and developments schedule using values of a, b, c, and d corresponding to the types or modes of a project.

The *intermediate* COCOMO model is an extension of the basic COCOMO model. The basic COCOMO estimates are not as accurate because the basic model uses only two cost factors: the size of the project (in KDSI) and the level of project development (organic, embedded, or semidetached). In intermediate COCOMO, the same basic types of formulae for the model are used, but the coefficients for the effort equation

Table 12.2 Estimating Development Effort and Development Schedule

Project type	Effort (in person months)	Schedule (in months)
Organic	$2.4 \times (KDSI)^{1.05}$	$2.5 \times (effort)^{0.38}$
Semidetached	$3.0 \times (KDSI)^{1.12}$	$2.5 \times (effort)^{0.35}$
Embedded	$3.6 \times (KDSI)^{1.20}$	$2.5 \times (effort)^{0.32}$

change. An additional 15 cost factors or *cost drivers* are used as cost predictor variables. These new cost factors presumably increase the precision with which effort and cost can be estimated.

The factors involve the product characteristics, characteristics of the development personnel, nature of the computing environment, and project factors. The complete list of these factors is as follows. Under the product attributes, Boehm (1981) included the complexity of the product; the size of its data base; and its required software reliability. Run-time performance and memory or storage constraints; volatility of the virtual environment; and required turnaround time fall under hardware attributes. Personnel attributes include analyst and software engineer capabilities; application and language experience; and machine experience. Under project attributes, the factors are the use of software tools; engineering methods; and development schedule. These additional cost factors are quantified and then multiplied to give an effort adjustment factor (EAF) whose typical values are in the range from 0.9 to 1.4. The effort equation for the intermediate model becomes:

$$Effort = EAF \times a \times (KDSI)^b$$

The effort equations for the different modes of the intermediate COCOMO model are given in Table 12.3. Notice the difference in the linear constant multipliers between the EAF table and the basic COCOMO table. The coefficient changes (which appear to move in the opposite direction to what one might expect) are compensated for by the estimated EAF factor.

Under the intermediate COCOMO model, the estimator assigns a rating to each cost factor on the scale of "very low," "low," "nominal," "high," "very high," or "extra high." These ratings are given in a table provided by COCOMO, which is not discussed here in detail but correlates each rating with a numeric value. For example, under product attributes, the complexity scores range from 0.70 ("very low") to 1.65 ("extra high"). Under personnel attributes, the capability of the team analysts ranges from 1.46 to 0.71. Under programmer capability, the factors range from 1.42

Table 12.3   Intermediate COCOMO Model

Project type	Effort (in person months)
Organic	EAF × 3.2 × (KDSI)$^{1.05}$
Semidetached	EAF × 3.0 × (KDSI)$^{1.12}$
Embedded	EAF × 2.8 × (KDSI)$^{1.20}$

("low") to 0.70 ("high"). Incidentally, whether the factors increase or decrease in numerical value as one ranges from "very low" to "extra high" depends on the nature of the factor's effect. Thus, "low" complexity should obviously decrease the expected EAF, so the corresponding numerical value should be relatively low.

On the other hand, for programmer capability, a "low" skill rating for capability would imply a relative higher value for the expected EAF, at which the numerical values start off with higher numerical values (the "low" rating is 1.42) and end up with lower numerical values (the "high" rating is 0.70). This is as should be expected because the less capable a programmer team is, the longer the project will take. Normal or nominal values are all 1.0.

The overall adjustment factor is obtained by multiplying all the numerical values. If it is assumed that the additional cost factors were nominal, then all adjustment factors would become 1. This would mean that the EAF would be equal to 1 and the effort equation would become the same as in the basic COCOMO model. Obviously, the model provided by intermediate COCOMO is more complex than the basic model. Despite this greater modeling detail, some researchers, such as Kemerer (1987) and Fenton & Pfleeger (1997), argue that the increased model complexity does not necessarily lead to better estimates because many of the factors are interdependent and are difficult to estimate objectively.

The detailed COCOMO model represents a further enhancement and builds on the intermediate model by using different effort multipliers for each phase of the project. The life cycle is assumed to have six phases: requirement gathering and analysis; product design; detailed design; coding and unit testing; integration; and test and maintenance. Estimates for the requirements analysis phase and for the maintenance phase are carried out separately using a method different from those for the estimates for the first four phases—product design through integration and testing (which are collectively called the development phases). The detailed COCOMO model provides more accurate estimates because it takes into consideration the fact that cost factors vary from one phase of the product life cycle to another. Two elementary examples of COCOMO-style calculations follow.

Sample Problem

Suppose a project requires building a Web development system estimated at 25,000 lines of code. Using the Basic COCOMO model, calculate how many man-months of effort this would take under the following scenarios:

1. The project complexity is simple and its size is relatively small.
2. The project size is large and the project must be developed under a set of complex hardware, software, and functional constraints.

Solution

1. The estimate for the relatively small, simple project is:

$$\text{Effort} = 2.4 \times \text{KDSI}^{.05} = 2.4 \times (25)^{1.05} = 70.5 \text{ staff-months.}$$

Observe that the value 25 is used rather than 25,000 because the size metric is in thousands of lines of code.

2. The estimate for the large project is:

$$\text{Effort} = 3.6 \times \text{KDSI}^{.20} = 3.6 \times (25)^{1.20} = 171.3 \text{ staff-months}$$

Sample Problem

Suppose the project in the previous example (simple project) is rated as "extra high" for the cost factor of "complexity" (effort multiplier = 1.65), and "low" for the cost factor of "programmer capability" (effort multiplier = 1.17), and all the other cost factors are rated as nominal. Calculate the effort.

Solution

This uses the intermediate COCOMO model in which the effort multipliers are used to calculate the EAF, which is subsequently applied in the effort equation. Thus:

$$\text{EAF} = 1.65 \times 1.17 = 1.93$$

The effort equation for the intermediate model is given by:

$$\text{Effort} = \text{EAF} \times a \times (\text{KDSI})^b$$

Because the complexity factor is "high," the project is assumed to be of embedded mode. For embedded projects, effort equals:

$$\text{Effort} = \text{EAF} \times 3.2 \times (\text{KDSI})^{1.20}$$

$$\text{Effort} = 1.93 \times 3.2 \times (25)^{1.20}$$

$$= 288.5 \text{ staff-months}$$

In the last decade or so, software development techniques have changed significantly. These changes have made application of the original COCOMO model presented above more problematic and less suitable. In the 1990s, an expanded model, COCOMO II, was developed (Boehm et al. 1997). This model reflects process developments in software practice since the original 1981 model was presented and is based on the data from 83 projects. It reflects the new emphasis on software reuse, object-oriented development, and the use of off-the-shelf components. COCOMO II has three staged models for estimation:

- The application composition model (for example, at a prototyping stage) can be used to clarify risk, particularly as pertaining to performance, system interaction, and technology maturity. It is based on measures such as the number of screens and objects used and their complexity.
- The early design model (for use when architectural alternatives are considered) can be used to clarify the choice of system and software architecture and the overall operational concept of the system.
- The postarchitecture model (when the project is to be developed) is used during the development and subsequent maintenance phases of the project.

The COCOMO model is critically dependent on the estimated size of the project in terms of the number of lines of code. This arguably just exchanges one problem (effort estimation) for another (size estimation). An approach called *function point analysis* can be used to estimate size on the basis of the number and type of functions that the system implements (Bell 2000). Function points can be identified as follows. For example, in a system with a graphical interface, a particular screen may display information about an inventory part: its price, functionality, manufacturer, the number in stock, etc. Such a screen represents what might be thought of as a unit of functionality provided by the system. This function point is an example of what is called a user-provided *output unit of functionality*. Other output functional units could be system reports, error messages, etc.

In function point analysis, each element contributes a count of one to the functional complexity of the system. The user outputs are triggered by user queries. Each different type of *user query* also contributes to the function count. Similarly, the back-end *files* that the system accesses contribute one count per file. Each distinct type of *user input* that provides application data to the system also adds to the function count. Finally, each *system interface* with an external system is counted. In COCOMO II, each separate type of function count is weighted depending on its complexity, which is evaluated as simple, average, or complex, with a numerical score assigned to each.

For example, user inputs are rated as simple (weight 3), average (weight 4), or complex (weight 6) and then their counts are scaled accordingly. There are similar weights for each of the other types of function counts. An overall weighted function count, *FP*, is then calculated using the formula:

$$FP = \text{(weighted total count)}* 0.01 \; C + 0.65)$$

where the variable C is an estimate of the overall technical complexity of the function points to be defined.

To calculate C, one sums the estimates of the technical complexity of each individual function, rating each function type on a scale from 0 to 5. The rating is guided or determined by factors such as the system's expected reliability and recovery requirements; performance criticality; complexity of the system inquiries; whether the software product is expected to be reusable; ease-of-use requirements; etc. Finally, to estimate the number of lines of code, one multiplies *FP* by a factor that depends on the programming language used. Conversion tables such as those in Jones (1996) can be used to map function points to the number of programming language lines, for example. Other software cost estimation techniques are available. These include:

- Making an estimate based on the judgment of an expert in the area of development
- Estimation on the basis of analogy with related applications that have been previously completed
- Bottom-up estimation based on estimates of the cost of components of the system
- Top-down estimation based on the overall logical functions provided by the system rather than by analyzing the components that implement those logical functions

Each of these approaches has certain advantages and disadvantages. See Boehm (1981) and Shaw (1995) for further discussion. Regardless of the method used, the cost estimation process is an ongoing one that must be continued and clarified as the project progresses to ensure that the project stays within budget, or to understand what factors may require the budget to be realigned.

References

Bell, D. (2000). Software Engineering—a Programming Approach. Reading, MA: Addison–Wesley.

Boehm, B. (1981). *Software Engineering Economics*. Englewood Cliffs, NJ: Prentice Hall.

Boehm, B., Abts, C., Clark, B., & Devnani–Chulani, S. (1997). COCOMO II *Model Definition Manual*. Los Angeles: University of Southern California.

Boehm, B. & Sullivan, K.J. (1999). Software economics: status and prospects. *Inf. Software Technol.* (special millennium issue), 41, 937–946.

Erdogmus, H., Boehm, B.W., Harrison, W., Reifer, D.J., & Sullivan, K.J. (2002). Software engineering economics: background, current practices, and future directions, In *Proceedings of the 24th International Conference on Software Engineering*, Orlando. International Conference on Software Engineering Archive, 683– 84.

Fenton, N.E. & Pfleeger, S.L. (1997). *Software Metrics: a Rigorous and Practical Approach*. London, U.K.: International Thomson Computer Press.

Hamlet, D. & Maybee, J. (2001). *The Engineering of Software*. Reading, MA: Addison–Wesley.

Jones, C. (1996). *Applied Software Measurement*. New York: McGraw–Hill.

Kemerer, C.F. (1987). An empirical evaluation of software cost estimation models. *Commun. ACM,* 30(5), 416–429.

Morrissey, J. & Wu, L.S. (1979). Software engineering...an economic perspective. In *Proceedings of the 4th International Conference on Software Engineering,* Munich, International Conference on Software Engineering Archive, 412–422.

Sharpe, W.F. (1972). *Economics of Computers*. New York: Columbia University Press.

Shaw, M. (1995). Cost and Effort Estimation. CPSC451 Lecture Notes. The University of Calgary.

Chapter 13

Specialized System Development

13.1 Introduction

Software development is a complex process driven by problem- and solution-related factors. The problem-related factors determine the criteria for the characteristics of the expected solution and help system designers tailor solutions to specific problems. The solution-related factors delineate possible options, assist in making projections, and facilitate scaling and mapping the solutions to problems. It remains an open issue as to whether the preferred software engineering approach should be to develop *generic prescriptions* for common problems (*generalization*) or derive *domain-dependent solutions* to specific problems (*specialization*). Generic approaches can be thought of as general-purpose strategies intended to give overall development guidance for an unrestricted range of applications. In contrast, specialized approaches are closely tailored or adapted to a specific type of application. They provide development guidance that is closely related to the kinds of problems that are prominent, essential, or difficult in that category of application.

According to one viewpoint, software engineering should be understood as a standardized response to software development based on the use of generic methodologies and strategies. It thus stands in contrast to the nonsystematic, informal approaches that characterized early software development. Standardization implies that one uses generic rules, procedures, theories, and notations. These are characteristics that mark milestones in the development of any scientific discipline.

267

With the advent of standardization, software development underwent a paradigm shift. It moved from trial-and-error experimentation to the beginnings of scientific maturity; from the nonstandardized representation and implementation of concepts to unified modeling and cross-platform independence; and from vaguely stated economic considerations to well-defined, software-driven business models. However, a one-size-fits-all viewpoint has not proved practical in real software development (Glass 2000). No single methodology is appropriate for every case. No strategy works perfectly for every problem. No off-the-shelf prescription is directly applicable without addressing scalability, tailorability, or customization. Approaches that fit specific situations do not necessarily fit them all the time because change is a constant and organizational and business needs evolve alongside innovation and emerging technologies. Thus, a balanced approach between generalization and specialization seems to be the best way to achieve effective software development.

This chapter examines specialized system development, an increasingly important approach that has been generally overlooked in the software engineering literature since the discipline's inception. Generic software development provides only an incomplete strategy (Vessey & Glass 1998) for solving problems because it only supplies guidance for solving problems but not actual solutions to problems at hand. Scalability, tailorability, and specialization have become key issues in the software industry and software engineering research. Furthermore, even general applications are not actually generic, with many current applications supporting customization features.

Additionally, these systems are released in different versions that range from the standard release to professional and enterprise editions suitable for a broad range of needs and problem complexity. Such applications also evolve over time to reflect changes in business requirements and technological capabilities. This chapter defines specialized system development, discusses its drivers, describes its advantages and disadvantages, and explores the different types of specialized system development. It also considers the need for specialized system development.

13.2 Principles of Specialized System Development

According to the Merriam–Webster dictionary, to *specialize* means to concentrate one's efforts on a special activity or field or to modify in an adaptive manner. Concentration provides greater attention to detail—in principle, allowing more efficient problem solving. Specialization links theory with practice, making the theory more meaningful. Specialized system development involves developing software systems within the context of a relatively narrow focus, although the focus can vary.

The focus can be an application domain, a phase of the development life cycle, or a specific software development methodology. An example of an application-domain focus is software development for pervasive computing applications, including wireless and portable systems. An example of a development phase focus is systems development with a special emphasis on project management, requirements analysis, or architectural design—as opposed to generic software engineering. An example of a methodology focus is systems development using structured or object-oriented strategies. This last specialization in methodology can span a wide range of approaches and tools, including software development process models (problem-solving strategies), CASE tools, and implementation techniques.

Application-focused software development is currently the most frequently used type of specialized system development in the software industry. It broadly falls under two categories: application-oriented development and infrastructure-oriented development, each of which may have a problem focus or a solution focus. The problem focus can be based on the industry involved or the application domain. The solution focus can be based on custom development, package development, or development aid (Glass & Vessey 1998).

13.2.1 The Roots of Specialized System Development

The history of specialized system development is closely coupled with the evolution of computer hardware and technological advancement. It spans four distinguishable eras:

- Domain dependent, which preceded the development of software methodologies
- Domain independent, which saw the emergence of software development methodologies
- Generic applications, which was marked by methodology-intensive software development
- Return to application-focused development, which represents a postmethodology software development period

13.2.1.1 Domain-Dependent Era: Before Software Development Methodology

In the period from 1955 to 1965, computer hardware depended on the specific application domain. Thus, it was virtually impossible to develop business and scientific or military applications on the same machine.

Problem-oriented languages like FORTRAN, COBOL, and ALGOL were developed during this period to provide software with a measure of platform independence compatible with the requirements of new computers. The domain-specific focus was a major element in building successful software systems. Entire new computing disciplines emerged to support these applications, including numerical analysis programming for military and scientific applications and information retrieval for business applications (Vessey 1997).

13.2.1.2 Domain-Independent Era: Early Software Development Methodology

In the period from 1964 to 1980, more powerful machines such as the IBM 360 were introduced, including the lower mid-range model 40 and the model 67, shipped with hardware to support virtual memory. The IBM 360 allowed scientific and commercial or business applications—previously restricted to different hardware platforms—to coexist on a single machine, partly through the implementation of multiple types of arithmetic instructions in the hardware. The sociology of software development was strongly influenced by the 360's ability to eliminate the machine-based separation between scientific and business applications. Generic applications became possible when the software business became independent of hardware vendors. Competitive advantage in software development became directly proportional to the interdependency of standards, hardware, and platforms. This period also saw many attempts to institutionalize application-independent software development strategies (Vessey 1997) and provided the foundation for the next era of methodology-intensive software development.

13.2.1.3 Generic Applications Era: Methodology-Intensive Software Development

The period from 1980 to 1995 saw the birth and evolution of desktop PC and laptop computing. With the increasingly widespread availability of computers and their increased user-friendliness, user involvement became more prevalent. The availability of technology also facilitated automation efforts in software implementation and nontechnical users became more active participants in the process (Glass 1998). Intuitive, user-friendly graphical use interfaces (GUIs) replaced the obscure demands imposed by JCL (job control language), thereby moving human computer interaction (HCI) to a higher level. Attempts at developing application-dependent software (such as fourth-generation languages, rule-based languages, and simulation languages) were also carried out (Vessey 1997).

13.2.1.4 Return to Application-Focused Development Era: Software Development Postmethodology

In the period from 1995 to the present, networked hardware architecture became the dominant driver. The development of Web-based applications was the milestone distinguishing this period. This was correlated with:

- Emergence of Web-driven tools and programming languages (HTML, Java, Java Script, XML, VML)
- Introduction of user-friendly Web interfaces such as Internet browsers and email agents
- Emergence of Web-based software engineering as a software development methodology
- Increased demand for software that balanced speed and quality
- Closer synchronization between business processes and software evolution

13.2.2 Generic versus Specialized Development

The shift from domain-specific to application-independent computers was a decisive event in the history of software development. The subsequent deployment of application-independent computers in desktop and notebook computing represented yet another milestone, marking a shift towards generic infrastructure systems, applications, and components. This deployment led to several notable advantages:

- *Portability.* Software applications can be accessed virtually anytime and anywhere because of the development of generic Web-based downloading and installation protocols.
- *Compatibility.* A single operating system can now host a vast number of applications regardless of their originating vendors. Generic operating systems are a central repository for shared components across applications.
- *Reusability.* One application or one module can be used across computer models, organizations, and user groups. It can be distributed over an organizational network or the World Wide Web. It can also be reused to develop new releases of software implementations. Furthermore, with modifications through built-in preferences and options, the same application can be customized or tailored to a variety of individual needs.
- *Ease of training.* Generic applications are easier to learn because of their availability, and training material is inexpensive (or even free) due to the use of mass production techniques.

■ *Cost effectiveness.* Because operational costs are generally lower with mass production and sales volume is usually high, products can be sold at competitive prices to end-users.

Generic applications also have noteworthy disadvantages. For example, such applications are based on the assumption that individuals and organizations have no significant differences that require special adaptability or scalability. This assumption applies also to generic methodologies or strategies for software development. Generic methodologies are rarely adapted to the type or size of the project, the technological environment, or organizational settings. These methodologies are one-dimensional approaches, often not mirroring a particular organization's social, political, and organizational development dimensions (Avison & Fitzgerald 2003). Generic applications also assume that businesses or individuals should be able to adapt to the infrastructure and functionalities of the generic application with limited provision for change. Although this assumption may be valid within one application domain, it may be highly ineffective for another.

Additionally, the assumption that business processes can be easily modified to fit a generic software product is unrealistic and can prove costly. The diversity of goals, market demands, stakeholder requirements, architectural specifications, nonfunctional requirements, and organizational cultures across business domains and specializations can make generic development strategies impractical. Indeed, for some organizations, the effect of adopting a particular generic methodology that fails to yield expected outcomes may be a wholesale rejection of methodologies in general (Avison & Fitzgerald 2003). Agile software development is one reaction to this phenomenon.

13.2.3 The Problem-Solving Context in Specialized System Development

Because software development tries to solve problems, it is important to view specialized system development in a problem-solving context. Solving problems always involves two elements: the ability to comprehend the problem and the ability to solve it. Accordingly, specialized system development may be problem focused or solution driven. The types of problem and the solution strategies in software engineering vary, so it is essential to have an effective understanding of this variety for successful specialized system development.

Specialized system developers face several challenges (see Figure 13.1). One is to understand how specialization in identifying problem characteristics can help in evaluating existing options, in selecting the most

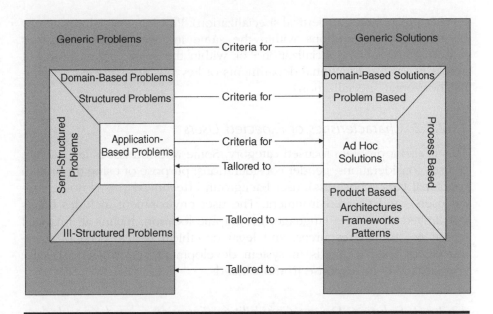

Figure 13.1   Generic and specialized software development in the problem-solving context.

appropriate options, and in using domain analysis and requirements engineering to develop effective solutions. Another challenge is how software products or solutions can be adequately used, reused, customized, personalized, reengineered, or redeveloped based on application-driven or domain-specific specialization. How specialization in the problem, method, product, or domain analysis can assist in the proper selection or successful construction of computer-based solutions that utilize suitable methods, process models, techniques, and tools is yet another challenge.

Examination of problem and solution diversity reveals three factors decisive in specialized system development: the characteristics of the system to be developed and of its anticipated users; solution-driven capabilities, experience, and knowledge; and the characteristics of system developers.

13.2.3.1 Characteristics of System

This is a problem-focused category. The diversity of software systems in terms of size; complexity; time constraints; scope; underlying technology; business goals; and problem environment are determinative for this category. The problems with which one deals range from structured problems at the operational levels of organizations to semistructured ones at the tactical level to ill-structured problems at the top-management or strategic level (corresponding to vertical specialization). Problem specialization may be between organizations within the same industry; across industries (external horizontal specialization); or within the same organization but across its various functional departments or key business processes (internal horizontal specialization).

13.2.3.2 Characteristics of Expected Users

This is also a problem-focused category. Some relevant issues are the age of user considerations; gender considerations; purpose of using the system (personal versus business); user background (technical versus nontechnical users); and user environment. The user environment includes but is not limited to culture; language; geographic location; technical; financial resources; human resources; and legal or ethical issues. Each of these introduces specific needs in system development and triggers specific specializations in response to those needs.

13.2.3.3 Solution–Driven Capabilities, Experience and Knowledge

System specialization in this category is based on tools and resources rather than on the application domain. These include capabilities affecting numerous specializations in the solution area:

- Capabilities and experience in project management tools
- Requirements analysis techniques
- Architectural models
- User interface approaches
- Database management strategies
- Implementation languages
- Development tools
- Development methodologies
- Process models

13.3 Application-Based Specialized Development

Several examples of specialized development are considered in this section: pervasive computing; real-time software; Web-based applications; and security-driven software.

13.3.1 Pervasive Software Development

Pervasive computing has arisen as the result of the convergence of three traditional computing specializations (personal, networking, and embedded systems). This has introduced the era of mobile computing, wireless devices, PDAs, pocket PCs, and tablet PCs, all of which are examples of pervasive computing products. Software applications are important components of these products and the distinctive nature of these applications presents new challenges to software development. Pervasive applications are distinguished by their ubiquity, interconnectedness, and dynamism. The applications are expected to be embedded, distributed, nonintrusive, and cost effective (Ciarletta & Dima 2000). As a result, system architecture, security, and software economics are especially significant issues in pervasive software engineering.

A conceptual model, proposed by Ciarletta & Dima (2000), partitions the aspects of pervasive systems development into four layers: physical, resource, abstract, and intentional. Table 13.1 illustrates the roles of each of these layers in specialized pervasive system development.

Effective m-commerce application can be deployed only if sufficient network reliability and redundancy are available. *M-commerce* (mobile commerce) applications require a unique blend of knowledge and need-specific networking support to be effective (Kalakota, Varshney, & Vetter 2000), including wireless quality of service (QoS); efficient location management; and reliable and survivable networking. Varshney and Vetter (2000, 2001) describe a four-level framework that may provide a process for developing effective m-commerce applications:

- *M-commerce applications.* These applications modify e-commerce applications for a mobile environment.
- *Wireless user infrastructure.* The new m-commerce applications should support the capabilities of user infrastructures. For example, such applications must be effective for mobile devices such as PDAs and cell phones.
- *Mobile middleware.* The new m-commerce applications must have superior response time and reliability when deployed because the middleware will be used to connect e-commerce applications with different wireless networks.
- *Wireless network infrastructure.* Networking requirements need to be satisfied by the m-commerce applications deployed. Such requirements include quality of service; network reliability; location management; roaming across multiple networks; and multicast support.

13.3.2 Real-Time Software Development

Real-time software development originated in the 1970s and continues to evolve today. The development of real-time systems requires consideration

Table 13.1   Roles of Pervasive Systems Development Layers

Layer	Rationale	Software Development Ramifications
Physical	The flow of control in pervasive applications may depend on signals received from or sent to the user's physical location. Excellent software architecture is ineffective in pervasive devices unless it is well supported by hardware design that mirrors the physical characteristics of human behavior.	Designing effective hardware architectures is crucial to software design because software effectiveness depends on hardware usability and hardware is irreplaceable (in contrast with desktop computing).
Resource	Corresponds to the infrastructure of pervasive software applications: operating systems, logical devices, system APIs, user interface, network protocol	ROM-based operating systems must be reliable at early releases because it will be prohibitively costly to make upgrades thereafter. System resources must be matched to user goals and needs. User interfaces must be intuitive and consistent. They must accommodate user languages and physical limitations. Networking features should be automatically available, self-configuring, and compatible with existing technology. System storage must enable users to access, retrieve, and organize information in a way that suits their requirements. The execution environment and volatile memory should be responsive and provide speed and sense of control via multithreading and multitasking.

Table 13.1   Roles of Pervasive Systems Development Layers (continued)

Layer	Rationale	Software Development Ramifications
Abstract	Represents the direct software application that the user will use	Maintaining compatibility between the user's mental model and expectations and the application logic "state" Shorter time frames are available to pervasive system users for learning about the system, compared with desktop users. More difficult physical conditions are encountered by mobile users of pervasive systems. User involvement and participation is much more critical in pervasive applications than traditional applications.
Intentional	Represents the user's goals and purposes in using the pervasive system	Analyzing the system to determine user goals and designing the system to fulfill these goals

of three basic issues (Felder 2002): the complexity of timing, which is recognized at the higher requirements specification level; resource constraints, which are addressed at lower design levels; and scheduling constraints, which are addressed at lower design levels.

Gaulding and Lawson (1976) described a disciplined engineering approach to real-time software development focused on a process design methodology. The basis of their approach was a process performance requirement, a document that described the interfaces to the software; software functional and performance requirements; operating rules; and the data processor hardware description. The objective of process design engineering was to develop an automated approach to the evolutionary design, implementation, and testing of real-time software. Gaulding and Lawson defined the crucial aspects of real-time software development as consisting of four core features:

■ Transformational technology for enabling traceable transformation from functional requirements to a software structure for a given computer

- Architectural approach, which required top-down design, implementation, and testing techniques supported by a single process design language
- Simulation technology, which provided the ability to evaluate trial designs for real-time software processes
- Supporting tools used to automate such functions as requirements traceability; configuration management; library management; simulation control; and data collection and analysis

Gomaa (1986) proposed an early software development life-cycle method for real-time systems that attempted to tailor generic software development methodology to the special needs of real-time software development. Table 13.2 overviews Gomaa's method and its phases and applications.

13.3.3 Web–Based Software Development

Web-based software development is growing faster than any other application domain. Software systems with Web capabilities are more likely to maximize added value for a business effectively because of the dramatically greater connectivity that they provide to customers and partners and because of their ability to enrich the business process with information (Evans & Wurster 1999). Hitt and Brynjolfsson (1996) identify the three key criteria for assessing the business value of IT-based systems as productivity, business profitability, and consumer surplus.

Web applications have caused traditional business goals to be broadened to encompass new measures of customer satisfaction, enhance internal processes, and elevate an organization's technological innovation activities. These measures are closely related to an organization's financial performance (Van Der Zee & De Jong 1999). Efficiency, quality, market share, and market penetration have emerged as important measures and goals of business (Singleton, McLean, & Altman 1988) upon which Web-based systems can have a significant impact. These developments have motivated businesses to adopt Internet/intranet information systems in their environments and to introduce management techniques that align the new technologies with their organizational structures.

13.3.3.1 E-business Software Systems

Web-based software development has intensified the demand for quality and reliability. Successfully configuring Web applications requires careful attention to several strategies that allow a business to leverage its Web engineering for a competitive advantage. Development teams, legacy systems, value chains, and business integration and management structures underlie these strategies. Thus:

■ *Skills, structure and management of the development team.* The availability of skilled staff for Web-driven software development projects is known to boost performance significantly. Training programs and availability of resources strongly affect the quality of e-business applications by helping to reduce the development time needed to tailor solutions to application needs. Effective management can compose the right team structure, capitalizing on the synergy of a diversified set of abilities.

■ *Legacy applications.* The scope and domain of legacy systems shape the strategies needed to solve e-business software problems. The existence of a negative correlation between organizational complexity and the impact of technological change is disputable (Keen 1981); the issue is obscured by the fact that the more complex an organization is, the more ill structured are its business problems (Mitroff & Turoff 1973). Even though this affects the ability to tackle such problems smoothly, information technology enables a complex organization to redesign its business processes so that it can manage business process complexity more effectively (Davenport & Stoddard 1994).

■ *Value chain and logistics management.* The value chain refers to the set of activities that a business implements in order to achieve its objectives through a process of adding values as activities progress from one business phase to another. E-business applications use Internet technology to support products and services that require the integration of business processes and the logistics of end-users and original suppliers. Effective management of the entire process can significantly enhance value for consumers by organizing, coordinating, and controlling supply chain activities and logistics (Turban et al. 2000). The context determines the requisite criteria for effective Web-based development, including its flexibility, level of quality, dependability, agility, and efficiency. The closeness of the process to optimality can be measured in terms of its ability to deliver the right product at the right time at each level of the supply chain (Vokurka, Gail, & Carl 2002). The value chain concept can be further applied to help design decision support systems, which enhance the decision-making process at the tactical and strategic management levels (Haavengen, Olsen, & Sena 1996). Electronic product development (EPD) is another aspect of e-business growth that relies on a holistic understanding

Table 13.2   Life-Cycle Phases for Real Time Software Systems

Phase	Phase Definition	Phase Application
Requirements analysis and specification	As in other approaches, the user requirements are analyzed, and system specifications are formulated that elaborate on these requirements.	State transition diagrams describe transitions between system states. Object-oriented UML-based state transition diagrams carry out this technique more effectively. Any operator interaction with the system should also be explicitly specified. Throwaway rapid-prototyping techniques have proven to be extremely effective in requirements analysis for real-time systems.
System design	Although the system is structured into tasks as in other software systems, real-time systems are designed with a specific focus on concurrent processes and task interfaces.	The asynchronous nature of the functions within the system is a key characteristic that affects decomposing real-time software systems into concurrent tasks. Data-flow and event-trace diagrams are effective techniques in mapping this phase.
Task design	Each task is structured into modules and module interfaces are defined.	Task-structure charts with intensive project and team management elements are essential to carry out task design efficiently.
Module construction	Detailed design, coding, and unit testing of each module are carried out.	This is similar to module construction in other system development approaches.
Task and system integration	Modules are integrated and tested to form tasks, which are in turn gradually integrated and tested to form the total system.	Incremental system development is used to achieve task and system integration.

Table 13.2 Life-Cycle Phases for Real Time Software Systems

Phase	Phase Definition	Phase Application
System testing	The whole system or major subsystems are tested to verify conformance with functional specifications. To achieve greater objectivity, system testing is best performed by independent test teams.	Automated testing is widely used for real-time systems.
Acceptance testing	This is performed by the user.	Extends user involvement to the validation and verification stages after system delivery.

of the entire product value chain (customers, designers, suppliers, manufacturers, and logistics providers) to help provide more successful mass customization (Helander & Jiao 2000).

■ *Aligning e-business applications with organizational goals.* E-business solutions can be very effective in serving organizational goals and marketing requirements. Strategies that integrate the Internet with traditional system capabilities can create advantages for existing corporations (Porter 2001). E-business software systems depend on the internal preparation of the company, as well as on the readiness of its customers and suppliers to engage in electronic interactions. An appropriate commitment of resources to a business problem can allow management to create value that boosts business readiness for e-commerce challenges (Barua et al. 2001). E-commerce solutions link customers, suppliers, partners, and interorganizational departments in one or more unified value chains. If these links are not properly managed and efficiently aligned in synchronized frameworks, delays will occur, costs may exceed profits, and financial loss and customer dissatisfaction may result.

Other factors that may indirectly affect the success of e-business applications are supply chain management (SCM) and enterprise resource management (ERM), which help explain the impact of legacy business applications on successful e-business development. By better understanding customer and supplier needs, as well as the effect of current business processes on the overall methods of supply chain and resource management, one can flexibly apply information technology to reengineer business processes (Daoud 2000).

13.3.3.2 Object-Oriented Development for Web Applications

Gellersen and Gaedke (1999) propose a Web composition model that uses an object-oriented approach to Web development based on Web implementation models. Their model is intended to provide object-oriented capabilities such as reusability, inheritance, improved modifiability, and extensibility to developers. Conallen (1999) addresses object-oriented Web application architecture using a UML-based approach, which facilitates managing complexity for Web applications and enhances reusability. Conallen's approach incorporates CASE tool support and integrates three models of Web application architecture: the business model, navigation model, and implementation model.

13.3.3.3 Customizable Web Applications

Several approaches have been proposed for modeling and implementing customizable Web applications; all of them share characteristics for Web development environments that explicitly consider user context for customization (Kappel, Retschitzegger, & Schwinger 2000). This reflects the attractiveness of personalization for individuals and classes of users and includes network and device contexts. The network context is related to network settings; the device context is based on multidelivery of different devices or classes of devices. However, these have different levels of location context (related to mobile computing and portability) and temporal context (based on time constraints).

13.3.4 Security-Driven Software Development

Software systems have evolved into global, networked infrastructures; multidimensional databases; and enterprise data warehouses that interconnect individuals; businesses; organizations; competing supply chains; numerous mobile and wireless applications; and even nations. Software engineering typically views security as one measure of quality and reliability in software products. It addresses the security issue as part of risk analysis, seeking to minimize the likelihood of intrusions, attacks, hacking, or fraud in information systems. The security of contemporary software applications is a critical element of business survival, given, for example, the need to protect organizational strategic assets such as information. In e-commerce, customers are more aware than ever of the ramifications of unsecured personal or private information and more likely to trust businesses with strong security measures, policies, and standards.

The area of information systems security has evolved across paradigms and strategies (Siponen 2002). These range from the generic, based on common sense, to the specific, which is based on organizational culture and needs, as summarized in Table 13.3. Security-driven systems are receiving greater attention in current software development strategies. Reengineering existing systems adds security features; creates security-based applications to ensure security in systems (such as antiviruses and firewalls); adds features that enhance the privacy of individuals; and builds surveillance-based applications that can help detect and protect against crime and terrorism. Computer vision, image processing, and multimedia-based technologies play a significant role in these applications.

As with all forms of software development, the design of such systems is not without challenges. The trade-off between open communication channels and the potential for security threats through these same channels is one example. The remaining parts of this section present a framework for dealing with security considerations in the software development process, particularly in terms of the analysis and design of such systems.

13.3.4.1 Security-Driven Requirements Analysis

Because most of the software engineering literature was written prior to the era of the Web, the investigation of system vulnerabilities was often not explicitly or carefully addressed. The rapid spread of Web-driven applications and infrastructures has changed this situation. For example, in terms of security, Web connectivity has increased public access to information, but has also exposed the same information and information systems to greater risks and vulnerabilities (Deswarte 1997). In updated software engineering methodologies reflecting the need for software systems to comply with internal and external security standards, the specification of security requirements is handled at the analysis phase as part of the nonfunctional requirements of the system.

Sommerville (2005) classified security requirements as external, nonfunctional safety and privacy requirements. Although this categorization is generally reasonable, it needs to be qualified to reflect the fact that even functional requirements should be guided by security metrics. Otherwise, an incorrect specification may even exacerbate system vulnerabilities. Furthermore, added or flexible requirements can also expose a system to unexpected risks (Smith 1991; Pfleeger 1997). Security-driven requirements analysis involves defining security objectives; setting their metrics;

Table 13.3 Four Generations of Information Systems Security Approaches

Generation	Drivers	Strategies	Techniques	Problems
First (early 1980s)	Generic thinking; common sense principles	Linking requirements (what to do) to capabilities (what can be done)	Risk analysis.	Gaps between generic strategies and special needs
Second (late 1980s)	Some focus on organization requirements	Formal methods	Control points and checklists	Considering natural, functional and technical requirements while ignoring the social nature of organizations
Third (early 1990s)	Business processes; focus on specific organization requirements.	Information systems modeling	Responsibility modeling; security semantics; logical approach; ERM, DFD, OO and business process modeling for security	Inadequate focus on social requirements of organizations.
Fourth (late 1990s up to recently)	Sociotechnical design; user participation; strong focus on specific organizational requirements	Domain-specific and application-driven design for information systems security	Responsibility modeling; viable information systems.	Still in its early phases

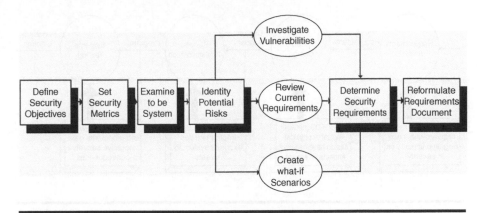

Figure 13.2   Security-driven requirements analysis process.

identifying potential risks; investigating vulnerabilities; creating what-if scenarios; reviewing current requirements; and reformulating requirements to reflect the input of the analysis phase. The output of the analysis becomes the guideline for designing a security-driven solution. Figure 13.2 shows an overview of a security-oriented requirements process.

Security objectives are usually defined on the basis of organizational standards; the nature of the underlying technology; the magnitude of the anticipated threat; and the risk to the organization of a given type of threat. Security breaches are highly unpredictable and their nature and scope change over time; thus, organizations need to adapt to new threats and be able to adjust their objectives to meet the demands of new challenges. Once the objectives have been determined, quantitative and qualitative measurements should be derived to establish evaluation metrics that can be used to verify the quality of software products in terms of the security requirements. The major task in security-driven analysis is to identify potential security risks or threats. Risk assessment is essential and must reflect the fact that an organization may be attacked from inside or outside its network (Swiler et al. 2001).

Identifying potential security risks involves investigating system vulnerabilities. Vulnerabilities can be associated with intentional and unintentional factors. Unintentional factors are related to human mistakes; exceptional hazards in the environment; system failures; gaps in hardware or software design; or bad requirements specifications. External factors contribute to the existence of vulnerabilities, but the analysis, design, implementation, and usability of the system enable the vast majority of security threats in most organizations. For example, a problem in data collection, data entry, data distribution, referential integrity, or authorization can result in breaches that put data at risk. The growing concern about infrastructure vulnerabilities, in which as much damage can be done

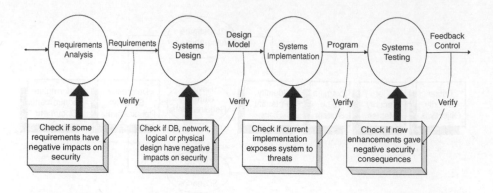

Figure 13.3   A software engineering approach to systems security via traceability analysis.

with a keyboard as with a bomb (Baskerville 1993), is an important issue for organizational management. Tracing and tracking leaks, security gaps, and security-related problems across the software development process are ways to ensure security in software systems. The traceability process shown in Figure 13.3 provides a strategy for a software engineering approach to system security via traceability analysis.

Intentional factors that threaten system security include data theft; data abuse; source code theft; deliberate data manipulation; data tampering; malicious damage; viruses and attacks; cyber crimes; terror attacks; and miscellaneous computer crimes. Computer crimes range from using the computer or computer network as a target to using a computer as a medium (i.e., giving misleading information) to using computers as planning or deception tools (Turban, Rainer, & Potter 2002). One of the current, serious challenges for information systems is to discover how information and communication technologies can contribute to public safety (Shneiderman 2002). Recent efforts focus on enhancing security at the technical level (network-based security) while paying some attention to security at the analysis and architectural levels.

Antiterror system development relies not only on solution-focused capabilities, but also on a deeper understanding of the problem domain by studying the attacker's behavior (Erland & Olovsson 1997). System vulnerabilities or security gaps in an information system provide opportunities to carry out attacks or steal critical information. Identifying and securing these gaps will minimize potential risks. Holmes (2001) points out the need to assess the motives for breaching system security in order to protect and then manage the systems infrastructure in accordance with the assessed vulnerabilities. Salenger (1997) relates the level of organizational Internet security to the relative "functional uses" of the Internet.

Demuth and Rieke (2000) emphasize that engineering secure systems requires managing infrastructure vulnerability.

Models suggested for designing a secure environment (Salter et al. 1998) include the adversary, vulnerabilities, and methodology models. The adversary model is based on understanding the motives for potential threats: what the perpetrators of the threat want to do and what they can do. The vulnerabilities model identifies three basic steps in any successful attack: analyzing the targeted system to identify its weaknesses; quietly gaining access to the system (stealth); and executing the security attack. The methodology model categorizes attacks based on their characteristics and aims to find effective, protective countermeasures. The adversary model is based on information gathering and the vulnerabilities model is driven by risk analysis. The methodology model depends on designing a procedure for response and recovery.

13.3.4.2 Security-Driven Systems Design

The design of security-focused solutions for software systems can be done at two different levels: conceptual and technical. The conceptual level provides the architectural foundation for the technical level. The key concept for security-focused architectures is the use of defense strategies. The ability of a software system to withstand threats is closely related to its ability to reduce vulnerabilities and provide protection shields that prevent, eliminate, or deal effectively with breaches and attacks. Figure 13.4 illustrates this approach in terms of a seven-layer conceptual model for defense strategies for security-focused system design.

In the layered model, five key defense strategies (prevention control, detection, limitation, recovery, and correction) are used separately or in combination to minimize system vulnerabilities or system weaknesses (Turban et al. 2002). Naturally, prevention control is the most effective strategy, whether it prevents human error, external attack, or unauthorized use. Access control also plays a significant role in this defense strategy. Figure 13.5 provides a basic taxonomy of the various types of security controls in software systems. An intrusion detection system (IDS) is a system that can distinguish authorized uses, misuses, or abuses of computers by authorized users or external perpetrators. Intrusions can be classified into three categories: single-intruder signal terminal (SIST), single-intruder multiple terminal (SIMT) and multiple-intruder multiple terminal (MIMT) (Puketza et al. 1996).

Object-oriented and component-based architectures have been shown to be maintainable structures. One key reason is that they allow easy replacement of defective components. Distributed-object architecture and

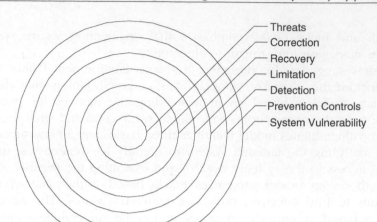

Figure 13.4   Seven-layer conceptual model for defense strategies in security-focused system design.

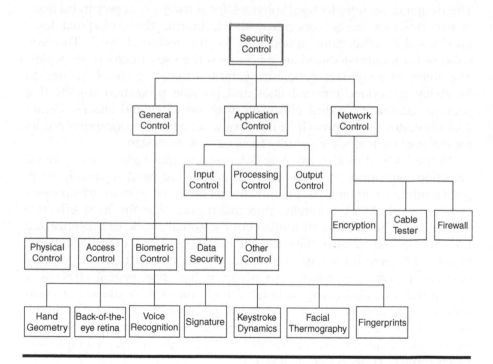

Figure 13.5   A basic taxonomy for security control techniques in software system. (Based on Turban, E. et al. *Electronic Commerce: a Management Perspective.* Englewood Cliffs, NJ: Prentice Hall, 2002.)

design standards provide an adequate level for generic distributed applications. However, these are only the first steps in building application-specific software architectures for achieving overall system development objectives. Although commercial enterprise application integration (EAI) tools and workflow management system (WFMS) products can help advance basic distributed standards to a commercial level, they remain far below the mission-critical needs of business and information security processes. System designers should employ security solutions that reinforce each other, define secure relationships based on trust, and use protective countermeasures to prevent attacks.

Effective database and network design play a crucial role in reducing system vulnerabilities. For instance, cryptographic protocol design is cited frequently in the literature as a source of distributed system vulnerabilities. Analysis and design techniques have proven useful in detecting protocol vulnerabilities (Stubblebine & Wright 2002). Cybenko and Jiang (2000) examined the vulnerabilities of the Internet and proposed a six-stage protection process to counteract malicious use.

- The first essential step in the process of protecting infrastructures and increasing awareness of emerging threats is the application of information-gathering techniques. These techniques include the use of intelligence reports, the analysis of unusual incidents, and automated information harvesting from the Web and Web news services.
- The second essential step in the process is a thorough risk assessment of the current system to identify vulnerable areas. This risk assessment includes modeling an attack, modeling failure of the main system, and modeling subsidiary failures due to main system failures.
- The third step is interdiction, which includes being able to make use of currently available prevention methods.
- The fourth step is detection of attacks through early warning systems and monitoring resources. Monitoring subsystems are able to take actions while an attack is underway, whereas a warning system can attempt to prevent an attack before it happens (Salter et al. 1998).
- The fifth step is implemention of a proper response procedure once an attack has been acknowledged. Response procedures are what Cybenko and Jiang (2000) call "forensic challenges"; they can only be implemented when an attack is already underway. Once an attack is detected, the system should be able to trace the attack.
- The final stage in the Cybenko–Jiang approach is recovery, which includes learning from the attack and documenting its characteristics in a knowledge base for future reference.

The importance of specialized system development has increased as the significance of scalability and tailorability in software development (as opposed to generic strategies and approaches) has been better recognized. The theoretical foundations of specialized system development will continue to evolve, providing new challenges and opportunities to the software engineering community. The future of R&D in this area is a matter of concern for government, industry, and academia alike. For example, the government's role in encryption of information on the Internet is crucial (Fox 2001).

Some of the intelligence issues and policies to be further addressed (Artz 2001; Wilson 2000; Zorpette 2002) include the human role in information analysis, gaps in technical intelligence, and cooperation between organizations and services that collect intelligence. It is necessary to define the role of government as well as to develop a clearer definition of organizational roles. Salenger (1997) claims that the level of security implemented by an organization is proportional to its size and income. This phenomenon is partly a result of the fact that larger companies have the human, technical, and financial resources required to establish and operate a secure Internet environment—resources that smaller companies may lack. Improved protocols for defining and enforcing security standards are expected to continue to emerge as security threats persist.

References

Artz, D. (2001). Digital steganography: hiding data within data. *IEEE Internet Computing,* 5(3), 75–80.

Avison, D. & Fitzgerald, G. (2003). Where now for development methodologies? *Commun. ACM,* 46(1), 48–72.

Barua, A., Konana, P., Whinston, A., & Yin, F. (2001). Driving e-business excellence. *MIT Sloan Manage. Rev.,* 43(1), 36–44.

Baskerville, R. (1993). Information systems security design methods: implications for information systems development. *ACM Computing Surv.,* 25(4), 365–414.

Ciarletta, L. & Dima, A. (2000). A conceptual model for pervasive computing parallel processing. *Proc. 2000 Int. Workshops Parallel Process.,* 9–15.

Conallen, J. (1999). Modeling Web application architecture with UML. *Commun. ACM,* 42, 63–70.

Cybenko, G. & Jiang, G. (2000). Developing a distributed system for infrastructure protection. *IT Prof.,* 2(4), 17–23.

Daoud, F. (2000). Electronic commerce infrastructure. *IEEE Potentials,* 19(1), 30–33.

Davenport, T. and Stoddard D. 1994. Reengineering: business change of mythic proportions? *MIS Q.,* 18(2), 121–127.

Demuth, T. & Rieke, A. (2000). Bilateral anonymity and prevention of abusing logged Web addresses. *21st Century Mil. Commun. Conf. Proc.,* 1, 435–439.

Deswarte, Y. (1997). Internet security despite untrustworthy agents and components. Proc. 6th IEEE Computer Soc. Workshop Future Trends Distributed Computing Syst., 53, 218–219.

Erland, J. & Olovsson, T. (1997). A quantitative model of the security intrusion process based on attacker behavior. *IEEE Trans. Software Eng.*, 23(4), 235–245.

Evans, P. & Wurster, T. (1999). Getting real about virtual commerce, *Harv. Bus. Rev.*, 77(6), 85–94.

Felder, M. (2002). A formal design notation for real-time systems. *ACM Trans. Software Eng. Methodol. (TOSEM)*, 11(2), 149–190.

Fox, R. (2001). Privacy trade-off fighting terrorism. *Commun. ACM*, 44(12), 9–10.

Gaulding, S.N. & Lawson, J.D. (1976). Process design engineering a methodology for real-time software development. *Proc. 2nd Int. Conf. Software Eng.*, 80–85, San Francisco.

Gellersen, H. & Gaedke, M. (1999). Object-oriented Web application development. *IEEE Internet Computing*, 3 (1), 60–68.

Glass, R. (1998). *In the Beginning, Recollections of Software Pioneers*. Los Alamitos, CA: The IEEE Computer Society Press.

Glass, R.L. (2000). Process diversity and a computing old wives'/husbands tale. *IEEE Software*, 17(4), 128–129.

Glass, R. & Vessey, I. (1995). Contemporary application-domain taxonomies. *IEEE Software*, 12(4), 63–76.

Gomaa, H. (1986). Software development of real-time systems. *Commun. ACM*, 29(7) 657–668.

Haavengen, B., Olsen, D., & Sena, J. (1996). The value chain component in a decision supports system: a case example. *IEEE Trans. Eng. Manage.*, 43(4), 418–428.

Helander, M. & Jiao, J. (2000). E-product development (Epd) for mass customization. Management of innovation and technology, *Proc. 2000 IEEE Int. Conf. ICMIT 2000.* 2(2), 848–854.

Hitt,L.M. & Brynjolfsson, E. (1996). Productivity, business profitability, and consumer surplus: three different measures of information technology value. *MIS Q.*, 20(2), 121–142.

Holmes, N. (2001). Terrorism, technology and the profession. *Computer*, 34(11), 134–136.

Kalakota, R., Varshney, U., & Vetter, R. (2000). Mobile commerce: a new frontier. *IEEE Computer Soc.*, (special issue on e-commerce). 33(10), 32–38.

Kappel, G., Retschitzegger, W., & Schwinger, W. (2000). Modeling customizable Web applications—a requirement's perspective. *Proc. Int. Conf. Digital Libraries: Res. Pract.* Kyoto, 168–179.

Keen, P. (1981). Information systems and organizational change. *Commun. ACM*, 24(1), 24–33.

Kelly, J. (1987). A comparison of four design methods for real-time systems. *IEEE Proc. 9th Int. Conference Software Eng.*, 238–252.

Mitroff, I. & Turoff, M. (1973). Technological forecasting and assessment: science and/or mythology? *J. Technol. Forecasting Soc. Change,* 5, 113–134.

Pfleeger, C.P. (1997). The fundamentals of information security. *IEEE Software*. 14(1), 15–16.

Porter, M.E. (2001). Strategy and the Internet. *Harv. Bus. Rev.*, 79, 63–78.

Puketza, N., Zhang, K., Chung, M., Mukherjee, B., & Olsson, R. (1996). A methodology for testing intrusion detection systems. *IEEE Trans. Software Eng.*, 22(10), 719–729.

Salenger, D. (1997). Internet environment and outsourcing. *Int. J. Network Manage.*, 7(6), 300–304.

Salter, C., Saydjari,O., Schneier, B., & Wallner, J. (1998). Toward a secure engineering methodology. *Proceedings of New Security Paradigms Workshop.* Charlottesville, VA. New York: ACM Press, 2–10.

Shneiderman, B. (2002). ACM's computing professionals face new challenges. *Commun. ACM*, 45(2), 31–34.

Singleton, J.P., McLean, E.R., & Altman, E.N. (1988). Measuring information systems performance: experience with the management by results system at Security Pacific Bank. *MIS Q.*, 12(2), 325–337.

Siponen, M. (2002). Designing secure information systems and software: critical evaluation of the existing approaches and a new paradigm. Unpublished Ph.D. dissertation. University of Oulu.

Smith, G.W. (1991). Modeling security-relevant data semantics. *IEEE Trans. Software Eng.*, 17(11), 1195–1203.

Sommerville, I. (2005). *Software Engineering, 7/E*, International Computer Science Press Series, Reading, MA: Addison-Wesley.

Stubblebine, S. & Wright, R. (2002). Authentication logic with formal semantics supporting synchronization, revocation, and recency. *IEEE Trans. Software Eng.*, 28(3), 265–285.

Swiler, L., Philips, C., Ellis, D., & Chakerian, S. (2001). Computer attack graph generation tool. *Proc. DARPA Inf. Survivability Conf. Exposition,* IEEE Computer Society Press.

Turban, E., Lee, J., King, D., & Chung, H. (2000). *Electronic Commerce: A Management Perspective.* Englewood Cliffs, NJ: Prentice Hall.

Turban, E., Rainer, K., & Potter, R. (2002). *Introduction to Information Technology,* 2nd ed. New York: John Wiley & Sons.

Van Der Zee, J.T.M. & De Jong, B. (1999). Alignment is not enough: integrating business and information technology. *J. Manage. Inf. Syst.*, 16(2), 137–158.

Varshney U. & Vetter, R. (2000). Emerging mobile and wireless networks. *Commun. Assoc. Computing Machinery,* 43(6), 73–81.

Varshney U. & Vetter, R. (2001). A framework for the emerging mobile commerce applications. *Proceedings of the 34th Hawaii International Conference on System Sciences.* Washington, D.C: IEEE Computer Society, 9014.

Vessey, I. (1997). Problems versus solutions: the role of the application domain in software. *Proc. 7th Workshop Empirical Stud. Programmers,* Virginia, 233–240.

Vessey, I. & Glass, R., (1998). Strong vs. weak: approaches to systems development. *Commun. ACM*, 41(4), 99–102.

Vokurka, R., Gail, M., & Carl, M. (2002). Improving competitiveness through supply chain management: a cumulative approach. *Competitiveness Rev.*, 12(1), 14–24.

Wilson, C. (2000). Holding management accountable: a new policy for protection against computer crime. *Natl. Aerospace Electron. Conf. Proc. IEEE 2000,* 272–281.

Zorpette, G. (2002). Making intelligence smarter. *IEEE Spectrum,* 39(1), 38–43

Glossary

4GL Acronym for *fourth generation language*. A 4GL is designed to be more accessible to nonprogrammers, require less programming skill, be easier to learn, and be more graphical than 3GL tools. 4GLs may provide database access, query languages, screen definition capability, graphics generation ability, and spreadsheets. Languages like C++ are called 3GL. The GL level of a software product tends to be used to indicate how leading edge a product is in a marketing sense. 5GL tools include knowledge-based capability, expert system behavior, and inference engine capability. See the NASA software engineering site study brief by Amy Parra for a useful discussion.

Actor UML terminology for a role a user plays in a system. The role is like a hat that the user wears. The user may wear many hats.

Actual Return The return that actually takes place at the end of a period of time as opposed to the expected return that was anticipated to be made.

Agile Development This model emphasizes people with skilled expertise and their interactions and ongoing collaboration with customers, rather than formal development processes. Refer to the *Agile Manifesto* of Beck (2001)—www.agilemanifesto.org—for a statement of purpose.

Aging Symptoms Degenerative characteristics caused by the changes in systems as a result of long-term, repeated maintenance that complicates ongoing maintenance and degrades system performance.

Algorithm A well-defined, step-by-step procedure for solving a problem. According to the NIST dictionary, a computable set of steps to achieve a desired result. Algorithms may be deterministic, probabilistic, heuristic, on-line, etc.

ASCII Acronym for *American Standard Code for Information Exchange.* An ASCII code is the standard bit representation for a list of alphanumeric, special, and control characters. The alphanumeric characters are for modern English Roman alphabet upper and lower case letters and decimal digits. ASCII was established as a standard in order to achieve character level interoperability or compatibility between different types of data processing equipment. The *Unicode* representation is used to represent characters in all human languages.

AS-IS Business Model This refers to the current state or practices of a business system or to a view or understanding of an existing system, as opposed to a prospective or TO-BE system.

Aspect-Oriented Development Addresses the difficulties caused by *aspects*, which are system properties that exhibit a lack of locality (such as occurs in phenomena like coordination, scheduling, fault tolerance, etc.), which in turn undermines the separation of concerns that is critical to object-oriented design.

Baldridge National Quality Award National award given to manufacturing and services businesses, healthcare and educational organizations for outstanding accomplishments in the areas of "leadership, strategic planning, customer and market focus, information and analysis, human resources focus, process management, and business results" (NIST Web site) and administered by the National Institute of Standards and Technology. It is intended to encourage organizations to improve their competitiveness by "delivering ever improving value to customers and improving overall organizational performance" (NIST).

Best Practice Proven practices in a particular field or in a given context like software engineering that experience has shown are most effective at achieving a desired result. Best practices are assumed to be widely used by the relevant community and evolve over time. The CMM model is intended as a measure, reference model, or standard recognizing and certifying the application of best practices in software development. An example of a promising best practice is the use of design patterns in OO design.

Black Box A view of a system in which only inputs and their corresponding output responses are known and define the system behavior. The box that represents the system is called *black* because there is no internal view into how the system operates. Black boxes are one of several types of *boxes*, such as clear boxes and state boxes, used in the Cleanroom model.

Breadboard A type of prototype used to determine if the proposed technical characteristics of a system work.

Break-Even Point Analysis (BEP) The point at which profits equal losses or at which expenses equal revenues, or total costs and revenues are equal. How much income a business needs to stay at a given level of profit. Break-even point analysis is different from the payback period, which is the period required to recover an investment.

BPR Acronym for *Business Process Re-Engineering*. The idea comes from the business management literature. It refers to the critical examination, analysis, restructuring, and radical redesign and reorganization of business processes in order to achieve dramatic improvements in performance.

Business Process Modeling The business process can be modeled graphically with flowchart like diagrams that include symbols for activities, object and control flows, and split or join and merge operations. The objective is to describe the logic of a business operation carefully. UML activity diagrams can also be used for this purpose. Business models are used to document the as-is system in BPR and to specify workflows for workflow management systems.

Capital Budgeting This refers to a management technique or approach that organizations use to make decisions on long-term investments. Capital budgeting projects are expected to produce positive cash flows at some future point. The decision to accept or reject a capital budgeted project depends on the outcome of an analysis of the projected capital cost of the project and cash flows generated by it.

CASE Acronym for *Computer Aided Software Engineering*. This refers to the use of automated computer support tools in the different phases of the software development process. Many CASE tools are commercially available. A comprehensive collection of CASE tools is used in the Rational Unified Process model supported by Rational Rose.

Class Diagrams A type of UML diagram used to describe the relations between the classes (objects) in a problem. The box elements in the diagram indicate the name, attributes, and methods of a class. Instead of the attributes and methods, a more conceptual approach will list just the responsibilities of the named class, as is done in the so-called Class Responsibility Collaborator approach.

Cleanroom Model The Cleanroom Model of software development combines incremental development with statistically tested modules and formal correctness techniques to ensure validity of the system developed. It can be applied to new and existing systems. The objective is to produce certifiable systems with zero defects in the field.

CMM The Capability Maturity Model (CMM or SEI-CMM) is a model for judging the maturity of the software processes of an organization and for identifying the key practices required to increase the maturity of these processes. This was developed by the Software Engineering Institute at Carnegie Mellon University.

COCOMO Model Acronym for *Constructive Cost Model*. Project cost, time, and schedule estimation model developed by Boehm, based on estimates of program size and complexity, and later on the proposed functionality.

Code and Fix Primitive presoftware-engineering approach to software development based on a succession of write-code or fix-code steps.

Cognitive Fit The idea that the external representation of a problem and the problem-solving task together affect how a problem is solved; also, an approach in which the goal is to match, as closely as possible, the representation to the task and the user. The expectation is that there should be a harmonious fit among three parameters: the user's cognitive skills, the task, and the representation of the task (as presented to the user).

Collaboration This refers to working collectively with others in order to achieve an objective. In a software development context, the collaborators include stakeholders, users, developers, affiliates, process owners, and external agencies.

Collaboration Diagram UML diagrams that visually depict the interaction between objects in terms of the sequenced messages between the objects. They combine information in the class, use case, and sequence diagrams. Unlike sequence diagrams, they do not explicitly indicate time, but numerically sequence messages in their order of execution.

Compensating Feedback A systems dynamics effect in complex systems according to which potentially beneficial changes, like the application of a new technology, produce feedback effects that counteract or undermine the anticipated impact of the intervention.

Conditions and Constraints Qualifying factors that must be taken into consideration when solving a problem. Conditions tend to be logical restrictions, and constraints tend to be quantitative restrictions or restrictions on how or when things can be done.

Continuous Quality Improvement (CQI) A management approach to improving development processes by analyzing their capabilities using quality assessments and improving the processes repeatedly and incrementally to increase customer satisfaction. When defined standards are met, new goals are established to further enhance quality, but if standards are not met, corrective strategies are devised and executed to meet standards and to make improvements.

COTS Acronym for Commercial Off-the-Shelf Software. This development model is based on the use of ready-made, commercially available software components that can be integrated to form a complete system and are delivered with the system.

Coupling This refers to the degree of connectedness between components, modules, or subsystems of a system. A low level of coupling is preferred in the design of a system because it tends to reduce the ripple effect of changes made in one subsystem, as well as allowing the parallel development of the subsystems. The converse concept is cohesion, which refers to the internal functional coherence of a subsystem.

Danger This refers to a type of development risk due to factors beyond the control of the participants.

Data Abstraction In imperative programming languages like C, this refers to the functional definition of modular operations on data structures like (linked list) insertion or deletion without regard to how the function is actually implemented. In object orientation, an object encapsulates the data and the methods associated with the object, with the data representation and method implementation details hidden and inaccessible except through the protocol provided by the object's public methods.

Data Dictionaries A dictionary with the definitions of all the data elements in a system. It should be arranged alphabetically or with an appropriate search engine; the terms should be defined in natural language in nontechnical terms; the legal values of elements should be defined.

Data Flow Diagrams (DFD) Directed graph-like diagrams that show the flow of data or information between processes or data transforms (depicted as bubbles) that functionally transform the data (depicted as labels on the directed edges). The diagrams also show sources, sinks, and stores of information. This is the fundamental modeling tool in the classic structures' analysis or design methodology. As opposed to flowcharts, which emphasize flow of control, DFDs emphasize the flow of data, with the execution order of processes resolved only later in the design.

Degree of Liquidity A fundamental characteristic of a healthy business firm is the ability to pay its accounts payable as they become due using its funds or resources. This is called the firm's degree of liquidity.

Design by Contract An approach that views a software system as a set of communicating components whose interaction is based on precisely defined specifications of the mutual obligations among the components, which are known as *contracts*.

Design Patterns Generic, reusable design templates or types of proven, successful, standard software architectures for solving certain classes of regularly recurring problem; introduced by the Gang of Four.

Design Specification   The detailed planning of the solution for a given problem.

Differences   The distinctions underlying diversity. So-called positive differences should be integrated or included in a problem analysis or solution. Negative differences should be excluded. Differences viewed as a potential source of added value are called optimizing differences. Differences that are merely accepted or tolerated are called neutralizing differences. Differences that are viewed as a source of problems or difficulties are called activating differences.

Disintermediation   The elimination of intermediaries between a server of resources and a client requesting resources. This design tactic is a decisive factor in the productivity improvements that have resulted from computerization and is prominently exemplified in many Internet business applications.

Disruptive Technology   A technological development that emerges from outside the mainstream of scientific development and radically challenges the existing technological paradigm. Open source development is arguably such a paradigm in the field of software development.

Diversity   Diversity is the organizational asset that embodies the hidden value of interdisciplinary, experiential, cultural, social, and psychological differences. Utilizing diversity is the key to incorporating interdisciplinary thinking in software engineering to enable a broad-based approach to development problem solving.

Diversity in Software Engineering   Integrative or diversity-driven problem-solving approaches capitalize on beneficial differences in order to obtain optimized solutions, in contrast to conventional problem solving, which addresses problems that try to eliminate sources of contradiction.

Divide and Conquer   The problem-solving strategy in which a problem is separated or partitioned into subproblems, which are more readily solved separately and whose solutions can be combined to solve the original problem.

DoD   Acronym for Department of Defense.

Domain Model   This term is used in many different ways. A common use is to refer to a conceptual, object-oriented model of an application domain. Requirements for a system can be thought of as composed of a domain model combined with use cases and a user interface definition. The model identifies the scope of the domain and its information objects. The domain model is built as the result of a domain analysis. Refer to the CMM http://www.sei.cmu.edu/domain-engineering/ for useful discussion.

EBIT Acronym for *Earnings before Interest and Taxation*. This is a financial measure defined as the profit of an organization including operating and nonoperating earnings, before subtracting interest and income taxes. It is also known as operating leverage.

Embedded Knowledge A term used in reengineering. It refers to the fact that the knowledge or understanding of a legacy system's behavior has become embedded in the system rather than being available through the system documentation.

Embedded Prototype Refers to prototyping when it is considered as a component of another software development strategy.

Enterprise Resource Management (ERM) Software that helps manage an organization's resources, including basic applications such as general ledger, accounts payable and receivable, manufacturing, inventory, and human resources.

Equivocality Uncertainty about the meaning of information. A common technique for resolving the uncertainty is to use negotiation to identify a consensus interpretation.

Evolutionary Development A reaction to limitations of the waterfall model in which increments of system capability are released and the successive stages of development are based on user and developer experience with earlier stages; the initial release provides enough capability to serve as a basis for user evaluation.

Executable Specifications Formal specifications that can be executed and dynamically extended by step-wise refinement, as in Zave's operational specification model.

Expected Return This refers to the return an investor anticipates occurring at the end of a period of time viewed from the investor's perspective at day zero.

Experimental Prototype The use of *prototyping* as a testing or evaluation technique to verify whether a proposed system will meet user or customer expectations, to determine system feasibility, or to explore alternative solutions.

Exploratory Prototype The use of prototyping as a technique for gathering and clarifying requirements.

Extreme Programming A type of agile development that places a strong emphasis on pair programming. The approach is described in Beck's well-known book, *Extreme Programming Explained.*

Feedback Control Loop A situation in which signals or controls caused by a system are fed back into the system to govern, control, or modify its dynamic behavior. In a software model, the comparison between an existing, intended outcome and a desired outcome, especially between successive stages of the life cycle, used to modify or correct the development.

Forward Engineering The use of the process results from reverse engineering to develop a new system. One of the most common adaptations is the development of new interactive interfaces, which may use new styles of interaction instead of the existing style of interface.

Freeware Software provided free by its author but on which the author retains the copyright.

Frequential Simplification The cognitive effect by which infrequently taken interactions or effects tend to be forgotten.

Function Point Units of functionality in a program or system used in estimation models like COCOMO to estimate project size.

Gang of Four A famous group of four software engineers who compiled over 20 design templates that have proven to be effective, reusable design patterns.

Glueware Internally developed software that allows the correct integration of COTS-based software systems by resolving mismatches between components or with the application and platform. For example, wrappers that encapsulate a data source to make it more compatible with a COTS component are a type of glueware.

Goal An objective to accomplish. Elicitation and continuous clarification of stakeholder goals is central in software development.

Gold-Plating The inclusion in a system design of overly elaborate functions that are not significantly connected to stakeholder goals.

Happy Path The scenario in a use case that follows a normal, unexceptional flow of events.

HCI Acronym for *Human Computer Interaction*. The study of how humans interact with computers. HCI is a discipline now that deals with the design, evaluation, and implementation of interactive computing systems for human use and the study of the major phenomena that surround them.

High-Fidelity Prototyping Intended to mimic the look and feel and responsiveness of a system including its delay characteristics.

Horizontal Prototyping A type of prototyping in which most system functions are at least nominally accessible but only a few are actually operational.

Horizontal Specialization Specialization across various functional departments or business needs within an organization or across various domains of an industry or between industries.

IBM 360 System IBM computers introduced in the period from 1966 to 1980, which allowed scientific and business applications to be done on the same machine by providing binary as well as decimal arithmetic instructions.

Identification of Business Goals The most appropriate context for viewing, evaluating, and utilizing software. These provide the criteria and framework in reference to which software systems can be assessed.

IEEE Acronym for *Institute of Electrical and Electronics Engineers*, a U.S.-based organization that defines standards for electronics and computing; also, professional organization to promote development and application of electrotechnology.

Ignorance In the context of software development, this refers to lack of data or to inaccurate data that prevents business and human problems from being well defined or well understood. Ignorance in this sense includes lack of knowledge about available, adequate, or effective tools.

In-Breadth Ignorance Refers to an assumption that development issues can be adequately captured using only one or two paths of knowledge with other aspects of the problem not considered for possible relevancy.

In-Depth Ignorance The case in which, although the relevant aspects of an issue may be considered, they are not studied adequately enough to capture the aspects effectively.

Incorporated Prototype A prototype intended to be included eventually in some fashion in a real product. In such a case, prototype development should follow normal development standards including maintenance of appropriate documentation, testing, and so on.

Incremental Development Similar to iterative development, but successive iterations tend to be understood as adding new, incremental functionality to the product—as building a *part of the intended system* in each of a sequence of partial releases until the entire system is completed.

Inferential Simplification The cognitive process by which similar interactions or event series are merged into single, prototypical rules in which differences between the similar cases are blurred.

Infrastructure Vulnerabilities Points of weakness and security gaps in the physical or logical architecture of an information system that create open opportunities for intrusion or theft of critical information.

Initial Operational Capability A milestone in Boehm's spiral model at the end of the development cycle that includes software preparation (software support, documentation, licensing, etc), site preparation (off-the-shelf vendor arrangements), and user and maintainer preparation.

Intangibles Nonmonetary benefits that may lead to an indirect financial return on an original investment, in contrast to tangible benefits. However, even though intangibles are nonfinancial, they may be measurably related to important business objectives.

Intent Specifications Specifications based on the psychological and cognitive factors involved in how people use specifications to solve problems.

Inverse Transition Diagrams Transition diagrams that display the *impossible* transitions in a system, as opposed to ordinary transitions that depict the allowed transitions in a system. These can be useful as a data visualization tool.

ISO 9000 Standards The ISO refers to the *International Organization for Standardization*, which is a consortium of the national standards institutes from over 140 countries with a central organization in Geneva, Switzerland, that coordinates the system and publishes finished standards. Its basic purpose is "to facilitate the international coordination and unification of industrial standards" (www.iso.org).

Iterative Development This development model creates a product in a series of development iterations beginning with a prototype of the entire product at the first iteration and then successively refining the partial product in subsequent iterations.

Iterative Enhancement The development model of Basili and Turner (1975), which develops a system as a series of subsystems with the emerging system and the originating problem more thoroughly understood as the process proceeds—similar to what happens in a learning process.

Kaizen Japanese for *improvement*. This refers to the Japanese business version of continuous improvement in the processes and practices of managers and workers. Its maintenance objective aims to maintain existing technological and managerial standards at their current level, but requires management establishment and enforcement of Standard Operating Procedures (SOPs). Its improvement objective seeks to improve the current standards continuously via kaizen-level adjustments (small, repeated, incremental changes) or by innovation (major change).

Key Process Areas (KPA) Related sets of software practices associated with each of the successive layers of the Capability Maturity Model.

Killer Apps Applications so effective that they potentially alter a market. Hardware killer apps have ranged from the light bulb and Xerox copier to the PC. In software, they must be customizable, interactive, dynamic, and stylish. Software examples are Web tools like Google and GUI Web browsers, sites like e-bay, and user environments like Windows. Lotus 1-2-3 was the software killer app that drove the market for the PC in the early 1980s.

Knowledge-Based Expert Systems Expert systems that use the encoded human knowledge or expertise in their databases as rules or data that can be automatically and appropriately invoked by an inference engine when solving a problem.

LAN Acronym for *Local Area Network*. A network of computers interconnected for geographically local communication. A LAN usually spans a small area like a single building or group of buildings.

Legacy Systems Established computer systems (hardware and software applications) in a company. Legacy systems typically perform mission-critical operations in organizations over a period of many years with the result that replacing them can be detrimental or disruptive to a company's routine work flows. Legacy systems can be updated particularly by using reengineering techniques.

Life-Cycle Architecture Spiral model milestone that elaborates on the life cycle objective elements, including system and software components, mediators between these components, and constraints, off-the-shelf or reusable software components, attributes like response time and reliability, and likely architectural trends over time. This milestone should lead to stakeholder agreement on the feasibility of the architecture and its compatibility with the stakeholder life-cycle objectives.

Life-Cycle Model This refers in an encompassing way to the entire, cradle-to-grave, software development process and recognizes the natural separate stages in this process.

Lightweight Models Models like agile development that are intended to reduce the perceived unwieldy process overhead in other approaches.

Lower CASE Tools Computer support tools for the implementation, testing, and maintenance phases of the software life cycle. Also called back-end CASE tools.

Low-Fidelity Prototyping Type of prototyping that simulates the proposed product in some very rudimentary way—even by pencil and paper or by slides.

Make-versus-Buy Decision The decision as to whether some desired application functionality should be purchased as a prebuilt product from a vendor or developed in house.

Metcalfe's Law The idea that the value of a network increases in value with each additional node (or user) in proportion to the square of the number of users.

Metrics Business goals when they become quantifiable as positive or negative indicators of business success. These can include product or services quality, customer satisfaction, etc. These supplement backward-looking financial measures like ROI and are expected to be related to factors that drive future performance.

Mockup A prototype used to determine the usability of a system such as the span and access to the prospective system's potential functions.

Modular Programming In this programming paradigm, a programming task is subdivided into logical subtasks or modules. Each module's function and interface are carefully defined before detailed programming is begun. The program is viewed as a set of interacting functions, each of which performs a single, well-defined, cohesive task, with low coupling (or side effects) between the functions. The approach is basically procedural rather than object oriented.

Moore's Law The empirically observed phenomenon that, because of technological developments, digital chip density doubles every 18 months, but cost remains constant, thus increasing computing power but not price.

NPV Acronym for *Net Present Value*. Based on the standard financial method for calculating the present value of a financial stream, compares the value of money now with the value of money in the future by discounting that future value. It is applied in capital budgeting as the present value of a project's cash in-flow minus the present value of the project's cash out-flow.

Object-Oriented Design (OOD) The methodology used to develop an object-oriented model of a software application.

Old Factory Model The approach to problem solving in a manufacturing environment that consisted of breaking a manufacturing problem into small units and allocating each unit to a separate human actor or resource (Smith, 1776).

Open Source Development Software development philosophy that encourages use and improvement of software written by volunteers that allows anyone to copy and modify the source code.

Open Systems A system whose interface specifications are completely defined, publicly available, and maintained through an open group consensus. Systems that constantly interact with the external environment.

Operating Leverage The effect of a change in total sales on earnings before interest and taxes (EBIT). Operating leverage also refers to the portion of a business's costs that are fixed rather than variable. The higher a business's operating leverage is, the greater is the impact of an increase in sales on income (after the break-even point has occurred).

Pair Programming Extreme programming technique in which a pair of programmers shares the same computer and collaborates in real-time.

Pareto Distribution A probability distribution followed by many social phenomena. Zipf's law is a discrete version of this. Related to the so-called *80–20 rule*, according to which 80 percent of the cases are driven by 20 percent of the causes for many economic phenomena.

Named after Pareto, a 19th century Italian economist who noted that in Italy, 80 percent of the land was owned by 20 percent of the population. A similar exhibit would be that 80 percent of sales are to 20 percent of a company's clients.

Pareto Improvement A change that improves the utility of one participant without decreasing the utility of any other participants. This is frequently used as a metric for measuring the effectiveness of an economic situation.

PDA Personal digital assistant.

People Capability Maturity Model An organizational change model designed to guide systems and software organizations in attracting, motivating, and retaining technical staff.

Personal Software Process A stage-wise model for improvement of developer behavior originated by Watts Humphrey of the SEI, which attempts to guide individual developers in sharpening the discipline and practices that they apply in software development.

Pervasive Computing The convergence of three traditional computing specializations (personal, networked, and embedded) to produce a new computing model marked by wireless and portable hardware and software. Numerous computing devices that can be easily accessed and are mobile or embedded in an environment and part of a ubiquitous network are characteristic.

Pilot System A type of prototype that provides essential system functions and, after some evolutionary iterations, can develop into a complete system.

Point Solution A solution optimized around an original problem statement and that therefore may be inadequately robust to changes in the problem definition.

Presentation Prototyping Provides users a concrete, first look at a real version of the intended system. It can serve a marketing purpose by exhibiting the expected system behavior to potential users.

Probability Expresses risk in a quantitative fashion, letting statistics be used intensively to weigh, prioritize, and manage risks.

Problem The difference between an existing situation and a desired situation.

Problem Engineering Refers to correct problem definition. Problem definition entails gathering necessary problem-related data, processing this data effectively, and then generating a statement that accurately characterizes a business problem.

Problem Givens A representation of the specific facts that must be identified prior to solving the problem.

Problem Solving The process by which a situation is analyzed and solutions are formed to solve a problem, with steps taken to resolve, eliminate, or mitigate the problem.

Problem-Solving Model An understanding of the problem, devising a plan, carrying out the plan, and looking back.

Problem-Solving Schema An organized body of knowledge or information that problem solvers build about the properties of a particular type of problem and the operations or steps required to solve it.

Problem Unknowns The detailed, particular things about a problem that must be discovered to accomplish the problem-solving goal.

Process Series of actions or operations directed toward a particular result.

Process Design Engineering The use of an automated engineering approach for the evolutionary design, implementation, and testing of real-time software.

Process Model A specification of a real-world software process.

Productivity Paradox Refers to the real or perceived lack of improvement in software development productivity despite the application of powerful new development techniques and automated support such as CASE tools.

Program A sequence of syntactically and semantically correct instructions forming a solution for a problem.

Programming by Imitation An approach in which an AI-based system is expected to generate an algorithm and its code on the basis of a worked specific example of the algorithm to be implemented.

Project Management The management of the people, budget, and money resources, schedule, and scope of a project. The project manager is responsible and accountable for the project success and must have the authority to direct the project so that it achieves its intended result.

Protocol Analysis The technique of eliciting verbal descriptions of thought processes (thinking out loud) from problem solvers in order to analyze and understand objectively what is happening in those processes. The subjects do not explain what they are doing or why. They merely verbally express what is going on in their minds as they solve a task.

Prototyping An approach that usually involves building a small version of an intended system prior to building the proposed complete system, thus allowing developers to work out kinks in a specification and design before full-scale development to reduce development risk significantly.

Rapid Application Development (RAD) A development paradigm that allows higher quality products to be developed faster, though often requiring compromises in adherence to requirements.

Rapid Prototyping A prototyping approach in which rapid development is achieved with the use of tools like code generators or 4GL languages.

Rational Unified Process A visual modeling tool from Rational Software that lets developers model the solution of a problem throughout the life cycle, from analysis, design, and implementation, through testing and configuration management using the UML notation.

Reach Refers to the degree of customer involvement or productivity.

Reengineering A development approach that reimplements existing legacy maintenance characteristics. The system may be redocumented, restructured, and retranslated to a more current language or platform, and data may be migrated to a newer database system. Automated tools are required to make the development cost effective.

Refactoring Modifying the structure of the code of a system without changing the system's functional behavior by using small incremental changes that are meticulously tested at each step.

Referential Integrity Term used in Cleanroom Model that requires that the design and specification correspond to the same mathematical function. If referential integrity is satisfied, then the design is a provably correct implementation of the specification.

Release Used in various ways. The first release of a software product that has been tested just by its developers is called alpha software. Software that has been alpha tested, is expected to have more bugs than a regular release, and is released to only a particular set of users who will test it is called a beta release.

Requirements Engineering The process of identifying, organizing, and accurately representing the user requirements so that these can be correctly implemented into systems built to meet those requirements.

Return on Investment (ROI) This financial ratio is the ratio of net profit to investment. It is a commonly used fiscal metric or figure of merit for guiding capital investment decisions. It compares the net benefits of a project to its total cost.

Reverse Engineering The process of analyzing a subject system to identify its components and their interrelationships in order to create representations of the system in another form or at a higher level of abstraction (Buss & Henshaw, 1991). The process of extracting and abstracting design information from an existing system's source code. The process aims to recover the design implemented in the code, taking as its point of departure information about the system's scope and functionality provided by a system inventory analysis.

Risk A state or property of a development project that, if ignored or left unresolved, will increase the likelihood of project failure; or in Boehm's terms: potential loss × probability of loss. Risk may be generic (such as confusion about requirements) or project specific (such as vendor failure to deliver a COTS component).

Round-Trip Engineering The idea in this paradigm is that changes to the model of a system should be automatically reflected in the source code and, conversely, changes to the source code for a system should also automatically update the design model for the system. This reduces the tendency to make ad hoc changes directly to the code rather than through the model. Automated tools that support this kind of change management process are available.

Scalability The ability to increase the number of users, volume of transactions, or demand on a system greatly without needing to make changes to the architectural design of the system, though supplemental hardware may need to be added to the environment. This is an especially important consideration for evaluating hardware and software for rapidly expanding enterprises.

Scenario See also *use case*; a basic tool informally expressed in English used to structure user requirements. A set of scenarios can be combined to form a use case. For example, one of the scenarios in a use case is the *happy path*, in which the expected actor goal is obtained without complication. Failure scenarios are also included, as well as scenarios that represent exceptional situations requiring special handling to complete the use case.

SCRUM A model of agile development in which work is broken into a series of steps called *sprints*. Prior to each sprint, developers meet with the customer to identify and prioritize the work to be done in the upcoming sprint. During the sprint, teams meet daily. On the completion of a sprint, the development team delivers a potentially shippable product increment.

SEI Acronym for *Software Institute of Engineering* at Carnegie–Mellon University, which developed and updates the Capability Maturity Model.

Semantic Distance The cognitive gap between the model of a system specification and the mental model of the system in the minds of its users.

Separation of Concerns Partitioning a problem in such a way that the separate parts can be discussed relatively independently of one another. This is one of the most basic principles of effective problem solving and of software engineering.

Sequence Diagrams UML *sequence diagrams* are used to illustrate the interactions between objects arranged in a time sequence (the sequence of messages between objects) and to clarify the logic of use cases. They are similar to collaboration diagrams, but accentuate the message sequence more than the objects involved in the messages.

Shareware This is so-called try-before-you-buy software. It is usually delivered digitally free of charge to the user, but the user is expected (on the basis of an honor system) to pay some small amount for the product after a trial usage period. After payment, the user's copy is typically registered with the distributor. At purchase, a more complete version of the product may be supplied. Updates and some level of assistance may be provided. The shareware product is copyrighted so the user cannot redistribute it as his or her own. An important advantage of this business model is the direct relationship between the user and the developer, rather than through an intermediary in a retail outlet.

Software Development Life Cycle (SDLC) This is about the process and model used to develop software systems. It describes the route that leads developers from problems to solutions. SDLC describes stages involved in an information system development project, from an initial feasibility study to the completed project onto maintenance stage.

Software Development Life-Cycle Models These are strategies that represent pretested patterns for successful software development under different conditions. The strategies share the same objective but reach their goal by different approaches.

Software Engineering According to the *IEEE Standard Computer Dictionary* (1990), "The application of a systematic, disciplined, quantifiable approach to development, operation, and maintenance of software, that is, the application of engineering to software."

Solution The final step in the problem-solving process.

Specialize According to the Merriam-Webster dictionary, to "specialize" is to concentrate one's efforts in a special activity or field or to change in an adaptive manner.

Spiral Model Development model due to Boehm that builds a product in cycles of development with an emphasis on risk reduction. Each cycle consists of analysis, design, code, test—just like the entire waterfall model. The model repeatedly cycles back to a go or no-go decision based on repeatedly revised understandings of the risk of the development. It relies heavily on prototyping and software engineering economics to understand and minimize development risk.

Standard Framework Framework that could be used as a common basis for solving the business problems encountered.

Stealth Technology Transfer The risk that a customer uses the product and knowledge acquired in the first stage of a thin requirements development merely to acquire the developer's expertise rather than evaluate the continuance of the project in good faith.

Structured Programming   A style of implementing programming control logic approach that restricts the flow of control to sequences, structured loops like while's, repeat's, and for-loops, and if–then–else statements; this avoids or dramatically reduces the use of arbitrary branches such as in unrestricted goto's. In the Dijkstra version of structured programming, programs are decomposed into parts that have a single entry and a single exit. Dijkstra's paradigm was used particularly to establish the formal correctness of programs.

Subgoals   The restatement of the problem goal in terms of subproblem goals.

Successive Refinement   The successive refinement of the functions or modules of a system until elements are reached that perform single coherent functions and can be coded as single units.

Supply Chain Management (SCM)   The process of efficiently coordinating the flow of resources like material, information, and money as they move from an original source to an end user (such as from supplier, to manufacturer, to wholesaler, to retailer, to user). This involves overseeing relationships with vendors and consumers, controlling inventory, forecasting demand, and keeping a close vigil at every link in the supply chain, from supplier to manufacturer to wholesaler to retailer to consumer.

System Dynamics   A computer simulation approach to understanding the behavior of complex systems of interacting components, with a particular emphasis on feedback loops, delay effects, and recursive or circular causality.

System Sequence Diagram   UML diagrams depict events input from a source external to a system that generate a system response. Thus, they show the system events that *actors* generate and their order during a scenario, and the system responses to the events and their order.

System Specialization   The concentration on unique problems and the techniques for comprehending and solving them.

Tangibles   Direct financial benefits on an original investment. Indirect benefits are usually called intangibles.

Taylorian Approach   The time-and-motion analysis and decomposition of industrial tasks into their smallest constituent components, introduced to improve manufacturing efficiency by Frederick Taylor in studies that established scientific management. This type of analysis is a basic paradigm in the field of industrial engineering.

Testing   Process of reviewing what was produced and done to solve the problem. Software testing establishes the correctness, reliability, usability, etc. In addition to testing expected cases, a classic way to test code is to stress it by testing at its limits or boundaries. Types of testing include system function testing, unit and integration testing, and user acceptance testing.

Thin Requirements A term used in Lott's variation of the waterfall model that refers to the use of limited, sparse system requirements that, when implemented, constitute the completion of the product up to that point. Further development can then be vetoed by either of the parties—the developer or the client.

Throwaway Prototyping In this approach, the prototype is discarded when development of the actual system begins. The prototyping is employed to simulate the product under development and to refine the design during the development cycle.

Time Sharing An operating system capability that allows multiple users to run different tasks concurrently, on a single processor (via time-sliced process scheduling) or in parallel on many processors. It allows the appearance of simultaneous service to the concurrent users. It differs from multitasking (which refers to tasks as its reference) and instead refers to the support provided to multiple simultaneous users.

Time Value of Money (TVM) Refers to the fact that money received in the present moment is more valuable than the same amount received at some future period by a factor that reflects the amount of interest that could be earned on the money by that time. It reflects the impact of expected inflation and the risk of default. Related terms are present value (of a future amount) and the future value (of a present amount).

TO-BE Business Model The intended or desired state of a business system.

Total Quality Management (TQM) A structured set of management practices followed throughout an organization aimed at satisfying all the stakeholders, internal, and external customers, by striving for continuous improvement, integrating the business environment with development, focusing on quality assurance and building quality into products in accord with customer wants, even changing the organizational culture. It requires continuing improvement of processes, services, and products.

UML Acronym for *Unified Modeling Language*. UML is the leader in modeling languages used for specifying and documenting the artifacts of software development process and has become the de facto standard. The set of tools available from Rational software are the most widely used.

Uncertainty The type of risk that refers to lack of knowledge of the future.

Unprocessed Data Data that is not transformed into useful information, in the correct form, at the right time, and to the right people is unprocessed data.

Unused Data When data is not used to solve problems, it amounts to an absence of data.

Upper CASE Tools Computer support tools for the requirements, specification, and design phases of the software life cycle. Also called front-end CASE tools.

Usage Profile Term used in the Cleanroom model in which the test cases are selected to be a statistically representative sample of a system's expected usage, so the testing is expected to be as reliable as a statistical sampling process.

Use Case A single task performed by a user of a system that produces a result useful to the actual goals of the user. The outcome must satisfy some user intent, not merely be a partial step along the way towards a user goal. For example, just logging onto a system is not a use case because the logon merely represents a means to an end. The actual objective is to do something useful on the system. The *use case diagram* is a UML tool for specifying the user goals of a system. The use case diagram graphically depicts the use cases and the *actors* (see beginning of glossary) where the actor can be another system.

User Action Notation (UAN) Description of the cooperative behavior manifested between a user and an interface during an interaction. The UAN descriptions can utilize scenarios, screen displays, and state transition diagrams to characterize the interaction.

V-Shaped Model Modified version of the waterfall model that added validation and verification processes by associating testing activities with the analysis and design phases.

Vague Data Data that is too low in quality. Such data may be uncertain, unconfirmed, unclear, undefined, or need proper translation or adequate clarification.

Validation Process of determining whether a proposed system was correctly implemented as opposed to determining whether the system proposed was the correct system to solve a problem.

Verification Process of determining whether a proposed system is the right system to satisfy stakeholder goals.

Vertical Prototyping Type of prototyping in which a narrow vertical slice of the system functions is implemented.

Vertical Specialization Specialization in the different levels of problem complexity across the intraorganizational pyramid from operational to top management.

WWWWWHH Principle An organizing principle of Boehm that addresses the why, what, when, who, where, how, and how much of software development.

Waterfall Model The most fundamental version of a software development life-cycle model used in software engineering. The waterfall is a generally linear, sequential development model with distinct goals and deliverables for each stage of development: analysis, design, coding, testing, and maintenance. Once a stage is completed, the development proceeds to the next stage with an expectation of minimal loop-backs to earlier completed stages.

Weak Strategy Generic approaches in problem solving that are not tailored to specific problem domains.

Well-Defined Problem Statement This statement contains three principal elements: goal, givens, and unknowns, which are shaped by the process of problem solving into a solution.

Win–Win Spiral Model Version of spiral model based on using so-called stakeholder win–win approach to determine the objectives–constraints–alternatives for each cycle of the spiral. This entails identifying the stakeholders of the system, determining their (win) conditions, and negotiating an agreed upon set of objectives–constraints–alternatives.

Workflow Enactment Coordinated execution of workflow activities supported by a *workflow metamodel*.

Workflow Engine Software in a workflow management system that interprets the requests for execution of different types of workflow activities and interacts with the processing entities to ensure the activities are executed as prescribed according to the workflow type.

Workflow Management System Systems that support the automatic enactment of business processes based on formal descriptions of those processes. They also address the distribution of workload to processors, availability of processors, rework requirements when activities are implemented incorrectly, etc.

Workflow Model An information systems model that views an enterprise as a network of collaborating agents in which informational transactions or tasks are passed between participants according to a set of procedural rules.

Author Index

Subject Index

T - #0097 - 101024 - C0 - 234/156/19 [21] - CB - 9780849339394 - Gloss Lamination